The Coming of the Son of Man

The Coming of the Son of Man

New Testament Eschatology for an Emerging Church

Andrew Perriman

PATERNOSTER

First published in 2005 by Paternoster Press

10 09 08 07 06 05 7 6 5 4 3 2 1

Paternoster Press is an imprint of Authentic Media,
9 Holdom Avenue, Bletchley, Milton Keynes MK1 1QR, UK
and
P.O. Box 1047, Waynesboro, GA 30830-2047, USA

www.authenticmedia.co.uk

British Library Cataloguing in Publication Data
A catalogue record for this book is available from the British Library

ISBN 1-84227-299-3

Cover Design by FourNineZero
Typeset by Textype, Cambridge
Print Management by Adare Carwin
Printed by J. H. Haynes & Co. Ltd, Sparkford

Contents

1. Storytelling	1
Reading New Testament Eschatology	3
The Daniel Narrative	9
Eschatology and an Emerging Church	13
2. A Voice Against Jerusalem	16
When Will These Things Be	17
The Structure of the Discourse	21
The Beginning of the Birth Pains	23
Harassment of the Disciples	26
The Jewish War	30
3. The Coming of the Son of Man	38
Signs in the Heavens	38
The Coming of the Son of Man	47
The Coming of the Christ in Acts	70
4. Life and Death in the Age to Come	74
The Gathering of the Elect	74
Being Watchful	77
The Sheep and Goats	80
The End of Their World	82
Images of Judgment	87
5. The Suffering of the Saints	98
The Present Distress	100
The Imitation of Christ	102
The End of the Age	113
A Day of Wrath	118
Where is the Promise of his Coming?	128

6. The Man of Lawlessness 130
The Man of Lawlessness 133
The Rebellion 139
The Restraining Force 142
The Daniel Typology 150

7. The *Parousia* of the Lord 153
Rescue and Retribution 153
The Firstfruits to be Saved 166
The Defeat of Christ's Enemies 176

8. The City which Is Sodom and Egypt 182
The Opening of the Scroll 184
The Vision of the Lamb 186
The Seven Seals 187
The Seven Trumpets 198
The Little Scroll 203

9. The Fall of Babylon the Great 211
The Beast from the Sea and the Beast from the Land 213
Judgment on Rome 216
The Defeat of the Beast and the Binding of Satan 219
The Word of God on a White Horse 220
Satan is Bound for a Thousand Years 221

10. The Church in the Age that Has Come 224
The Heart of Salvation 227
Final Judgment 237
New Heavens and New Earth 243

Bibliography 246
Scripture Index 253
Index of Ancient Sources 270

One

Storytelling

What we are looking for is a story within a story within a story within a story. The outer layer in this Russian doll of a sentence is a complex, disorderly, incomplete historical narrative about the Jews in the Hellenistic-Roman world from, say, the Maccabean revolt around 166 B.C. to the suppression of the Bar Kokhba uprising in A.D. 135. Within that setting we find the New Testament story about Jesus and the emergence of the church in the first century A.D, which in turn contains a more or less coherent apocalyptic drama, acted out across a stark visionary landscape, at the climax of which a human figure appears, coming on the clouds of heaven, invested with power and glory, accompanied by the hosts of heaven. This story is the one that we mainly need to disentangle and then tell in this book. But, if we shake this third doll, we hear a rattling sound – there seems to be still another story inside it. The narrative that holds together the various insights, prophecies, warnings, and arguments that make up New Testament eschatology is itself the product of a prior story, one that was told with increasing desperation as Jews struggled to come to terms with their powerlessness in the ancient world.

The historical development of this fourth story and how it came to be found at the center of our Russian doll is beyond the scope of this book. We will, instead, make two straightforward assumptions: first, that it is most clearly expressed and probably originated in the later chapters of the book of Daniel; and secondly, that one of the many streams of apocalyptic reinterpretation that arose from this source flowed through the creative, prophetic mind of Jesus and became a sort of template for New Testament eschatology.[1]

Two technical terms have made an appearance in this paragraph that require explanation. The more general one is "eschatology," which has traditionally signified the study of the "last things" – the theological categories of death, judgment, heaven, and hell. In a book, however, that is looking not primarily for ordered categories but for narratives, and in particular for the interplay between narrative and history, we will need a working definition of eschatology that is both *narrative* and *historical*. For our purposes, eschatology deals essentially and quite simply with the believing community's expectation that God will intervene decisively in the course of history to bring something to an end and start something new. It is theology oriented towards the future but *within a certain context and from a certain perspective*, which may not be ours.[2] The significance of this qualification will become apparent as we go along. The term "apocalyptic" denotes a particular form or style of eschatology – a way of speaking about the end, a way of imagining the future. What gives apocalyptic literature its rather acrid flavor is that it is often
Bitter
the product of a state of religious or political crisis: it

[1] C. A. Evans has recently argued that "to understand how Jesus perceived his role in the proclamation and advancement of the kingdom of God it is necessary to take very seriously Daniel's visions, not least the vision of ch. 7" ("Defeating Satan and Liberating Israel: Jesus and Daniel's Visions," *JSHJ* 1.2 [2003], 162). In effect, this study develops this broad argument in relation to the whole of the New Testament.

[2] Cf. N. T. Wright's definition of eschatology as "the climax of Israel's history, involving events for which end-of-the-world language is the only set of metaphors adequate to express the significance of what will happen, but resulting in a new and quite different phase *within* space-time history" (N.T. Wright, *Jesus and the Victory of God* [London: SPCK, 1996], 208).

expresses the concrete and urgent hope that God will bring the crisis to an end and inaugurate a better state of affairs.

Reading New Testament Eschatology

This is not primarily a book about method, about *how* we should read New Testament eschatology. A too self-conscious and fastidious approach to the subject is as likely to obscure the nested narratives that make up our Russian doll as to elucidate them. Nevertheless, certain broad hermeneutical commitments have been made that should be exposed and explained at the outset – recognizing that in practice, of course, these commitments are as much the product of our reading as they are the prior condition for it. Essentially they are an expansion of the point just made, that we wish to explore the lived interplay between narrative and history.

1. We will try to read forwards from the first century rather than backwards from the twenty-first century. One of the reasons why the apocalyptic language of the New Testament can be so puzzling to the modern interpreter is that we cannot help but read it retrospectively and with the advantage, which more often than not turns out to be the disadvantage, of hindsight. It is rather like words written on a glass door. Once we have gone through the door, the text is reversed and becomes difficult to decipher. To make sense of it, we must at least *imagine* how it must have appeared from the other side of the door – as it would have been viewed by those for whom it was written. We must also make an attempt at a much harder task, which is to imagine that we share their ignorance about what lies in the future, on the other side of the door. A fundamental characteristic of genuine apocalyptic discourse is that it *speaks about that which is unknown*, things not seen, which must have significant implications for how it carries meaning: we would expect it to have something at least of the indirectness and inventiveness of metaphor. The language I use to describe what sort of person I think my

daughter will be in twenty years must be more tentative and more imaginative than the language I might use to describe her now. The danger with taking a historical approach to interpretation is that we think we know, or ought to know, what the stories and images actually came to refer to, and we are tempted to read them *after the event* not as prophecy but as actual description. Paula Fredriksen rightly observes that "our knowing what Christianity's future would be makes its past harder to see."[3] Interpretation too easily becomes a crude exercise in matching the details of the texts against what is known from history. This is necessary insofar as we need to take into account the historical relevance of apocalyptic, but it should not be pursued to the extent that the essential (and quite realistic) uncertainty of prophetic reference is removed.

2. We will work from the assumption that New Testament apocalyptic relates meaningfully to the world as it was seen from the first century. When you travel along a road, you pass signposts that give information about what is coming up ahead: an intersection, a freeway, the risk of falling rocks, for example. It is the relation between the sign and the physical feature that makes the sign meaningful. It does not normally (or literally) *make sense* to take a sign that informs the driver of an imminent turnoff to Birmingham and place it just before the exit to Manchester. Nor does it make sense to collect signs from random points along the road and place them all at some hypothetical super-intersection in the future. Nor does it really make sense for theologians to compile exhaustive catalogues of road signs and then argue over the proper method of classification. It is the road – or better the journey along the road – that gives the signs meaning.

We will need to ask ourselves repeatedly, therefore: Why has this sign been placed *here*, at this juncture, for these people to see and take note of? We will assume that apoca-

[3] P. Fredriksen, *Jesus of Nazareth, King of the Jews: A Jewish Life and the Emergence of Christianity* (London: Macmillan, 2000), 10.

lyptic language, even in its more obscure and mythical formulations, relates meaningfully to historical events as experienced or foreseen by the community which generated the apocalyptic visions. Eschatology is not just *said* – it is *said about something*. It tells us something about a world that is experienced and spoken about in other ways – in the way, for example, that the Jewish historian Josephus experienced and wrote about the war against Rome. This is why it is so important that, as far as possible, we allow narrative – the story of the journey along the road – rather than developed dogmatic interests to provide the structure for our interpretation. Narrative will help us to preserve the connection with history, to safeguard the referentiality of apocalyptic language, to keep us grounded in the concrete and uncomfortable experience of following Christ. We have lost sight of the pain and fearfulness – and with that the faith – that gave meaning and urgency to these visions.

Pick up a study by evangelicals on the nature of hell, for example, and you are likely to find that the exegetical section is structured according to the debate between two well dug-in and well-armed theological camps. On the one side are those who believe that the unsaved will suffer endless conscious torment; on the other side are those who prefer to think that the end awaiting the unsaved will be, sooner or later, annihilation. The approach is then to take the various New Testament texts that are supposed to say something about hell and ask which argument they support best. This book does not have a chapter about hell – or about heaven, for that matter – because the texts on which the doctrine is based belong in stories and arguments. They are not, in the first place, snippets of doctrinal data that someone has unhelpfully scattered through the pages of the New Testament. They are things that people said and wrote at particular moments in a historical narrative, in response to particular developments, drawing on particular memories and traditions, correcting particular misconceptions, encouraging particular attitudes and actions. Fillet the teaching from the narrative spine of the fish and you have a mass of ideas that can be chopped up and served as fish fingers or something more imaginative, but you no longer have a fish.

3. New Testament apocalyptic is thoroughly allusive: much of its phraseology and imagery has not been minted new for the purpose but has been *borrowed* from the Old Testament, especially from the Psalms and the Prophets, with perhaps a looser dependence on Jewish apocalyptic tradition. In this regard our road signs metaphor needs to be modified. It may well be that as we approach the intersection to Birmingham, for example, the sign actually says "Brighton" or "Berlin" or even "Babylon." How do we make sense of this oddity? We might conclude that the highway agency has simply put up the wrong sign. We might take the sign at face value, read it literally, ignore the fact that our map shows that Brighton, Berlin, and Babylon are nowhere near here, and conclude that this is not the intersection for Birmingham after all. Or we might more sensibly ask: In what way is the intersection to Birmingham *like an* intersection to Brighton or Berlin or Babylon? Why might someone want us to interpret the one in terms of the other? The misplaced signpost, borrowed from some earlier intersection, has come to function *as a metaphor* that tells us something about our journey that the literal signpost to Birmingham would not.

The assumption that we will make, then, in reading New Testament apocalyptic, is that borrowing language and imagery is not inconsequential but must be taken into account in at least three important respects.

First, it brings into view a surrounding argument or narrative that is likely to have a significant bearing on how the New Testament argument or narrative is to be interpreted. A well-known example is Jesus' quotation of Psalm 22:1 shortly before he died: "My God, my God, why have you forsaken me?" (Matt. 27:46; Mark 15:34). These words are despairing, but the Psalm as a whole expresses the hope of one who believes that God will rescue him from his enemies – from those who mock him, pierce his hands and feet, and cast lots for his clothing. The context is not passive – not merely a repository of colorful metaphors and phrases – but an *integral part of the argument* and must be read along with the foreground text. New Testament apocalyptic does not only tell a story: it invokes, elicits, and raises to consciousness a multiplex background narrative from Jewish belief and tradition.[4]

Secondly, the very fact that language is borrowed from a prior, highly significant literary source raises immediate questions about how the New Testament depicts future events.[5] We look over here in order to understand what is over there. The object about which we speak is not exactly where the words appear to place it; we must allow for a certain *refraction* of meaning – just as water refracts light and gives misleading information about a submerged object. The borrowing is virtually an admission on the part of the author that the future is not seen clearly, is not known directly: it will be like, or it will have the significance of, some other event. If we find, for example, that Jesus describes what is going to happen in terms of what has already taken place, this is surely because he is less concerned to give a literal account of events than to draw attention to certain underlying theological continuities. We cannot anticipate here all the implications of this principle of biblical intertextuality, but we need to keep it in mind as we work through the texts.

Thirdly, what may look like the fulfillment of Old Testament prophecy is often better understood as its

---

[4] Wright regards the echo of Micah 7:6 in Mark 13:12 as a "classic example of an entire passage being invoked by a single reference" (Wright, *Victory*, 348).

[5] Gospel "no clear textual prods" to push us in the direction of a non-literal interpretation (D. C. Allison, "Jesus and the Victory of Apocalyptic," in C. C. Newman [ed.], *Jesus and the Restoration of Israel* [Downers Grove: InterVarsity Press; Carlisle: Paternoster, 1999], 131). It raises the question, however, of whether New Testament apocalyptic should be read differently to other Jewish apocalyptic texts (cf. 138–39).

reapplication: the prophecy is borrowed in order to say something about a new and as yet unexpressed state of affairs. If at the Birmingham intersection we see a sign to Brighton, it is not because there was no earlier intersection to which it referred. Brighton was a real place with its own intersection and its own sign, but the sign has been *borrowed* – prophetically redeployed – in order to make better sense of the Birmingham intersection. So when Jesus tells the disciples that they will see the abomination of desolation, the desolating sacrilege, standing in the holy place (Matt. 24:15; Mark 13:14), he is not denying that the thought in Daniel originally referred to events in the second century B.C. Rather, he borrows it, exploiting its affective power, the story around it, and perhaps a certain intrinsic openness to another future, in order to characterize the coming judgment as a comparable event and, most importantly, to assimilate the new narrative into the old.

4. Finally, we will endeavor to construct an *integrated and consistent* apocalyptic narrative for the New Testament. The primary authors (Jesus, Paul, John) will be read separately: they have very different perspectives on the future. But we will be looking for what holds their visions together. In this we will inevitably collide with, and no doubt sometimes transgress, the boundaries imposed by a proper literary-critical methodology. We are in the rather difficult position of having to make sense of the parts and of the whole at the same time. We are dismantling a piece of equipment that we suspect has not been properly assembled. (Here is one important respect in which this is an "emerging church" project: we are not simply gathering data and building from scratch; we are consciously rethinking an older paradigm.) But in order to reassemble the machine we have somehow to get at least the main pieces in roughly the right place and then push the whole thing together until it clicks. There is too much interdependence of parts: the meaning of a text is determined in part by its context, but this context is only the product of this and other "texts."

Which comes first, the texts or the context?

In the end we must rely a great deal on a sense of narrative coherence – both internally, within the body of New Testament apocalyptic, and across its various interfaces: with New Testament teaching as a whole, with the background of religious and political thought, and with the historical circumstances of those for whom this future mattered. This is primarily an exercise in *macro*-exegesis – in storytelling. It will be based on a careful examination of the texts, but not every interpretation can be properly defended on intrinsic grounds, either because we lack space or because texts out of context are often irreducibly ambiguous. It is important that we do not lose sight of the wood because we have our noses up against the bark of the trees. The Russian doll metaphor suggests that we have another approach to the question available that will help us in this respect. If there is an older story behind the story, centered around Daniel's vision of a human figure coming on the clouds of heaven, then this will naturally provide an integrating framework for the disparate material that is scattered through the writings of the New Testament.[6] Before we begin to read the New Testament, therefore, it will be helpful to preview the story that emerges in the later chapters of Daniel.

The Daniel Narrative

First, something needs to be said regarding the texts of the Old Testament and of Daniel in particular. Modern English translations of the Old Testament are based on the Hebrew text (also known as the Masoretic text). The writers of the New Testament, however, frequently make use of the Greek translation of the Jewish Scriptures known as the

[6] In a more limited way Evans speaks of a "Danielic template" for Jesus' self-understanding (Evans, "Defeating Satan," 168). For the general popularity of Daniel's prophecies in first-century Judaism see Jos. *Ant*. 10.11.7 §267–9; cf. C. F. D. Moule, "'The Son of Man': Some of the Facts," *NTS* 41.2 (1995), 277–79.

..gint (LXX). Daniel presents a more complex situation. in addition to the fact that the original text is partly in Aramaic, partly in Hebrew, we will find especially in our discussion of 2 Thessalonians 2:1–8 that we need to take into account not only the Septuagint version, but also Theodotion's translation (Theod.). Although this dates from around A.D. 180, there are strong grounds for thinking, not least in the case of Daniel, that it is based on an earlier version that was known in the New Testament period.[7] We will not attempt here to resolve the uncertainties that exist, but some flexibility will be required in the way in which the dependencies and interconnections are explored. Unless otherwise indicated, the English Standard Version (ESV) has been used for biblical quotations.

The book of Daniel begins with an account of how the Lord gave Jehoiakim, king of Judah, into the hands of Nebuchadnezzar, king of Babylon, how vessels from the Jerusalem temple were installed in the pagan temple in Shinar, and how a number of young high-ranking Jews were taken to serve and be educated in Nebuchadnezzar's palace. Among these well-endowed youths were Daniel, Hananiah, Mishael, and Azariah of the tribe of Judah (Dan. 1:1–7). Chapters 1 to 6 relate a number of incidents that illustrate the determination of Daniel and his friends to perform their duties and demonstrate loyalty to the king (first Nebuchadnezzar, then his son Belshazzar, then

---

[7] See J. J. Collins, *Daniel* (Minneapolis: Fortress Press, 1993), 10–11. Aus notes expressions in 2 Thess. 2 that are closer to the Hebrew OT than to the LXX (R. D. Aus, "God's Plan and God's Power: Isaiah 66 and the Restraining Factors of 2 Thess. 2:6–7," *JBL* 96.4 (1977), 541–44); also J. T. Townsend, "II Thessalonians 2:3–12," *SBLSP* 19, (1980), 234–35; C. A. Wanamaker, *Commentary on 1 & 2 Thessalonians* (Grand Rapids: Eerdmans; Exeter: Paternoster, 1990), 245. See generally J. E. Goldingay, *Daniel* (Dallas: Word, 1987), xxvi–xxvii; M. Silva, "Old Testament in Paul," in G. F. Hawthorne, R. P. Martin and D. G. Reid, *Dictionary of Paul and His Letters* (Downers Grove/Leicester: nterVarsity Press, 1993), 630–42; J. Barr, "Paul and the LXX: A Note on Some Recent Work," *JTS* 45.2 (1994), 593–601; C. D. Stanley, *Paul and the Language of Scripture* (Cambridge: CUP, 1992), 252–64.

Darius the Mede) without compromising their religious identity as Jews, even at risk of death. In the process we discover that Daniel is exceptionally gifted in the interpretation of dreams and visions (cf. 1:17, 20). A key theme that emerges from the royal dreams that he decodes is that at some point in the future the Most High God, who is sovereign over the kings of the earth, will "set up a kingdom that shall never be destroyed, nor shall the kingdom be left to another people" (2:44; cf. 3:29; 4:2–3, 34–35; 5:21, 26; 6:26–27).

The second part of the book develops this theme. Three visions that come to Daniel while he is in Babylon describe a future political-religious crisis that will threaten the people of Israel. In the first vision four terrifying beasts come from the sea; a little horn on the head of the fourth beast makes war against the holy ones of the Most High; but judgment is given in favor of the oppressed people and the fourth beast is destroyed (Dan. 7). In the second vision a he-goat defeats a ram in battle, and then a little horn on its head becomes exceedingly arrogant, destroys the people of the saints, and brings about the desolation of the temple of God; the ram is said to represent the kings of Media and Persia, the he-goat the king of Greece (Dan. 8).

The appearance of the little horn at the "time of the end" (cf. 8:19) comes as the climax to a period of "wrath" against Israel that stretches back to the Babylonian exile (8:19; 9:16, 24–26). Having read in the prophet Jeremiah that the devastation of Jerusalem would last for seventy years (cf. Jer. 25:11–12; 29:10), Daniel confesses the sins of the people (9:4–15) and prays that God's anger may be turned away from Jerusalem (9:16): "we do not present our pleas before you because of our righteousness, but because of your great mercy" (9:18). Jeremiah's period of seventy years is converted by Daniel into a longer period of seventy weeks of years, or 490 years – a good example of how prophecy may be extended and reapplied. This, according to the angel Gabriel, is the time decreed for Israel and Jerusalem "to finish the transgression, to put an end to sin, and to atone for iniquity, to bring in everlasting righteousness, to seal both vision and prophet, and to anoint a most holy place" (9:24). It is during the last week of this period that a foreign ruler will bring devastation on the people and on Jerusalem (9:26).

In the third vision, an angelic figure appears to Daniel and reveals to him "what is inscribed in the book of truth" (10:21). What follows is a lengthy and detailed account of the political game played by the kings of Persia, Greece, Egypt, and Rome that will culminate in the crisis depicted in the first two visions. Eventually a king from the north – the "little horn" of the first two visions – will set his heart "against the holy covenant" (11:28). His forces will desecrate the temple, removing the continual burnt offering and setting up the "abomination that makes desolate" (11:31). He will "speak astonishing things against the God of gods" (11:36). At "the time of the end" he will invade the "glorious land"; tens of thousands will fall (11:40–41); it will be a time of unprecedented trouble for the people of Israel (12:1). Some of the Jews will be seduced by this blasphemous intruder and will abandon the covenant (11:30, 32; cf. 9:27). Their fate will be "shame and everlasting contempt" (12:2). Others, however, will remain faithful to their God and will stand firm against the slide into apostasy. The angel calls them the "wise": they will give understanding to many, they will lead many to righteousness (11:33; 12:3). They will be persecuted for their intransigence, but as a result they will be "refined, purified, and made white" (11:35), so that in the end they will "shine like the brightness of the sky above . . . like the stars forever and ever" (12:3). These are the oppressed saints of the Most High who will be vindicated and who will receive the kingdom when "one like a son of man" is presented before the Ancient of Days (7:13).

Within the frame of reference of Daniel's prophecy this last king from the north is the Syrian Antiochus IV, who invaded Judea in 168 B.C. and set about a comprehensive program of Hellenization, which included the reconstitution of Jerusalem as a Greek city with the name Antioch. The contrast between the two groups is reflected clearly in the Maccabean writings. There were the "lawless men" (*paranomoi*), who at the time of Antiochus' accession "came forth from Israel and misled many" by advocating a "covenant" with the Gentiles (1 Macc. 1:11 RSV). Having received authorization from Antiochus to observe Gentile practices, they "built a gymnasium in Jerusalem . . . and removed the marks of circumcision, and abandoned the holy covenant" (1:14–15 RSV). But there were also those in Israel who "stood firm": "They chose to die rather than to be defiled by food or to profane the holy covenant; and they did die. And very great wrath came upon Israel" (1 Macc. 1:63–64 RSV). This was the great contest through which victory was won over tyranny and evil (4 Macc. 16:16–19; 17:11–15).

It is no coincidence, then, that it is the angel Gabriel who appears to Mary and announces that she will bear a son who will be called "the Son of the Most High," who will "reign over the house of Jacob forever, and of his kingdom there will be no end" (Luke 1:32–33). The stage is set for some sort of enactment, or reenactment, of Daniel's prophetic narrative.

Eschatology and an Emerging Church

Before the curtain goes up, however, we need to offer some justification for what may seem a rather presumptuous claim: that what we have presented here is a contribution to the development of an "eschatology for an emerging church." There is undoubtedly a far-reaching re-evaluation of what it means to be church currently under way in the West. Whether "emerging church" is the best label for that layer of the church that is engaged most consciously in this process (or for any new consensus that may arise from it) is not important. There is an undercurrent of dissatisfaction with what is increasingly felt to be an outmoded paradigm and a sense that something new is slowly coming to birth that not only is more congenial to a *post*-modern mentality but also – much to our surprise – may have a better claim to be biblical. This book is in different ways self-consciously both a product of this process and an attempt to give some form and direction to it. It is probably already clear enough that it owes much to the achievement of N. T. Wright (and others) in rethinking the historical origins of Christianity. But it has also been motivated by a sense that what his work has done is provide access to an unfamiliar territory that has massive implications for how we understand the New Testament and ourselves as the church. This study is an expedition – perhaps a rather headstrong and impulsive expedition – into that territory.

Having said that, in its attention to exegetical detail this will no doubt appear to be a rather lumbering and pedantic adventure to many postmoderns, who generally prefer their truth to be pithy, laconic, playful, and salted with irony. But at its heart there is a concern to tell a story that should resonate with the emerging church's interest in more dynamic and versatile structures of knowledge. Stories are inexact, inventive vehicles of information and understanding: they invite retelling, the participation of communities; they invite interpretation, but they are too volatile to be pinned down. Ancient stories in particular may require careful and disciplined interpretation, but if this dispels the sense of wonder in the telling, the extraordinary power of narrative and argument to create meaning out of nothing, to make things appear in the darkness of the future, then too high a price has been paid.

We are also looking for a reading of New Testament eschatology that flies close to the surface of history – not because the past is more important than the present, or because the worldly is more important than the supernatural, but because real human experience is at all times more important than abstract theology. It is fundamentally a matter of theological integrity that we take seriously the outlook of the authors of the New Testament, even if that means restricting, or at least redefining, our own interest in their view of the future. Built into this respect for the contingency of New Testament teaching is a resistance to the universalizing tendency of modernism. We have become too accustomed to speaking in abstractions; we have lost touch with reality. So now we are learning to make truth difficult for ourselves by going back to the restricted, short-sighted, uncertain vision that struggled to bring it to light. Once we have done this, once we have recovered a sense of how distant and alien the story is, we will be in a position to make it simple again and retell it for ourselves, for our communities, for the world.

Finally, I hope that as we come to understand differently – and I think more exactly – how the future appeared to the early followers of Jesus, we will also understand more clearly what it means to be the people of God. I want to argue very strongly that eschatology is not irrelevant to the present existence of the church. On the contrary, it is definitive for it. Classic evangelical definitions of the church have tended to look to static New Testament models such as "temple," "body," "vine." An emerging church, however, will come to understand itself much more as the product of a narrative – one which stretches back to Abraham, and which runs right through the heart of the crisis of judgment and renewal that we call New Testament eschatology, the birth pains of the new age, the vindication of an exceptional vision. Within this narrative I think that we will then find a grounding for the sort of earthy, holistic, creational notions of community, spirituality, and mission that characterize the thinking of the emerging church. There is undoubtedly an important "escapist" element to New Testament eschatology, which needs to be understood properly; there is also a highly resilient hopefulness for the whole of creation. But the main thrust is not to lure us away from the world with the hope of heaven but to refocus the question of the very existence and purpose of a "people of God" in the world.

Two

A Voice Against Jerusalem

The war against Rome began in A.D. 66. Four years earlier a man called Jesus, the son of Ananus – one of the rural peasantry, as Josephus describes him – had come to Jerusalem during the feast of tabernacles (*J.W.* 6.5.3 §300–309).[1] At a time of relative peace and prosperity in Judea the words that he proclaimed day and night through the streets of the city – much like the modern prophet of doom with his sandwich board and megaphone, wandering up and down Regent Street or Madison Avenue – seemed uncomfortably out of place: "A voice from the east, a voice from the west, a voice from the four winds; a voice against Jerusalem and the sanctuary, a voice against the bridegroom and the bride, a voice against all the people!" Bothered by his antisocial attitude, some of the leading citizens had him arrested and flogged. When this failed to drive the demon from him, they dragged him before the Roman procurator, Albinus, who could only recommend a more vigorous application of the same remedy. As each stroke stripped the flesh from his body, the poor wretch made no complaint but cried out repeatedly in a piteous voice, "Woe to Jerusalem!" In the end Albinus dismissed him as a madman.

For another seven-and-a-half years this prescient misfit wandered the streets, answering both charity and physical

---

[1] See also Fredriksen, *Jesus of Nazareth*, 228; E. P. Sanders, *The Historical Figure of Jesus* (London: Penguin, 1993), 267; B. D. Ehrman, *Jesus: Apocalyptic Prophet of the New Millennium* (Oxford/New York: Oxford University Press, 1999), 158–59.

abuse with his familiar dismal refrain, until in the end the Romans laid siege to the city and inadvertently silenced him. He was prowling one day along the city wall, crying, "Woe once more to the city and to the people and to the temple." Suddenly his lament changed: "and woe to me also." At that moment, we are told, a stone from one of the siege engines struck him and he was killed.

The story of Jesus, son of Ananus, is an uncanny transposition of the story of Jesus, son (as was believed) of Joseph: an outsider publicly warns of a catastrophic disaster that is about to come upon Jerusalem and the temple, is arrested by the Jewish authorities, is beaten, passed on to the Roman overlord who dismisses him as an innocent fool, and in the end is killed by the callous instrumentality of Rome.[2] There is no reason to think that the parallel is in any way contrived, but it is certainly instructive. Viewed through the disturbing filter of the story of Jesus son of Ananus, the career of Jesus of Nazareth stands out in stark and intriguing relief.

When Will These Things Be?

From its inception, the messianic movement that centered on Jesus of Nazareth was oriented towards certain critical future events. John the Baptist set the eschatological alarm bells ringing out in the desert regions of Judea with his announcement that God would soon intervene decisively in the internal affairs of the nation of Israel: the kingdom of God was at hand, the ax was already laid to the root of the trees, and one was coming who would baptize with the Holy Spirit and with fire. These three simple predictions constitute, in fact, a concise digest of the gospel of Jesus – a framework into which much of his teaching can be easily slotted. But they also set boundaries to it; they draw the eschatological horizon within which it becomes meaningful.[3]

---

[2] Note also the prediction of Rabbi Johanan ben Zakkai, a contemporary of Jesus, in B. Yoma 39b (see M. D. Hooker, *The Gospel according to Mark* [London: A & C Black, 1991], 304).

[3] Cf. Wright, *Victory*, 322–23.

This orientation towards the future runs right through the Gospels. Jesus does not simply teach people how to live; he teaches them how to live *in the light of what was about to happen*. For example, he answers the disciples' question about fasting with reference to the days to come when "the bridegroom is taken away" (Luke 5:35). The wisdom of building one's house on the rock rather than on the sand only becomes apparent when eventually a storm comes (Matt. 7:24–27). The kingdom of God is like seed scattered on the ground that grows, produces fruit, and then is harvested (Mark 4:26–29). Blessed are those servants whom the master finds awake when he returns from the marriage feast (Luke 12:37). The disciples are entrusted with the task of preaching the good news of the kingdom throughout the towns and villages of Israel, but they will not have time to complete the task before the Son of Man comes (Matt. 10:23). This pattern reaches a climax in a section of teaching given in Jerusalem a few days before his death commonly known as his "apocalyptic discourse." The immediate occasion for the discourse, and in effect the logical starting point for apocalyptic in the New Testament, emerges in two questions put to Jesus by the disciples: "Tell us, when will these things be, and what will be the sign when all these things are about to be accomplished?" (Mark 13:4).

According to the traditional reading of the prophetic narrative that follows, these are questions about *our* future. We imagine that in response Jesus discloses or *unveils* – that is the etymology of "apocalypse," an unveiling – the sequence of events that will signal the end of all things, the termination of cosmic history. If he was also thinking of events that would take place in Judea in the first century, these would serve only as a historical foreshadowing or partial fulfillment of the greater apocalyptic end-game that still awaits us. This is our perspective as we look down the wrong end of the telescope of history. But the questions put by the disciples are not *our* questions. Jesus is not – on the face of it – addressing the concerns of a later Gentile church impatient for, or skeptical about, the second coming. If we allow the historical dimension to be collapsed in this way, we risk severely damaging the delicate tissue of significance that connects the discourse with the actual historical circumstances that it both presupposes and predicts. The narrative setting in the Gospels must be taken seriously. It is not merely an inconsequential literary device, a pretext for a universal homily that rapidly abandons the outlook and interests of the earliest communities of believers – any more than World War II was a pretext for Churchill to offer abstract reflections on the need to "wage war against a monstrous tyranny, never surpassed in the dark, lamentable catalogue of human crime."[4]

As Mark tells the story, Jesus is seated on the Mount of Olives[5] with four of the disciples – Peter, James, John, and Andrew – who have approached him privately, troubled by some remarks that he had made earlier as they were leaving the temple (Mark 13:3; cf. Matt. 24:3).[6] One of the disciples – with the earnest enthusiasm of a sightseer from the provinces – had marveled at the splendor of this monument to Herod's megalomania. But Jesus' response had been abrupt and shocking: "Do you see these great buildings? There will not be left here one stone upon another that will not be thrown down" (Mark 13:2).[7]

The anger, though startling, is not unmotivated. Jesus

---

[4] In his first speech as Prime Minister, May 13, 1940, to the House of Commons.

[5] Note Zech. 14:4. Cf. Wright, *Victory*, 344–45.

[6] Luke appears to have Jesus give this teaching in the temple, directly following on from his dispute with the scribes and chief priests (Luke 21:5, 37).

[7] In Matthew the question is phrased rather differently (Matt. 24:3). The destruction of the temple is regarded, whether by the disciples or by Matthew, not merely as a historical event but as an event with eschatological significance. It is linked at the start with the *parousia* of an absent Jesus and the end of the age. The basis for this is probably to be found in 23:37–39, where the pronouncement of judgment upon Jerusalem for having rejected God's prophets and spurning Jesus' compassion is followed by the affirmation: "you will not see me again until you say, 'Blessed is he who comes in the name of the Lord.'"

appears to have spent the whole of that day in the courts of the temple, teaching the people and debating with the temple authorities, the chief priests, and others who regarded him as a threat to the established order. A story that he told about some tenants who managed a vineyard for an absent landlord was a barely disguised denunciation of the leaders of the nation – those to whom care of the vineyard of Israel had been entrusted by God (Mark 12:1–12; Matt. 21:33–46; Luke 20:9–19). The point of the story was certainly not lost on the chief priests and the scribes, who would have arrested him had they not feared the reaction of the crowd. Matthew includes two other parables in this context, both of which underline the failure of these leaders to respond appropriately to the demands of the kingdom of God: they are like the son who told his father that he would work in the vineyard and then failed to go (Matt. 21:28–32); they are like guests invited to a royal marriage feast who, when everything is prepared, refuse to come because they have their own business to attend to (Matt. 22:1–14). These men sit on Moses' seat, Jesus told the crowds; they are teachers of the law of God, "so practice and observe whatever they tell you" – but they are hypocrites, their lives are not worthy of imitation (Matt. 23:2–3). The kingdom of heaven is given not to those who seek status and public acclaim but to those who make themselves least; those who exalt themselves will be humbled (23:5–12).

Then, according to Matthew, Jesus pronounces an angry litany of "woes" upon the scribes and Pharisees, culminating in the accusation, already prefigured in the parable of the vineyard, that they had aligned themselves not with the righteous but with those who throughout Israel's history murdered the prophets. There is an echo of John the Baptist's virulent indictment: "You serpents, you brood of vipers, how are you to escape being sentenced to *geenna*?" (Matt. 23:33; cf. 3:7). Jesus knew – and the foreknowledge, even if not quite unique, is extraordinary[8] – that the current

[8] Cf. N. T. Wright, "Jerusalem in the New Testament," in P. W. L. Walker (ed.), *Jerusalem Past and Present in the Purposes of God* (Cambridge: Tyndale, 1992), 58–59.

generation would suffer the consequences of the nation's persistent and violent rejection of the prophets and wise men sent by God to call the people to righteousness.

The last word in the temple (Matt. 23:37–39[9]) is more elegiac, but conclusive nonetheless. Jesus would have gathered together the inhabitants of Jerusalem as a hen gathers her brood under her wing; but the earlier confrontations had confirmed that official Judaism was hardly ready to countenance such an outcome. The prospect instead, as Jesus saw things, was ruination: "see, your house is left to you desolate." Perhaps, as R. T. France suggests, the journey that Jesus makes from the temple to this mountain east of the city was a deliberate reenactment of the departure of the glory of the Lord from the temple, leaving it for destruction, in Ezekiel 11:22–23.[10] How and when this would come about, what impact it would have on the disciples and the preaching of the gospel, and what it implied for the position of Jesus himself as Messiah, become the subject of his teaching shortly after on the Mount of Olives.

The Structure of the Discourse

The discourse can be divided into four main narrative sections, to which are added some general exhortations and, in Matthew's Gospel, a number of parables relating to readiness and judgment. The three versions of the discourse have much of their material in common but diverge quite significantly at certain points. Luke, for example, inserts a large section of the teaching at an earlier juncture while Jesus is on his way to Jerusalem, as a reaction to a question about the coming of the kingdom of God put to him by the Pharisees (Luke 17:20–37). In Luke,

---

9 Luke has Jesus utter this paragraph on the journey to Jerusalem but in a similar thematic context (Luke 13:31–35).

10 R. T. France, *The Gospel of Mark* (Grand Rapids/Carlisle: Eerdmans/Paternoster, 2002), 507.

too, the apocalyptic tone is less strident than in Mark and Matthew, and the language runs closer to the track of realistic historical narrative. These differences do not prevent us from constructing a reasonably coherent composite text – they are mostly a matter of omission or rearrangement rather than of contradiction. But we have no way of knowing how closely such a synthetic discourse would correspond to the words that Jesus actually spoke on the Mount of Olives on that occasion. At one level this is a simple literary dilemma: how do we reconstruct the original speech from these three divergent transcriptions? At another level it becomes a more disconcerting historical problem: to what extent is this "discourse" to be regarded not as a more or less veracious record of Jesus' teaching about the future, but as the product of hindsight? Many scholars would argue that the prophecy about the invasion of Judea and the destruction of the temple must have been fabricated by the evangelists after A.D. 70.[11]

These are important questions and should not be carelessly dismissed. Our aim, however, is the more straightforward one of determining what the Jesus of the Gospels might have meant *if* he had indeed spoken this composite apocalyptic discourse to a small group of his disciples shortly before his arrest. There is an evangelical preference built into this method, but at the same time we freely admit that the texts present literary and historical difficulties that invite a more cautious and critical evaluation. This is a limbo between the urge to believe and rigorous historical method into which we cannot help falling.[12]

The historical fulcrum upon which the vision is levered is the destruction of the temple and the devastation of the city by the armies of Titus in A.D. 70. The prophecy of this event forms the third part of the discourse. If we are to grasp the scope and significance of what Jesus is saying, this

---

[11] See discussions in Fredriksen, *Jesus of Nazareth*, 225–32; Wright, *Victory*, 340, 348–49.

[12] In the same way we will assume the integrity of the Pauline corpus, recognizing that for scholarship this is a much-contested assumption.

circumstance must be kept firmly in view.[13] The events of the first two sections should be ascribed to the years preceding this crisis – at least, we are given no reason to believe that any of this is expected to take place *after* the fall of Jerusalem. The fourth section, which we will come to in the next chapter, describes the coming of the Son of Man on the clouds of heaven. This will be the most difficult part of the discourse to resolve, but it cannot be prized away from the historical frame of the narrative simply because Christ has not yet apparently come again – this is precisely the *weight* that is levered against the central historical event. If we are to take the organization of Jesus' teaching seriously, we must allow the Roman invasion of Judea and its outcome to make sense of the prophecy about the Son of Man.

The Beginning of the Birth Pains

The first section (Mark 13:5–8; Luke 21:8–11; Matt. 24:4–8) speaks of certain occurrences that will constitute the beginning of the "birth pains." On the one hand, false messiahs will appear and will mislead many of the Jews; the disciples should take care, therefore, lest they also be deceived. On the other hand, they should not be alarmed by the threat of wars, by natural disasters such as earthquakes and famines, or by "terrors and great signs from heaven" (Luke 21:11). These "birth pains," as elsewhere in Jewish apocalyptic literature, refer to the period of upheaval and affliction that is expected to accompany the onset of divine judgment (e.g., Isa. 13:7–9; Jer. 22:23; 48:40–42; 49:22; Micah 4:9–10) or the inauguration of the messianic age (e.g., 1 Enoch 62:4; 4 Ezra 4:42).[14] In the framework of Jesus' discourse,

---

[13] Cf. K. E. Brower, "'Let the Reader Understand': Temple and Eschatology in Mark," in K. E. Brower and M. W. Elliott (eds.), *"The Reader Must Understand": Eschatology in Bible and Theology* (Leicester: IVP, 1997), 140, quoting Geddert: "Mark 13 is an anti-temple speech; it is not a speech introduced by a few unimportant references to the temple and then proceeding with total disregard for the temple and its fate."

[14] See N. T. Wright, *The New Testament and the People of God* (London: SPCK, 1992), 277–78; Wright, *Victory*, 577–79.

they may be interpreted for the most part literally in terms of the turmoil and suffering associated with the Roman invasion of Judea. Many of the details can be paralleled in Josephus. He is especially scornful of the activities of religious imposters. For example, the Egyptian who led a crowd out to the Mount of Olives, claiming that the walls of Jerusalem would fall down at his command, was a "false prophet" (*J.W.* 2.13.5 §261–263; *Ant.* 20.8.6 §169–170; cf. Acts 21:38); many others deceived the people "under the pretense of divine inspiration" (*J.W.* 2.13.4 §259); and six thousand died when the last colonnade of the outer temple was burned, having been led on to the roof by a "false prophet" who had promised that they would receive "miraculous signs of their deliverance."[15] Rumors of the inexorable and brutal progress of Vespasian's armies through Galilee and into Judea would have reached the inhabitants of Jerusalem. And Josephus describes in horrific detail the extreme state of famine in Jerusalem during the siege, which in the end accounted for the deaths of 600,000 of the poor in the city (*J.W.* 5.13.7 §569; cf. 5.12.3).

Josephus also refers to marvelous signs that preceded the desolation: a star resembling a sword over the city, a bright light around the altar, a heifer that gave birth to a lamb in the temple, a temple gate that opened of its own accord, visions of heavenly armies (cf. 2 Macc. 5:2–3; *Sib. Or.* 3:796–808), a quaking and a great noise (*J.W.* 6.5.3 §288–300; cf. 4.4.5). A similar report is found in the account of the Roman historian Tacitus:

---

[15] See D. A. Hagner, *Matthew* (Dallas: Word, 1995), 690–91. There is no evidence that these men aspired to messianic status until the Bar Kokhba revolt in A.D. 135. Note also Tacitus' remarks: "Some few put a fearful meaning on these events, but in most there was a firm persuasion, that in the ancient records of their priests was contained a prediction of how at this very time the East was to grow powerful, and rulers, coming from Judaea, were to acquire universal empire. These mysterious prophecies had pointed to Vespasian and Titus, but the common people, with the usual blindness of ambition, had interpreted these mighty destinies of themselves, and could not be brought even by disasters to believe the truth" (Tacitus, *Hist.* 5.13).

> Prodigies had occurred, which this nation, prone to superstition, but hating all religious rites, did not deem it lawful to expiate by offering and sacrifice. There had been seen hosts joining battle in the skies, the fiery gleam of arms, the temple illuminated by a sudden radiance from the clouds. The doors of the inner shrine were suddenly thrown open, and a voice of more than mortal tone was heard to cry that the Gods were departing. At the same instant there was a mighty stir as of departure. (Tacitus, *Hist*. 5.13)

Whether or not we regard these reports as being in any way credible, it is evident that supernatural signs, including signs in the heavens, were regarded as fitting portents of such events.

Jesus' language, however, also evokes earlier visions of divine intervention, especially Nebuchadnezzar's invasion of Judah in 588–587 B.C. to crush a misguided rebellion against Babylonian rule. In Jeremiah 10:22 LXX, for example, the warning is given: "behold, there comes a rumor of a noise (*phōnē akoēs*) and a great earthquake (*seismos*) from a northern country, to appoint the cities of Judah for destruction and to be a bedding-place of ostriches."[16] And the prophet is told that the people "shall be cast out in the streets of Jerusalem, victims of famine and sword" (Jer. 14:16). Such echoes suggest that these imagistic details serve a dual purpose: both to depict the actual nature of the disaster and to bring into view, through allusion to the prophetic interpretation of analogous events in the past, the eschatological significance of the political crisis. How we differentiate between the two entails a difficult interpretive judgment, which we will address in Chapter 3. But the effect of the conventional apocalyptic imagery is to set the coming crisis on a par with the Babylonian invasion in terms of its theological and covenantal significance. What

---

[16] All translations from the LXX, unless otherwise indicated, are mine. Cf. Jer. 23:19 LXX; Isa. 29:6, though in this instance the destructive force is directed against Israel's enemies (cf. Ezek. 38:19). The rumor or report of impending catastrophe is also found in Jer. 4:16; 6:24; 10:22; 27:43 LXX; 30:8 LXX; 30:29 LXX; Hos. 7:12; Obad. 1:1–2.

we have, then, is a quite deliberate reorientation of Old Testament eschatology towards a new, and as yet unrealized, state of affairs. This, essentially, is how metaphorical language *recasts* or *redescribes* its referent: the Roman invasion of Judea, when eventually it takes place, should be *seen as*, or interpreted in terms of, the Babylonian invasion. In this way, the net of salvation history is thrown out into darker waters: not only Israel's past but also Israel's future must be brought within the reach of divine purpose.

Harassment of the Disciples

In the second part of this narrative (Mark 13:9–13; Luke 21:12–19; Matt. 24:9–14) Jesus tells the disciples what they can expect to face on a more personal level in the period leading up to the destruction of Jerusalem.[17] They will not be merely passive victims in all of this; they have been appointed to proclaim the good news of the kingdom of God, and this will inevitably provoke opposition. They will be arrested and brought before both Jewish and Gentile authorities on account of their allegiance to Jesus, in many instances having been betrayed by their own families and friends (Mark 13:12; Luke 21:16; Matt. 24:10–12).[18] The outcome will be beatings, imprisonment, and, for some, death (Mark 13:9; Luke 21:12; Matt. 24:9; cf. 10:17–18); and they will be hated by all nations (Mark 13:13; Luke 21:17; Matt. 24:9). But their arraignment will also be an opportunity to speak about what they have seen; and the effectiveness of their testimony will lie in the fact that their

[17] The same teaching is found in Matt. 10:17–23. The disciples are told that they "will not have gone through the cities of Israel before the Son of Man comes" (10:23). The teaching generally in this chapter, with its emphasis on the threat of conflict (10:34–39) and the assurance of divine care (10:26–31), relates to the circumstances of the church in Judea prior to A.D. 70.

[18] Cf. Micah 7:6, which "speaks of judgment coming upon Israel and the need to wait patiently for YHWH's deliverance" (Wright, *Victory*, 347).

words will not be premeditated but will have the spontaneity and power of divine utterance (Mark 13:11; Luke 21:13–15). This will be concrete evidence, at a time when it matters most, that the Spirit of Jesus is with them. As a result of this persecution, the faith of the church will be shaken; false prophets will cause confusion and "the love of many will grow cold" (Matt. 24:11–12). The disciple, however, who does not succumb but remains faithful, who "endures to the end" (Mark 13:13; Matt. 24:13) in the face of rejection by the Jews and hatred from the Gentiles, will be saved – as Luke puts it, he will gain his life (Luke 21:19).

Let us remind ourselves of the historical context. The "end" in view here is specifically the end of the period of suffering associated with the judgment upon Israel and the coming of the Son of Man (cf. Matt. 10:22–23): it is the end of the tribulation whose beginning is described in Matthew 24:8 (cf. Mark 13:8).[19] The possibility that the sufferings might end in death is certainly envisaged, but to be "saved," for these Jewish disciples of Jesus, meant in the first place to escape the very worldly and bloody fate that was to befall the rest of the people. The assurance that Jesus gives, therefore, has to do not primarily with attaining a post-mortem salvation – his concern is that they should not be swept into oblivion by the political catastrophe which he predicted.

This period of turmoil will not reach its climax, however, until the gospel has been preached "throughout the whole world as a testimony to all nations" (Matt. 24:14; cf. Mark 13:10). The preaching of the gospel to all the nations has often been taken as a goal for the church today and as a means of hastening the return of Christ: the sooner we get the work finished, the sooner he will come and take us into his kingdom. In the context of Jesus' discourse, however, this accomplishment is made part of the nexus of events associated with the persecution of the Jewish church and the invasion of Judea. This is especially clear in Mark 13:10,

---

[19] Cf. 4 Ezra 6:25; 7:27; Dan. 12:12 Theod.

which connects the preaching of the gospel to "all nations" with the witness of the disciples "before governors and kings." The reason for the urgency, therefore, is probably quite pragmatic – that the gospel should be internationalized and the church established beyond the boundaries of Israel before the destruction of Jerusalem and the dispersal of the disciples in Judea.[20] Jesus is anxious that the church should not go down with the sinking ship – a metaphor, ironically, that Josephus uses to describe the desertion of Jerusalem by its eminent citizens (*J.W.* 2.20.1 §556). This makes good historical sense and provides a more credible rationale for the statement than the very artificial idea that the end of the world will be triggered by the preaching of the gospel in the last nation on earth. As a stimulus to world mission today, this argument is altogether too contrived and gives too much weight to evangelism as a narrowly conceived and mechanical program.

The concern on Jesus' part for the well-being and "salvation" of the disciples during this period of upheaval in Judea has implications for the interpretation of other teachings in the Gospels which have usually been taken in a more generalized and universal sense. One example is the judgment of the sheep and the goats, which Matthew places at the end of the apocalyptic discourse (Matt. 25:31–46). We will examine this passage more closely in Chapter 4, but we may note in passing, at least, that judgment has to do with how people respond to the circumstances of "these my brothers" (25:40). The hardships envisaged are, in the first place, just those that the disciples could expect to face as they proclaimed this new and very controversial gospel (a "pernicious superstition" as Tacitus called it[21]) in the world. They would be hungry, thirsty, strangers, destitute, sick, and imprisoned – and very much dependent on the charity of others.

---

[20] Cf. France, *Mark*, 516–17.

[21] Tacitus, *Ann.* 15.44.

The same theme emerges in the parable of the dishonest steward (Luke 16:1–9). This story has always puzzled commentators because Jesus appears not only to commend the Machiavellian self-interest of "the sons of this world" but also to make "unrighteous wealth" a means of gaining entry to *tas aiōnious skēnas* ("the eternal dwellings" in 16:8–9). We could read this as irony,[22] but if Jesus has in mind the social and material hardships that the disciples will face in Israel's "last days," a more literal understanding seems appropriate: by making friends with the wealthy the disciples may make some provision for their material needs in times of insecurity. The chief difficulty with this reading lies in the expression *tas aiōnious skēnas* (16:9). The traditional interpretation of these words, however, is problematic: how will the *unrighteous* wealthy receive the disciples into "the eternal dwellings"? In view of the fact, therefore, that the wealthy are described as "the sons of this age" whereas the disciples are "sons of light," we should perhaps understand the expression as a reference to "the dwellings of *this* age" – in other words, the homes of the wealthy. This accords directly with the central point of the parable – that by his foresight the steward ensures that he will not be destitute and homeless when his present resources fail (16:4).

The plight of the disciples in these "last days" is also in view in the parable of the unjust judge in Luke 18:1–8. As the widow pleads with the judge to give her "justice against my adversary,"[23] so the disciples will cry out to God day and night for vindication against those who oppose and persecute them. The assurance given is that God will not delay but will "vindicate them quickly."[24] The parable immediately follows teaching about the coming of the kingdom of God and the judgment of a sinful generation in

---

[22] Cf. A. R. C. Leaney, *The Gospel According to St Luke* (London: A & C Black, 1966), 223.

[23] Cf. Isa. 41:11 LXX; Jer. 28:36 LXX. In 1 Pet. 5:8 Satan is the "accuser" (*ho antidikos*) of the brethren.

[24] Luke 18:7–8 (translation mine); cf. Sir. 35:12–20.

a manner analogous to the flood or the destruction of Sodom (17:20–37). It opens with a pointed reference to "a certain city" and concludes with a question: will the Son of Man find faith on earth when he comes? The story is told, therefore, not to a universal audience but to the few who had started down the narrow path that leads to life, who were about to enter the dark tunnel of Judaism's eschatological crisis, not knowing when – or even whether – they would emerge from the other end. It is not a general parable about prayer (although general lessons can certainly be drawn from it) but a parable about the vindication of Jesus' disciples.

The Jewish War

In the third part of the discourse we come to the heart of the judgment upon Israel (Mark 13:14–20; Luke 21:20–24; Matt. 24:15–22). Armies will encircle Jerusalem (Luke 21:20; cf. 19:43–44); and the "abomination of desolation" spoken about by the prophet Daniel will be set up in the holy place (Mark 13:14; Matt. 24:15; cf. Dan. 9:27; 11:31; 12:11). This cryptic and resonant phrase was imbued with horror for any first-century Jew. The allusion is to the erection of an altar to Zeus in the temple by Antiochus Epiphanes in 168 B.C., but this notorious event became for later generations the archetypal act of desecration, the inevitable culmination of religious failure.[25]

It is not difficult to find a fulfillment of Jesus' prophecy in the circumstances of A.D. 70. When the Romans finally broke into the temple, fire quickly spread through the buildings and colonnades. Titus had no desire to see the Holy Place destroyed and endeavored to have the flames put out. But one of the soldiers, driven by hatred of the Jews who still fought the Romans within the grounds of the temple, snatched up a flaming brand, climbed up on the back of another soldier, and tossed it through one of the golden apertures into the inner courtyard, setting fire to the

[25] See, e.g., 1 Macc. 1:54, 59.

rooms of the priests around the Holy Place. When Titus heard what had happened he ran to the scene, but he was powerless to prevent the frenzied troops from slaughtering the remaining Jews or from finally torching the sanctuary itself. It was the tenth of Loös, Josephus reports – the day on which, centuries before, Solomon's temple had been burned by the Babylonians. As the house of Israel's God was engulfed in flames, the Romans brought their standards into the temple area. They set them up opposite the East Gate and offered sacrifices to them, acclaiming Titus as *Imperator* (*J.W.* 6.4.1 – 6.6.1 §220–316).[26]

Josephus also saw the analogy between Antiochus' action and the Roman invasion: "And these misfortunes our nation did in fact come to experience under Antiochus Epiphanes, just as Daniel many years before saw and wrote that they would happen. In the same manner Daniel also wrote about the empire of the Romans and that Jerusalem would be taken by them and the temple laid waste" (*Ant.* 10.11.7 §276). He had a rather different perspective, however, on the manner in which Daniel's vision was fulfilled. In his view, it was not the Romans but, ironically, the Jewish rebels who committed the ultimate sacrilege: "For there was an ancient saying of inspired men that the city would be taken and the sanctuary burnt to the ground by right of war, whensoever it should be visited by sedition and native hands should be the first to defile God's sacred precincts. This saying the Zealots did not disbelieve; yet they lent themselves as instruments of its accomplishment" (*J.W.* 4.6.3 §388).

Some scholars have argued, therefore, that it was the barbaric and self-defeating activities of the Zealots, under John of Gischala, who occupied the temple area during the winter of A.D. 67–68, that constituted the appalling

[26] At this stage, of course, it was far too late for anyone to flee to the mountains. Hagner thinks, therefore, that the meaning is more general: "i.e., that the disciples should flee when events indicated that the desecration of the temple was inevitable" (Hagner, *Matthew*, 701).

[27] E.g., W. L. Lane, *The Gospel of Mark* (Grand Rapids: Eerdmans, 1974), 469; cf. France, *Mark*, 525.

sacrilege predicted by Jesus.[27] What especially upset the orthodox was the blasphemous presumption of the Zealots, who took it upon themselves to appoint a compliant high priest. A villager was chosen by lot, a man called Phanias, who was dressed up in the sacred vestments and taught to act the part. A former high priest, Ananus, complained bitterly at these events: "Truly well had it been for me to have died ere I had seen the house of God laden with such abominations and its unapproachable and hallowed places crowded with the feet of murderers" (*J.W.* 4.3.10 §163). No doubt any remaining Jewish Christians in the city would have shared his horror. Although it seems more likely that the "abomination of desolation" refers, albeit loosely, to the desecration of the temple by a Gentile power, we again see how well Jesus' prophecy matches the general circumstances of the Jewish War against Rome. Josephus is quite clear in his own mind that the Jews brought the disaster upon themselves (cf. *J.W.* 6.4.5 §250).

As these events unfold, the only hope for escape is to flee to the mountains, for this will be a time of retribution for Israel, a time of extreme affliction, when many Jews will fall by the sword or be taken into captivity.[28] The mountains were an obvious place of refuge. Ezekiel describes the wrath that will come upon Israel: "The sword is without; pestilence and famine are within. He who is in the field dies by the sword, and him who is in the city famine and pestilence devour." Any who manage to escape will be in the mountains, "all of them moaning, each one over his iniquity" (Ezek. 7:15–16). After Mattathias killed the royal official who sought to enforce the idolatrous decree of Antiochus – the incident that triggered the Maccabean revolt – he fled with his sons to the Judean hills,

---

[28] Josephus estimated that 97,000 were taken captive and 1,100,000 were killed during the siege (*J.W.* 6.9.3 §420).

[29] Wright sees in Jesus' words a deliberate allusion to the flight of Mattathias and his sons to the hills: "The way of loyalty was the way of flight. Such flight . . . would be undertaken with the intention of regrouping as a body, in order subsequently to be vindicated as the true people, indeed the true leaders" (Wright, *Victory*, 353).

leaving all that they had in the city (1 Macc. 2:28).[29] The only evidence that Jewish believers left Jerusalem before the war comes from the church historian Eusebius (ca. A.D. 260–340), who reports that they migrated to Pella in Perea, across the Jordan, in accordance with an "oracle" given to the church (Eusebius, *Hist. eccl.* 3.5.3). The historicity of this tradition has been disputed, but in general terms at least the story is credible.[30] We can imagine the disciples in Jerusalem and Judea reading the signs of impending national disaster without too much difficulty. Israel's house was left desolate. There was no point in staying.

At this point in the narrative, Jesus adds two comments regarding the duration of this state of affairs. First, there is the assurance that these "birth pains," though more appalling than anything that has gone before, will not last so long that the "elect" will not survive the catastrophe (Mark 13:19–20; Matt. 24:21–22). The thought is an echo of Daniel 12:1: "And there shall be a time of trouble, such as never has been since there was a nation till that time. But at that time your people shall be delivered, everyone whose name shall be found written in the book."[31] It is uncertain whether Jesus expected the "elect," for whose sake the days of affliction are cut short, to be among those who fled to the mountains or who had to endure the horrors of war in Judea.[32] The underlying concern, however, is clear: the survival of this vulnerable group of disciples in a period of indiscriminate, wholesale destruction. The language of unprecedented calamity, though apocalyptic in tone, is barely hyperbolic: Josephus was also of the opinion that "the misfortunes of all nations since the world began fall

---

[30] See J. Nolland, *Luke* (Dallas: Word, 1993), 985; Lane, *Mark*, 468, n. 79; B. van Elderen, "Early Christianity in Transjordan," *TynBul* 45.1 (1994), 104–109.

[31] Cf. Dan. 9:12. A similar formula is also found in Joel 2:2 with reference to the power of the army that comes against Zion.

[32] Cf. France, *Mark*, 522. Normally "all flesh" would have a universal reference, but in this context the phrase is undoubtedly restricted to those in Judea and Jerusalem (cf. Jer. 12:12).

short of those of the Jews" (*J.W.* Proem 4 §12; cf. 6.9.4 §429).[33] There is no reason, therefore, to think that Jesus now looks beyond the fate of Jerusalem to a global catastrophe at the end of all things. That the formula also has a future aspect ("and never will be") makes it clear that this "tribulation" at least will be an event in the midst of history, not at its climax.

Secondly, a limit is placed on the time that Jerusalem will be under foreign domination. The city, Jesus says, will be "trampled underfoot by the Gentiles, until the times of the Gentiles are fulfilled" (Luke 21:24) – an indefinite period of time that underscores the severity of the judgment.[34] The prophecy is realistic enough, but echoes of the Maccabean crisis are again especially strong. Daniel speaks of the "giving over of the sanctuary and host to be trampled underfoot" for a period of 2,300 evenings and mornings as a result of Antiochus' sacrilege (Dan. 8:12–14). In 1 Maccabees 3:45 we have a more graphic and concrete account of the city's devastation: "Jerusalem was uninhabited like a wilderness; not one of her children went in or out. The sanctuary was trampled down, and the sons of aliens held the citadel; it was a lodging place for the Gentiles" (RSV).[35] Jesus depicts the coming judgment as in some sense a repetition of the earlier, biblically interpreted disaster. Nothing is said about what will happen to Jerusalem following the fulfillment of the times of the Gentiles: this is beyond the horizon of Jesus' vision.

---

[33] The expression is a commonplace: Exod. 9:18; 10:14; 11:6; Joel 2:2; 1 Macc. 9:27; 1QM 1:11–12; *T. Mos.* 8.1; Rev. 16:18.

[34] Nolland takes *kairoi ethnōn* to refer to "the period for a judgment upon the gentile nations" (Nolland, *Luke*, 1002–3). Cf. Jer. 27:26 LXX. But note also 1 Chr. 29:30; Tob. 14:5; Acts 17:26; Eph. 1:10; 1 Tim. 2:6; 6:15. The *achri hou* clause serves only to mark the end of the period of Gentile domination. The idea of judgment on the nations is not required by the argument.

[35] Cf. Isa. 63:18; Dan. 9:26; 12:7; Zech. 12:3 LXX; 1 Macc. 3:51; 4:60; Tob. 14:5.

Looking for the Christ

The third section of the narrative concludes with a warning against being misled by false declarations about the presence of the Messiah (Mark 13:21–23; Matt. 24:23–26; cf. Luke 17:23). The fear, quite clearly, is that in a time of great suffering and confusion his followers might easily be persuaded to run after any prophet or demagogue brandishing the hope of salvation or escape. The fear was not unfounded. Both Menahem, son of Judas of Galilee, and Simon Bar-Giora presented themselves in Jerusalem during the course of the war as Israel's rightful king (*J.W.* 2.17.8 §433–438; 4.9.3–8 §503–544). Among the various "false prophets" whom Josephus denounced were those who promised an act of divine deliverance in order to keep the people from deserting the city during the war (*J.W.* 6.5.3 §285–286) – the contrast with Jesus' advice to flee Jerusalem at the onset of war is striking. Josephus comments: "In adversity man is quickly persuaded; but when the deceiver actually pictures release from prevailing horrors, then the sufferer wholly abandons himself to expectation" (§287).

What should alert the disciples most clearly to the spuriousness of such claims is the knowledge that the Christ, when he comes, will not be found in any *particular* location, whether out in the wilderness or in a private room. The *parousia* of the Son of Man, Jesus tells them, will not be spatially restricted in this way – as the presence of an individual in some place or other – but will be like lightning, which illuminates the whole sky (Matt. 24:27; Luke 17:24). This powerful image has usually been understood to describe the effulgence of Christ's bodily coming at the end of the age. The contrast, however, is not with the ordinariness of these imposters – after all, they will "perform great signs and wonders" – but with false announcements about a concrete, localized and embodied mode of being. A more careful reading of the simile suggests that it signifies the immaterial and universal nature of Christ's *presence*. The significance of the lightning is not so much that it is bright – though that is certainly a connotation – but that it "comes from the east and shines as far as the west."[36]

A similar contrast is made at the beginning of Luke's displaced apocalyptic discourse: the kingdom of God is said not to be a matter of physical observation, but is "in the midst of you" (Luke 17:21).[37] Jesus tells his disciples that they will long to see "one of the days of the Son of Man." But he will not be present in such a way that people will be able to point him out: "'Look, there!' or 'Look, here'" (17:23). "For as the lightning flashes and lights up the sky from one side to the other, so will the Son of Man be [in his day]" (17:24). What the form of the simile emphasizes is not the particular point at which the bolt travels from heaven to earth, the place of a physical descent, but the illumination of the *whole* sky. Again, it is the *extent* of the presence of the Son of Man that is at issue here. Jesus' argument directs the disciples' imagining away from the idea of a localized and material manifestation of the Son of Man to something global and intangible. How this "something" is to be understood will be the subject of Chapter 3.

At this point in the narrative, however, Matthew inserts an enigmatic remark about the vultures which gather around a corpse (Matt. 24:28). The saying is used in a non-figurative sense of the eagle's young in Job 39:30 LXX ("wherever the dead may be, immediately they are found") and may have been proverbial. In Luke it stands as a response to a question posed by the disciples regarding the whereabouts either of those who are taken or of those who

---

[36] Cf. B. Witherington, *Jesus, Paul and the End of the World* (Downers Grove: InterVarsity Press, 1992), 173. Lightning has a universal significance in *2 Bar.* 53:8–10; Ep. Jer. 60. There may also be some recollection of Ezekiel's account of the glory of the Lord returning to the temple (Ezek. 43:2). Elsewhere in the Old Testament lightning connotes the coming of the Lord to save the people and defeat Israel's enemies (e.g., Zech. 9:14). The biblical overtones suggest that the language is not simply descriptive but theological.

[37] For the meaning of *entos humōn* see Nolland, *Luke*, 853–54.

are left behind "on the day when the Son of Man is revealed" (Luke 17:30, 34–37) and would seem, therefore, to relate in general terms to the theme of judgment. This connection finds ready support in the Old Testament. Job: the ungodly man "has been appointed to be food for vultures, and he knows in himself that he exists as a carcass" (15:23 LXX). Jeremiah: on account of their idolatry "the dead bodies of this people" will become "food for the birds of the air . . ." (Jer. 7:33 LXX; cf. 15:3; 16:4; 19:7; 41:20). Habakkuk: the horsemen of the Chaldeans, recruited as instruments of divine judgment, "fly like an eagle swift to devour" (Hab. 1:8).

As Matthew has constructed the passage, however, the saying appears to be a comment on the manner of the *parousia* of the Son of Man; but the exact point of the analogy is hardly transparent. Strictly speaking, it is a statement about the location of the plural vultures rather than of the singular corpse – one should expect to find them where the body is – which perhaps suggests the reference is to the invading Roman army with their eagle standards (*aetos* can signify both an eagle and a vulture), or to believers who gather around the Son of Man, or even to the false Christs and false prophets mentioned in verses 24–26, who feed off the carcass of a spiritually corrupt people. It is unlikely, however, that the details are meant to be allegorized in this way. In the context of Jesus' discourse in Matthew, the saying simply reinforces the indeterminacy of the image of the lightning and the contrast with the false hope that the Messiah will be concretely, physically, present at a time of extreme need. The Son of Man will be found instead *wherever* there is that which attracts his presence: perhaps the community of believers, perhaps the people who are judged at the time of his *parousia* (cf. 24:37, 39), which brings us much closer to the use of the saying in Luke – and to the next part of the story.

Three

The Coming of the Son of Man

In the fourth section of Jesus' narrative (Mark 13:24–31; Luke 21:25–33; Matt. 24:29–35) the apocalyptic language intensifies and the question of what is actually being described becomes much more problematic. After the affliction there will be cosmic disturbances of a quite unnatural kind and terror upon the earth. The sun and the moon will be darkened; the stars will fall from the heavens, and the powers of the heavens will be shaken; on earth there will be great anxiety and fear among the nations at the prospect of what is to come (Mark 13:24–25; Luke 21:25–26; Matt. 24:29). The scope of the crisis has clearly expanded at this point to include both cosmic powers and the nations of the earth; and inevitably this presents the modern reader with a number of difficulties.

Signs in the Heavens

The first difficulty concerns the temporal relation between the escalation of the crisis and the preceding events. If the shaking of the heavens and the coming of the Son of Man were meant to follow on directly from the destruction of Jerusalem in A.D. 70, how is it that no one noticed? We can hardly avoid the conclusion that this is how the writers of the Gospels intended us to understand Jesus' narrative. Mark's phrase "in *those* days, after *that* tribulation," with its strong demonstrative pronouns, does not allow for an indefinite intervening period; and Matthew makes the reading quite unequivocal by adding "immediately."[1] The later statement that "this generation will not pass away until all these things take place" (Mark 13:30; cf. Luke 21:32; Matt. 24:34) also restricts the events described to a narrow time-frame.[2] In a similar statement in Matthew 10:23 Jesus tells the disciples, "you will not have gone through all the towns of Israel before the Son of Man comes." The "days of the Son of Man" – the day "when the Son of Man is revealed" – will be a time when judgment falls on a people too preoccupied with the mundane business of life to notice the storm clouds gathering on the horizon, a heaven loaded with fire and sulfur (Luke 17:26–32).

There is also an important thematic connection between what is said about the Son of Man coming in clouds and the preceding naturalistic account of the turmoil that will culminate in the Roman invasion. Jesus warns the disciples that people will encourage them to go *looking* for the Christ in this place or that, but these will only be false messiahs, false prophets (Mark 13:21–22). Verse 23 then begins with a strong adversative ("But (*alla*) in those days, after that tribulation . . ."), suggesting that we are meant to hear a deliberate correlation between *seeing* the false Christs with their "signs and wonders" and *seeing* the "Son of Man coming in clouds with great power and glory" (13:26).[3]

In order to preserve the traditional reading at this point the argument has sometimes been made that when Jesus says that "these things" (*tauta*) will take place within the lifetime of "this generation" (Mark 13:30), he is referring only to the events depicted in verses 5–23, which will precede the revelation of the Son of Man – that is, the sequence of events culminating in the besieging and

---

1 Hagner regards *euthōs* ("immediately") as a redactional insertion reflecting, in effect, a misunderstanding of Jesus' teaching about the *parousia* on the part of the disciples (Hagner, *Matthew*, 711–13).

2 See D. Wenham, *Paul: Follower of Jesus or Founder of Christianity?* (Grand Rapids/Cambridge: Eerdmans, 1995), 291, 295.

3 The contrast is even clearer in Matt. 24:26–27: do not go looking in the wilderness or inner rooms, *for* as the lightning comes from the east . . .

destruction of Jerusalem. Craig Blomberg, for example, thinks that "these things" in verse 30 must have the same referent as "these things" in verse 29, which expressly refers to events that *come before* the moment when "it is near, at the doors": "It makes no sense therefore for 'these things' to include Christ's actual return because then the parousia would no longer be simply near, close at hand; it would have arrived."[4] But there are difficulties with this line of reasoning. First, as France points out, "these things" in verse 30 constitutes an answer to the disciples' question in verse 4 regarding "when all these things are about to be accomplished," which is a question about the destruction of the temple.[5] Secondly, verse 30 refers not simply to "these things" but to "*all* these things," and one might suppose that the more emphatic and comprehensive form is meant to include the stupendous events described in verses 24–27. Thirdly, the argument of verses 28–29 is not simply that the events of verses 5–23 will occur before the climactic revelation of the Son of Man. Rather, they are signs of the *nearness* of this great dénouement. The appearance of leaves on the fig tree (13:28) does not mean that summer is *always* imminent but that it is imminent *at that moment*. This assurance of the nearness of the end corresponds to the statement in verse 20 that the period of suffering will be shortened for the sake of the elect. We cannot force a separation here: the revelation of the Son of Man marks the ending of the affliction; and in Paul it is precisely the event which brings the affliction to an end (cf. 2 Thess. 1:7; 2:8).

If this is the case, however, then we are faced with an age-old problem. Do we suppose that Jesus, like every apocalyptic fantasist before or since, was simply – and

---

[4] C. L. Blomberg, "Eschatology and the Church: Some New Testament Perspectives," in C. R. Trueman, T. J. Gray and C. L. Blomberg (eds.), *Solid Ground: 25 Years of Evangelical Theology* (Leicester: Inter-Varsity Press, 2000), 92, dependent on G. R. Beasley-Murray, *Jesus and the Last Days* (Peabody, MA: Hendrickson, 1993). Cf. Hagner, *Matthew*, 715; Witherington, *Jesus, Paul*, 42.

[5] France, *Mark*, 540.

tragically – deluded? Do we forcibly insert a delay into the apocalyptic timetable, clutching at the straw of Jesus' admitted ignorance about the precise hour or day (Mark 13:32; Matt. 24:36)? Or should we look for some other way of making sense of the close connection between the destruction of Jerusalem and the coming of the Son of Man?

The second difficulty is to know whether the crisis itself has become universal or whether these are merely the *effects* of the calamity that will come upon Israel. The language and imagery are drawn from the Old Testament. Similar disturbances presage divine judgment against Babylon (Isa. 13:9–11), Egypt (Ezek. 32:7–8), the nations generally (Isa. 24:21–23; 34:4; Joel 3:15–16; Hag.2:6–7; 21–22), and against Israel (Joel 2:10, 30–32). They are the garish neon signs on the highway of salvation history that mark the coming events as an act of God.[6] The "affliction" of Israel, however, would appear at this point to be finished, having been cut short for the sake of the elect: the desecration of the temple and the flight from Jerusalem have taken place, and Jerusalem is now trodden by the nations. An ensuing act of retribution against Rome would undoubtedly be accompanied by cosmic events of this nature; and the typical Old Testament pattern of judgment upon Israel followed by judgment upon Israel's enemy might lead us to expect this.[7] But in Jesus' narrative such a conclusion to the process is no more than implicit:[8] it is

---

[6] Cf. Brower, "Temple," 141; C. H. T. Fletcher-Louis, "The Destruction of the Temple and the Relativization of the Old Covenant: Mark 13:31 and Matthew 5:18," in Brower and Elliott, *"The Reader Must Understand,"* 147.

[7] Cf. Isa. 10; 13 – 14; 33; 47; Jer. 50 – 51; Dan. 9:26–27; Zech. 14. Also perhaps Ezek. 38; Hab. 1:1 – 2:3; *2 Bar*. 12:3–4.

[8] In Daniel's vision, the coming of the Son of Man follows on from the judgment on Israel's enemies. If the fourth beast is in any sense Rome, then the enthronement of the Son of Man presupposes the abrogation of Rome's "dominion." It seems unlikely that Jesus would have cast the Jerusalem hierarchy in the role of the fourth beast (against Wright, "Jerusalem," 61), not least because the Antiochus typology already allows for an unrighteous element within Israel which will collaborate with the enemy against the saints. The judgment of the sheep and the goats entails at least a limited judgment on the nations. We might also take the phrase "times of the Gentiles" in Luke 21:24 to refer to a period of judgment on Rome.

perhaps an indication of the finality of this judgment on Israel that there is no consequent destruction of her enemies and no restoration of peace. What the "signs" advertise then, instead, is that which is explicitly stated: the shaking of the powers of heaven, on the one hand, and the coming of the Son of Man, on the other. We look away from the affliction that will take place on earth as the judgment against Jerusalem reaches its climax, and we are shown the reordering of things that will take place in the heavens – a shake-up that will cause consternation on earth (and, according to Luke, rough seas) but, conspicuously, no destruction. The earth, as far as we can tell, continues to exist – buffeted, but otherwise intact.

The "powers in the heavens" appear to be spiritual forces associated with the heavenly bodies. They are represented in the Greek Old Testament and other Jewish writings as heavenly creatures subordinate to God, members of the divine entourage (cf. 2 Chr. 18:18; Ps. 33:6; *Odes Sol.* 16:14; Sir. 17:32); at times, however, Israel made the mistake of worshipping them (cf. 2 Kgs. 21:3, 5; 23:4, 5). Possibly we are meant to see here an allusion to the overturning of the old spiritual order – Paul, no doubt, would have attached much greater theological significance to these forces, recasting them perhaps as the "elementary principles of the world" by which humanity is enslaved (cf. Gal. 4:3; Col. 2:8, 20).[9] But Jesus refers to them only in passing. It is the coming of the Son of Man that constitutes the central climactic event, so alarmingly heralded by the apocalyptic hullabaloo. This will not be a matter of merely Jewish interest. Probably we are to think of it as having, literally or metaphorically, cosmic repercussions; but it will certainly have far-reaching implications for the "inhabited world" (*tēi oikoumenēi*: Luke 21:26).

The third difficulty concerns the nature of the language

---

[9] Luke, who rather dissociates the shaking of the powers of heaven from the visible "signs in sun and moon and stars," may be thinking along these lines.

used: how literally is it to be taken? Did either Jesus or the writers of the Gospels believe that people would actually see the sun and moon darkened and the stars falling from the sky? Did they imagine that there would really be panic across the world provoked by the fury of the sea and fear at what was about to hit the world? Or are these simply the idioms and conceits that the apocalyptic genre typically employs in order to disclose something of the eschatological meaning behind world events? This is the perennial dilemma of biblical interpretation and perhaps cannot be fully resolved. Metaphor, whatever form it takes, is inherently ambiguous. Although a writer may choose to indicate in some way whether or not a statement is metaphorical, he is not bound to do so.[10] Given a worldview that permits an almighty God to tamper with, and perhaps even decommission entirely, the machinery of cosmic history, it will always be logically possible to interpret the language of apocalyptic more or less literally.

One way to approach the question, however, would be to examine the Old Testament passages from which these images of cosmic turmoil appear to have been drawn.[11] If Jesus expected his hearers to recognize the allusions, it is reasonable – in the absence of any indications to the contrary – to suppose that he intended the language to be read in the same way. He was a Jewish prophet speaking like a Jewish prophet. In an oracle concerning Babylon Isaiah writes: "the stars of the heavens and their

---

[10] Luke is careful to diminish the literal force of the description and to draw attention to the underlying significance of the events: the cosmic disturbances are "signs" (cf. Ps. 65:8); people faint with fear and expectation of what is to come; it is not the physical earth that is affected but the "inhabited world," perhaps even specifically the Roman world; and the shaking of the powers of heaven is presented not simply as one further event but as an *explanation* (*gar*) for the turmoil.

[11] Cf. France, *Mark*, 531. Evans rejects this line of argument largely on the grounds that too many details in Mark 13:5–23 "do not fit the events between Pentecost and the Jewish revolt" (C. A. Evans, *Mark 8:27 – 16:20* [Nashville: Thomas Nelson, 2001], 328–29).

constellations will not give their light; the sun will be dark at its rising, and the moon will not shed its light" (Isa. 13:10). The Lord of hosts will summon an army "from the end of the heavens . . . to destroy the whole land" (13:4–5); sinners will be destroyed from the land (13:9); the heavens will tremble and the earth will be shaken (13:13). A massive catastrophe is envisaged, yet the earth is not destroyed. The agents of destruction are merely the armies of the Medes (13:17). Babylon, once the "glory of kingdoms," will be overthrown like Sodom and Gomorrah (13:19), but the uninhabited land will continue to exist (13:20–22). Similarly, Isaiah 34, a proclamation of God's anger against the nations and against Edom in particular, includes the predictions: "All the host of heaven shall rot away, and the skies roll up like a scroll. All their host shall fall, as leaves fall from the vine, like leaves falling from the fig tree" (34:4). But again the world is not destroyed, and in the end Edom is depicted as a wasteland overgrown with thorns and thistles, inhabited by wild animals.[12]

What the extravagant apocalyptic language suggests, in these instances, is that the impending national crisis is not an accident of history but the outworking of God's judgment in a manner precisely foreshadowed in the Old Testament. Perhaps behind this lies a polemic against paganism, whose manufactured gods cannot produce such signs (cf. Ep. Jer. 64–67; Jer. 10:2). Or the contrast may be with the "great signs and wonders" performed by the counterfeit saviors (Matt. 24:24). But there is more to it than this: these are *final* and irrevocable acts of judgment on the particular socio-political entity. The city or nation or régime that opposed the people of God does not simply suffer temporary harm; it ceases to exist, and in its place is a wasteland. The cosmic disorder is indicative of a fundamental disruption in the order of human society and

---

[12] Also Isa. 24:21–23; Ezek. 32:7–8: the destruction of Egypt by the king of Babylon is accompanied by darkness in the heavens.

a transition to a new state of affairs – the end of one age, the beginning of another.[13]

There are other texts, however, that apply the language of eschatological catastrophe not to the nations but to Israel, and these are likely to have a more direct bearing on the interpretation of this passage. While it is difficult to determine the intended historical reference of the events described in the book of Joel, the congruence of this vision of a coming Day of the Lord with early Christian understanding of the crisis facing Israel in the first century A.D. is clear and worth expounding – not least because it becomes less clear that Jesus depicts the destruction of Jerusalem in terms of Old Testament prophecies regarding the destruction of Babylon as has sometimes been argued.[14]

Joel warns of a Day of the Lord which will come "as destruction from the Almighty" (Joel 1:15). The Lord himself will lead a formidable army against Jerusalem, which will devastate the land like a swarm of locusts. "Before them peoples are in anguish; all faces grow pale . . . The earth quakes before them; the heavens tremble. The sun and the moon are darkened, and the stars withdraw their shining" (2:6, 10). Similar portents are said a few verses later to precede the coming of the "great and awesome day of the LORD" (2:30–31).[15] If the people repent and return to the Lord their God, then he will have pity on them and turn back the northern army (2:12–20). There will be a new sense of God's presence in Israel: "You shall know that I am in the midst of Israel, and that I am the LORD your God and there is none else. And my people shall never

---

[13] Cf. Lane, *Mark*, 475. The theoretical basis for this may lie in the belief that spiritual powers in the heavens correspond to political powers on earth. Cf. Judg. 5:19–20; Ps. 82; Isa. 24:21; Dan. 8:10; 10:13; 4 Ezra 5:5; but note the contrary thought of Wis. 13:1–3. See Goldingay, *Daniel*, 291–92.

[14] Against Wright, *Victory*, 340, 354–58; Wright, "Jerusalem," 61–2. The prevalence of the motif of God's people fleeing from Babylon before judgment comes upon the city (Isa. 48:20; 52:11–12; Jer. 50:6, 8, 28; 51:6–10, 45–46, 50–51, 57; Zech. 2:6–8; 14:5) may be significant.

[15] Cf. Isa. 5:30; Amos 8:9.

again be put to shame" (2:27). More importantly, God will pour out his Spirit on all flesh (2:28). In the face of impending catastrophe, "everyone who calls on the name of the LORD shall be saved. For in Mount Zion and in Jerusalem there shall be those who escape, as the LORD has said, and among the survivors shall be those whom the LORD calls" (2:32).

Whether directly or analogically, this prophetic narrative closely prefigures the crisis of salvation and judgment that confronted Israel, as it is interpreted in the New Testament. With John the Baptist there is a call to repentance. In the ministry of Jesus this appeal to the whole nation is superseded by the more narrowly focused task of gathering a group of disciples, a faithful remnant, "survivors . . . whom the LORD calls," who will invoke the name of the Lord and receive the Spirit of God. The nation then faces catastrophe, a "great and awesome day of the LORD," when a foreign army will besiege Jerusalem, bringing enormous suffering upon Israel and in the end demolishing the place of God's dwelling among his people.

In Joel's narrative, if we pursue the parallelism, it is in anticipation of this dreadful event that the heavens are shaken and the lights of heaven obliterated: the "great and awesome day of the LORD" is a day of devastation from which only a few escape (Joel 2:31–32). By quoting this text in his address to the astonished crowds on the day of Pentecost, Peter makes exactly the same connection between cosmic portents and national disaster: the indiscriminate outpouring of the Spirit upon Israel is in effect a sign of a coming "great and magnificent day," preceded by "wonders in the heavens above," from which the inhabitants of Jerusalem will be saved only by calling on the name of the Lord (Acts 2:17–21). In Jesus' discourse the focus is shifted away from the destruction of Jerusalem to the manifestation of the Son of Man, but there is perhaps the implication that these two events *coincide* symbolically. We should recall how in their original question to Jesus the disciples connect the *parousia* of Christ with the destruction of the temple (Matt. 24:3). The connection also appears in

John's Gospel, where Jesus claims that the Father has given the Son "authority to execute judgment, because he is the Son of Man" (John 5:27) – the vivid tableau of Daniel's vision is in the background. To make sense of this convergence we need to look carefully at the description of the "coming" of the Son of Man that follows.

The Coming of the Son of Man

The climax of the apocalyptic narrative depicts the coming of the Son of Man "in clouds with great power and glory" (Mark 13:26; Luke 21:27; Matt. 24:30). Matthew adds to this the appearance of "the sign of the Son of Man" in heaven, at which "all the tribes of the earth will mourn." This is a complex assemblage of Old Testament allusions: it may be more than the sum of its parts, but we cannot hope properly to understand its working without first discovering from where the various components have been borrowed.

The sign of the Son of Man in heaven

The raising of a sign and the blowing of a trumpet are conventional means by which an imminent action on God's part (the gathering of a scattered people or the mustering of an invading force) is advertised among the nations (cf. Isa. 18:3; 66:19; Jer. 28:27 LXX). In Isaiah 11:12 it is said that the "root of Jesse" – a Davidic messiah, on whom the Spirit of the Lord will rest – will raise up a signal for the nations and will "assemble the banished of Israel, and gather the dispersed of Judah from the four corners of the earth." The same connection appears in Matthew's version of the apocalyptic discourse: after the appearance of "the sign of the Son of Man" the angels are sent out to "gather his elect from the four winds, from one end of heaven to the other" (Matt. 24:31).[16] We will come back to this theme shortly.

[16] Note also Isa. 49:22. In Isa. 66:19–20 it is those who escape or are saved from the judgment who are sent to proclaim the Lord's glory among the nations and "bring all your brothers from all the nations as an offering to the Lord."

The question arises, however, as to what the "sign" might be. We can hardly doubt that the reference to the "Son of Man coming in clouds with great power and glory" (Mark 13:26) is meant to evoke Daniel's vision at night of "one like a son of man" coming with the clouds of heaven, who approaches the "Ancient of Days" – a periphrasis for God – and is given "dominion and glory and a kingdom" (Dan. 7:13–14).[17] But is the "sign" something distinct from, and prior to, the coming of the Son of Man – a banner or ensign raised to mark the imminence of the Day of the Lord (cf. Isa. 18:3; 49:22; Jer. 4:21; 1QM 2:15–4:17)? Or is the appearance of the Son of Man itself the "sign" – the "sign" *which is* the Son of Man (an appositional genitive), rather as Jesus earlier spoke of "the sign of the prophet Jonah" (Matt. 12:39; cf. 16:4; Luke 11:29)? It is difficult to be dogmatic, but two considerations weigh in favor of the latter interpretation.[18] First, no sign precedes the coming of the one like a son of man in Daniel's vision. Secondly, we are given no indication what this "sign" might otherwise be: the future tense with *tote* ("then there will be revealed") makes it unlikely that it is the cosmic disturbances described in the preceding verse.

In view of this, we may suppose that the revelation of the Son of Man in heaven is the "sign" which in Isaiah 11:12 heralds the gathering of the people from the four corners of the earth. But the parallel with the earlier statement about Jonah may point to a further level of meaning. In Luke's version of the altercation with the Pharisees and Sadducees over their demand for a sign, Jesus warns them, "For as Jonah became a sign to the people of Nineveh, so will the Son of Man be to this generation" (Luke 11:30). Although in

---

17 Jesus also casts himself in this role at his trial before the high priest, provoking the charge of blasphemy (Matt. 26:64–65; Mark 14:62–64).

18 Hagner argues that *tote* dissociates the "sign" from the "coming" as two consecutive events (Hagner, *Matthew*, 713). But this is not quite accurate. The appearance of the sign is dissociated not from the appearance of the Son of Man but from the reaction of the tribes of the earth.

Matthew the direct analogy between Jonah and the Son of Man is lacking (Matt. 16:4), it is possible that the revelation of the Son of Man in heaven is a sign of judgment for the current evil generation in the same way that Jonah was a sign of judgment for Nineveh.

Matthew tells us that "all the tribes of the earth" will mourn and will see the Son of Man when he comes (Matt. 24:30). The allusion here is to Zechariah's words concerning the mourning of the families of Jerusalem with compassion for the one whom they have pierced (Zech. 12:10–14). It is followed by forgiveness: "On that day there shall be a fountain opened for the house of David and the inhabitants of Jerusalem, to cleanse them from sin and uncleanness" (Zech. 13:1).

It is possible that Jesus is using this passage in a quite precise manner. In the Septuagint Zechariah 12:12 reads: "the land shall mourn according to tribes." The "land" (*hē gē*) is Israel, the "tribes" (*phulas*) are the families of Jerusalem: the houses of David, Nathan, Levi, and Shimei are listed. Jesus likewise speaks of the "tribes of the land" (*hai phulai tēs gēs*), and it could be argued that he is thinking here only of the tribes of Israel, and perhaps specifically of the people of Jerusalem. The focus, then, would be on the vindication of the Son of Man before those who failed to recognize the time of their "visitation" (Luke 19:44) and who condemned the Christ to death. The vindication, of course, is powerfully underlined – and in a sense brought about – by the destruction of the city and the end of the temple system. The phrase *hai phulai tēs gēs*, however, refers consistently in the Old Testament to the nations of the earth (Gen. 12:3; 28:14; Ps. 71:17 LXX; Ezek. 20:32; Amos 3:2; Zech. 14:17). We should perhaps see in this shift in usage a deliberate universalization of the narrower Jewish motif. But if this is the case, there is still no reason to think that in the process the basic meaning has changed. The mourning, therefore, is not at the prospect of judgment but over the ill-treatment of the Messiah, who was "delivered over to the Gentiles" and in the end killed by them. The "tribes of the earth" will recognize the significance of Christ's suffering – perhaps because they have seen it replicated in the suffering of his followers – and, as a result, they too will "see" the coming of the Son of Man.

At this point we are confronted with some more fundamental difficulties. One concerns the direction of this "coming": Where does the Son of Man come from? Where is he going to? Another can hardly be separated from this: What is the time of the coming? Where does it touch down on the runway of history? Is it still to come, perhaps even just around the corner? Or has it in some way happened already? What is the relation between this coming and the *parousia*? Do they refer to the same event, or should they be differentiated in some way? There are questions, finally, surrounding the identity of this person: Who is he? Is he in any sense real or is he, like the beasts, a symbol for some other reality in heaven or on earth? Is he singular or plural? And what happens at the moment of his coming? What is the purpose of his appearance?

The Son of Man coming in clouds

The Son of Man will be seen "coming (*erchomenon*) in clouds" (Mark 13:26); Luke has only one "cloud" (Luke 21:27); Matthew has "clouds of heaven" (Matt. 24:30; cf. 26:64). Mix them together, stir them up, and we have almost a verbatim quotation from Theodotion's translation of Daniel 7:13: "and behold, with the clouds of heaven one like a son of man was coming (*erchomenos*)."[19] At other points in the chapter Matthew uses the word *parousia* apparently in reference to the same event, and he is presumably responsible for its introduction into the discourse. The disciples ask Jesus, "what will be the sign of your *parousia*?" (24:3); and Jesus tells them that the "*parousia* of the Son of Man" will be, on the one hand, like lightning that comes from the east and shines as far as the

---

[19] LXX has "and behold, on the clouds of heaven one like a son of man came (*ērcheto*)."

west (24:27) and, on the other, analogous to the days of Noah (24:37, 39).

A huge amount has been written about Jesus' use of the expression "Son of Man." Although it would no doubt be great fun to survey that material here, unfortunately there is not space, so we will have to be satisfied with a rather cursory overview of the use of the phrase in the Old Testament – and there may be some benefit in simplifying matters.[20] The term is used in a number of instances as a synonym for "man," especially in idiomatic or poetic parallelisms such as Psalm 8:4: "what is man that you are mindful of him, and the son of man that you care for him?"[21] In a natural extension of this usage, Ezekiel is consistently addressed by God as "son of man" – but in ways that prefigure the stories about Jesus. He is a "son of man" who acts out judgment against Jerusalem, who is told to portray the city on a brick and lay siege to it, to lie on his side for more than a year to "bear their punishment" (Ezek. 4:1–7; cf. 5:1–4). He is a "son of man" who dwells "in the midst of a rebellious house, who have eyes to see, but see not, who have ears to hear, but hear not" (12:2; cf. Mark 8:18). He is a "son of man" who propounds riddles and speaks allegories to the house of Israel (17:2). He is a "son of man" who is told to set his face against Jerusalem (Ezek. 21:2; cf. 13:17; cf. Luke 9:51).[22] He is a "son of man" who will judge Jerusalem and the elders of Israel (20:3–4; 22:2). He is a "son of man" who prophesies to the "breath" (*pneuma*), and the breath gives life to the dry bones of the

---

[20] For a convenient survey see I. H. Marshall, "Son of Man," in J. B. Green, S. McKnight, and I. H. Marshall (eds.), *Dictionary of Jesus and the Gospels* (Downers Grove/Leicester: Inter-Varsity Press, 1992), 775–81.

[21] Cf. P. C. Craigie, *Psalms 1–50* (Waco, TX: Word, 1983), 108; T. B. Slater, "One Like a Son of Man in First-Century CE Judaism," *NTS* 41.2 (1995), 184. Cf. Num. 23:19; Job 25:6; 35:8; Ps. 144:3; Isa. 51:12; 56:2; Jer. 50:40. Used with this meaning the phrase is far more common in the plural.

[22] Ezek. 21:2 LXX has *stērison . . . epi*, whereas Luke 9:51, in the context of Jesus' final journey to Jerusalem, has *estērisen . . . eis*.

whole house of Israel (37:9–14). Although it would be wrong to suggest that Ezekiel understood "son of man" as "some mysterious or exalted title,"[23] we cannot ignore the powerful association of the term with one who, in dramatic and even eccentric fashion, prophesied judgment against Jerusalem in the form of military conquest and the restoration of the nation through the Spirit. Likewise, "one like a son of man" is only descriptive in Daniel 7:13: it simply denotes a figure *in human form* in contrast to the four beasts that have so far appeared, representing oppressed Israel.[24] But it is a descriptive term that has become inseparable from its visionary context.[25]

The meaning of the word *parousia* apart from its use in the New Testament with reference to Christ is not difficult to determine. It signifies, in effect, the *coming so as to be present of a person or group*. In other words, if it means "presence," it generally carries with it the thought that the one who is present has only recently arrived or might otherwise have been absent.[26] So, for example, when Judith turns up outside the tent of Holofernes causing considerable stir in the camp (Jud. 10:18), the phrase *hē parousia autēs* could equally be translated "her arrival" or "her presence"; it does not, however, refer to her "coming"

---

[23] Wenham, *Paul*, 110.

[24] In Ps. 79:16, 18 LXX "son of man" appears to refer to Israel oppressed by her enemies (for the use of *krataioō* ["strengthen"] in relation to Israel see Ps. 104:24 LXX).

[25] Cf. Slater, "Son of Man," 188. In the NT we nearly always have *ho huios tou anthrōpou*, but this form never occurs in the LXX, where it is invariably *anarthrous*; the articles are missing in John 5:7 and Rev. 1:13; 14:14, where there is a more indefinite reference to "one like a son of man" (cf. Moule, "Son of Man," 277–78). The reason presumably is that Jesus has given the "son of man" a definite identity, but the form may also *refer back* to the figure in Dan. 7. Slater thinks that the one like a son of man is the archangel Michael (189–90), but it seems unlikely that an angelic figure would be interpreted as the "holy ones of the Most High," even if these were themselves angels. In any case, our interest here is principally in how Jesus understood the prophecy.

[26] Cf. Wright, *Victory*, 341.

if by that we mean the journey that she made in order to be present outside the tent of Holofernes. In a letter to his generals, King Ptolemy Philopator recounts how, having arrived in Jerusalem, he "went up to honor the temple of those wicked people, who never cease from their folly." The Jews, he says, "accepted our presence (*parousia*) by word," but insincerely because, "carried away by their traditional conceit," they refused to allow him to enter the temple (3 Macc. 3:16–18 RSV). Paul tells the Corinthians that he rejoices in the *parousia* of Stephanas, Fortunatus, and Achaicus because it makes up for their *absence* (1 Cor. 16:17).[27] The word *parousia* appears especially suited to denoting the *presence* that is the immediate result of the *arrival* of a figure of significance. In the context of Paul's thought we may want to add to this a wider range of associations, but this is probably alien to Jesus' discourse.

The related verb *pareimi* has the same sense of coming in order to be present or of being present rather than absent. The Jews drag Jason and some other believers before the city authorities, complaining, "These men who have turned the world upside down have come (*pareisin*) here also" (Acts 17:6); Paul characteristically warns the Corinthians: "though absent in body, I am present (*parēn*) in spirit" (1 Cor. 5:3; cf. 2 Cor. 10:2, 11; 13:2, 10). Interestingly, *pareimi* also appears in the LXX of Daniel 7:13, though not with reference to the Son of Man figure: "behold, on the clouds of heaven (one) like a son of man was coming (*ērchetō*), and (one) like an ancient of days was present (*parēn*), and those standing by were coming (*parēsan*) to him."[28] Another motif that may have relevance appears in

---

[27] Cf. 2 Cor. 7:6–7; Phil. 2:12. Even in 2 Cor. 10:10 Paul's "bodily presence" stands in contrast to the impact of his letters *when he is absent*.

[28] The Theodotion text does not use *pareimi* but emphasizes the presence of the son of man figure before God: "behold, with the clouds of heaven one like a son of man was coming (*erchomenos ēn*) and arrived at (*ephthasen*) the ancient of days and was brought before him." Possibly between the two texts there is an argument for the use of *pareimi*/*parousia* to denote the coming of the son of man figure before the Ancient of Days.

Isaiah: "my people will know my name in that day because I am the one saying I am here (*pareimi*)" (Isa. 52:6 LXX); "you will cry, and he will listen to you; while you are still speaking, he will say to you, Behold, I am here (*pareimi*)" (58:9 LXX). These are passages that speak powerfully of the restoration of Zion (52:8; 58:12). Josephus, finally, uses *parousia* for the presence of God at Mount Sinai (*Ant.* 3.5.2 §80) and in the tabernacle (*Ant.* 3.8.5 §202), and for the presence of God with the servant of Elisha (*Ant.* 9.4.3 §55).

The meaning of the coming

The traditional understanding has been that Jesus is speaking of a coming of the Son of Man *from heaven to earth.* The action of Daniel's vision, however, is more complex, and it is important that we correctly visualize its topography and the development of the events described. Four beasts come out of the sea and cause havoc on the earth (Dan. 7:3–8); the fourth beast is especially dreadful on account of its blasphemies and aggression against the "saints of the most high" (7:8, 20–21, 25). Thrones are then set in place *on the earth* (if we were in heaven the throne of God would not need to be placed) and a figure advanced in years ("one that was ancient of days") comes – perhaps from heaven, but that is not made explicit – and takes his seat (7:9, 22).[29] The books are opened and a judgment takes place. The fourth beast is slain; the other three beasts are not destroyed ("their lives were prolonged for a season and a time") but "their dominion was taken away" (7:11–12). The survival of the first three beasts and the fact that the thrones are set on earth indicate that this is an event *within* history rather than at its end.

At this point Daniel repeats the formula with which the vision opened: "I saw in the night visions, and behold . . ." (7:13; cf. 7:1). Then a human figure appears, coming "with the clouds of heaven" to be presented before the Ancient of

[29] Against, for example, Wright, who locates the visionary action in heaven (Wright, *Victory*, 361).

Days and to receive "dominion and glory and a kingdom, that all peoples, nations, and languages should serve him" (7:13–14). The accompanying "clouds of heaven" may suggest that this figure is traveling from heaven to earth (cf. Rev. 10:1), but this is doubtful. The beasts are *earthly* creatures: the Ancient of Days has made the journey for the purpose of enacting judgment on the beasts and bestowing sovereignty on the "one like a son of man." The subsequent identification of the one like a son of man with oppressed Israel reinforces this impression. In this case, the clouds more likely signify, on the one hand, the exalted status of the "one like a son of man" and, on the other, the fact that he is being brought into the presence of the God who has come to judge the four kingdoms.[30] Within the context of the vision, however, the direction of travel is of little significance: movement plays no part in the explanation of the vision when the kingdom is said to be given to the holy ones of the Most High (7:22, 27). It is the *transfer of sovereignty* – judgment of the beasts and enthronement of the one like a son of man – that constitutes the central action in the drama.

It goes against the grain of the traditional interpretation, but we are bound to ask whether Jesus' words should not be read in the same way: the tribes of the earth, having come to understand the significance of the Messiah's suffering, will see what Daniel "saw," namely, the judgment in favor of the Son of Man and his enthronement. What they will literally *see* will be the destruction of the temple, the rejection of national Israel as God's chosen servant, the steady expansion of the gospel into the pagan world, and the eventual collapse of Roman imperialism – but they will *understand* from these developments that spiritual authority has been taken from the old powers and

---

[30] Cf. Wright, *Victory*, 632. In 4 Ezra 13:1–3 the man ("something like the figure of a man") flying "with the clouds of heaven" does not descend from heaven but *arises* "out of the heart of the sea": the clouds of heaven do not of themselves signify descent.

given to Jesus Christ.[31] This, after all, was an integral part of Daniel's vision: "to him was given dominion and glory and a kingdom, that all peoples, nations, and languages should serve him" (Dan. 7:14).[32]

Jesus' account is terse and probably selective. There is no reference to the throne of God, which has led William Lane to conclude that he is talking not about the coming of the Son of Man to the Ancient of Days but of his descent "as a sovereign in the celestial chariot of the clouds," on the one hand, to judge, on the other, to gather those who are scattered.[33] But we would still have to ask on what basis a figure designated "son of man" would play the divine part of descending to judge and deliver his people. The transfer of sovereignty that takes place in Daniel's vision must still be in the background. There is also no reference to the judgment and destruction of the fourth beast. The coming of the Son of Man in Jesus' narrative certainly coincides with the devastation of Jerusalem, but he does not himself appear to act as judge in this: the emphasis is on the fact that he has "power and great glory" and that he is responsible for the gathering of the elect. The imagery surrounding the judgment of the little horn and the beast is found elsewhere in the New Testament, but we will see that this comes at a time when Rome, not Jerusalem, is the problem. Within the typology of Daniel it is not the destruction of the fourth beast that corresponds to the judgment on Jerusalem but the aggression of the little horn towards Israel.

It appears, therefore, that Jesus has drawn upon Daniel 7 here to make a *rather limited point within the discourse as a whole* – principally regarding the circumstances under which he, and the disciples with him, will be vindicated in the world. But it is likely that a more complex series of events is in the background: (i) the assault of the beast on

---

[31] Cf. France, *Mark*, 535: "If this is not the prediction of a visible 'descent' . . . what is being 'seen' is a heavenly authority."

[32] Cf. Phil. 2:9–11; Eph. 1:20–23.

[33] Lane, *Mark*, 476.

Jerusalem and the desolation of the temple; (ii) the coming of God and the establishment of a court to pass judgment on the beast; (iii) the destruction of the beast and the ending of the oppression; (iv) the coming of the Son of Man to the throne of God to receive the kingdom; and (v) the inclusion of the saints within that kingdom. The term *parousia* most naturally denotes the "coming to be present" of Christ in the midst of eschatological crisis to defeat his enemies and deliver those who trust in him. But it may have come to function as a more general label for a story that centers around the vindication of the Son of Man. Possibly associations that attached to the related verb assisted this development.

This may have a bearing on how we understand the eschatological scope of Jesus' vision. Wright has insisted, for example, that there is no reference to a "second coming" in the traditional sense in the discourse. The announcement of the destruction of the temple was also an announcement of Jesus' vindication: "in other words, of his own 'coming' – not floating around on a cloud, of course, but of his 'coming' *to Jerusalem as the vindicated, rightful king*."[34] The coming of the Son of Man and the *parousia* are the same thing. The problem with this may lie less with the interpretation of Jesus' discourse than with how we understand the use of *parousia* elsewhere. The *parousia* of Christ that Paul describes in 2 Thessalonians 2:1–8, for example, certainly includes actions that are prefigured in Daniel's visions but which are not fulfilled in the destruction of the temple.

Against this, France has argued in his commentary on Mark that there is a distinct change of topic at 13:32, signaled by the change from "in those days" earlier in the passage (13:17, 19, 24) to "that day or that hour" here, and by the note of uncertainty introduced regarding the timing of the event.[35] At this point, he thinks, Jesus is talking about

---

[34] Wright, *Victory*, 342 (Wright's italics); cf. Wright, *New Testament*, 461–64.

[35] France, *Mark*, 501, 541–42.

the *parousia* as an event distinct from his vindication that is not subject to the same temporal constraints. The exegetical arguments, however, are not entirely convincing. It is very difficult *not* to read "that day or that hour" as some sort of reference back to the preceding events, and very difficult to understand what the objection is to reading "in those days" as a reference to the period leading up to "that day" when the Son of Man is revealed. France argues that Matthew differentiates between the *parousia* and events associated with the fall of Jerusalem in Matthew 24:27.[36] But the obvious contrast here is between the appearance of the false Christs and false prophets and the coming of the Son of Man on the clouds: this is what the disciples were waiting for. There is no reason for Matthew to insert at this point the thought of a subsequent coming and final judgment. He makes use of the word *parousia* not in order to introduce a new idea but because it has come to function as a convenient shorthand for this multifaceted prophetic scenario.

If the figure coming on the clouds in Jesus' restatement of the prophecy already has "power and great glory," it is because this is the *resurrected* Christ, who was "declared to be the Son of God in *power* . . . by his resurrection from the dead" (Rom. 1:4), who was "raised from the dead by the *glory* of the Father" (Rom. 6:4).[37] To this power and glory is then added the sovereignty that formerly belonged to the kingdoms of the world. This may also account for the apparent reversal of the sequence in Mark 14:62 (cf. Matt. 26:64; Luke 22:69): the Son of Man is seen first "seated at the right hand of Power" and then "coming with the clouds of heaven." It has been argued from this that Jesus must have been thinking of the "descent" of the Son of Man from heaven to earth.[38] But if the image of the Son of Man

---

36 France, *Mark*, 501.

37 The close association of the terms "power" and "glory" with resurrection is especially apparent in 1 Cor. 15:43.

38 Cf. Blomberg, "Eschatology," 99. Matthew and Luke both add "from now." Luke omits both "you will see" and the reference to "coming."

"seated at the right hand of Power" speaks of resurrection and exaltation, as Peter certainly understood it to do (Acts 2:33–34),[39] there is no difficulty with the order of events: Christ is first raised in power and glory and then *subsequently* – as representative of the "saints" who suffer for his sake – receives the kingdom. Jesus is probably less concerned here to outline a precise order of events than to warn the high priest of the imminent (Matthew and Luke have "from now") fulfillment of two *distinct* Old Testament texts.[40] He is saying to the high priest, in effect: you will see the Son of Man both as the one who is seated at the right hand of God, about to rule from Zion in the midst of his enemies (Ps. 110:1–2), and as the one who comes to receive sovereignty from the Ancient of Days (Dan. 7:13). We will see later, however, that the distinction between being seated at the right hand of God and exercising sovereignty is of some significance for Paul's understanding of the kingdom of Christ.

By way of a slight diversion at this point we may consider Jesus' cryptic warning that, while anyone who "speaks a word against" (*eipēi logon kata*), or blasphemes against, the Son of Man will be forgiven, anyone who "speaks against (*eipēi kata*) the Holy Spirit will not be forgiven, either in this age or in the age to come" (Matt. 12:32; cf. Mark 3:28–29; Luke 12:10). This comes at the end of his defense against the accusation made by the Pharisees that he casts out demons by Beelzebub (Matt. 12:24–32). It may be entirely coincidental, but in Daniel's vision of the coming of the Son of Man it is said that the arrogant little horn will "speak words against[41] the Most High" (Dan. 7:25). Since it is not difficult to read the metaphor of the binding of the strong man and the coming of the kingdom of God against the background of Daniel 7, it could be

---

[39] Cf. Acts 5:31; 7:55–56; Rom. 8:34; Eph. 1:20; Col. 3:1; Heb.1:3, 13; 8:1; 10:12; 12:2.

[40] Cf. Hooker, *Mark*, 362.

[41] LXX: *rhēmata eis . . . lalēsei*; Theod.: *logous pros . . . lalēsei.*

argued that this is a warning to the Pharisees not to align themselves – deliberately or otherwise – with the satanic power of the fourth beast, which is Rome. To speak against the Spirit of God by which the demonic is cast out is to speak against the Most High. By acting in effect as mouthpieces for the power of the beast, the Pharisees risk coming under the same judgment, which is a judgment both for this age and for the age to come.[42] Although the primary conflict in the Son of Man vision is between the people of God and the pagan oppressor, there is a secondary conflict that emerges later in Daniel between competing notions of what constitutes national interest – between the righteous and the wicked, between the wise and those not knowing God. In the Gospels this becomes the controversy between Jesus and the various alternative programs for survival or victory. The Son of Man will be vindicated not only before the overweening pagan powers but also before the wicked shepherds of Israel.

The Son of Man and the saints of the Most High

This line of thought must be taken a step further. In Daniel's prophecy the "one like a son of man" is no less an apocalyptic symbol than the four beasts.[43] The significance of the phraseology is that this figure, unlike the destructive chimerical creatures that preceded it, is in *human* form. Whereas dominion is *taken from* the four beasts (7:11–12), the one like a son of Man *receives* "dominion and glory and a kingdom" (7:14) from the Ancient of Days. In the explanation that is given to Daniel by one of those standing around the throne, however, the individual figure in human form has disappeared. Instead, this fifth divinely appointed kingdom is given to a group, the "holy ones of

---

[42] Mark has "blasphemes against" (*blasphēmēsēi eis*) in place of the "speaks words against" idiom (Mark 3:29). Luke has removed the saying from the Beelzebub controversy but has placed it instead very firmly in the context of the appearance of the Son of Man before the throne of God (Luke 12:8–9).

[43] Cf. Wright, *New Testament*, 291–93.

the Most High" against whom the fourth beast made war (7:18, 22, 27).

The identity of these "holy ones" (ESV has "saints") is unclear. Although Jewish usage generally supports the view that these are heavenly beings (cf. Ps. 89:5, 7), there is certainly a very close association with the people of Israel, and on the whole it is easier to accept the traditional understanding that the reference is either to the nation as a whole or to a righteous few within the nation. The drama takes place on earth – the "holy ones" are oppressed by the fourth beast. And although the idea that heavenly beings should come under attack from earthly powers is not unheard of (cf. Dan. 8:10–12; perhaps also 8:24; Isa. 14:12–15), we do not find in Daniel 7 the imagery of height or of casting down typically associated with this motif. More importantly, there is no precedent for a transfer of sovereignty in this momentous fashion to heavenly beings. What is foreseen in the prophecy, therefore, is not the coming of an individual messiah but the transfer of sovereignty from the kingdoms of the world to oppressed Israel.

There is no reason to think that Jesus did not understand this. If this is the case, what he predicts is not a coming in the sense of a quasi-physical descent from heaven to earth but a *transfer of authority*, perhaps specifically from the Roman imperium, to the "people of the saints of the Most High" (Dan. 7:27). The statement about the coming of the Son of Man is less a direct description of what will visibly take place at some point in the future than an affirmation that the nations will "see" the fulfillment of the prophecy of Daniel 7:13–14. It is perhaps not merely incidental that what is described here is the *seeing* of the Son of Man; there is no direct statement about his coming or the events surrounding it (cf. Matt. 26:64). We have, in effect, something much more like Jesus' statement to Nathanael: "you will *see* heaven opened, and the angels of God ascending and descending on the Son of Man" (John 1:51). The "visionary" aspect of the event is even clearer in Luke 17:30, where Jesus speaks of the "day when the Son of Man *is revealed*." In the end, what this may amount to is simply the *public* recognition in the ancient world that there has been some sort of transfer of spiritual authority from Rome to the people of the Most High.

The vision, however, has been reconstructed around a very different conception of this people – this is the audacity of Jesus' self-understanding. He has taken the tradition of persecuted Israel – so vividly portrayed, for example, in the accounts of martyrdom in the Maccabean literature[44] – and refocused it upon himself: it is the Son of Man alone who "will be delivered over to the Gentiles and will be mocked and shamefully treated and spit upon. And after flogging him, they will kill him, and on the third day he will rise" (Luke 18:32–33). Here we glimpse, in effect, something of the historical logic of the "salvation" offered to Israel. The nation had sinned and would suffer punishment from God at the hands of Rome, which is identified with the fourth kingdom of Daniel's vision, whether as a matter of direct fulfillment or by way of an analogical reapplication of the prophecy. By taking upon *himself* alone the symbolic role of the Son of Man, Jesus presented an alternative – a narrow and dangerous path that led to life. The Son of Man would suffer many things, but those "in him" (Paul's terminology) would escape destruction – by fleeing from Jerusalem, by being dispersed into the wider world, but also by being subsequently incorporated into the story about the Son of Man who suffers and on the third day is raised from the dead. The allusion to Hosea 6:2 is highly significant. Hosea describes the "resurrection" not of an individual but of a people – Ephraim and Judah – who have suffered under the judgment of God, "that we may live before him." Jesus suffers in the place of the nation, but his resurrection is also a sign, a precursor, an anticipation of the renewal of the people of God.[45]

---

[44] On this see R. Bauckham, *The Climax of Prophecy: Studies on the Book of Revelation* (Edinburgh: T&T Clark, 1993), 236–37.

[45] See N. T. Wright, *The Resurrection of the Son of God* (London: SPCK, 2003), 322.

The outcome of this is the vindication of the Son of Man.[46] This has implications for those whom he has called to follow him and imitate his life. They become the "people of the saints of the Most High," against whom the little horn on the head of the fourth beast makes war, and to whom dominion is given – in two important respects. On the one hand, if they "have strength to escape all these things that are going to take place," the disciples will at some point "stand before the Son of Man" (Luke 21:36).[47] On the other hand, the dominion given to the Son of Man is extended further to those who *continue with Jesus in his trials*: like him they will receive a kingdom, will sit at his table in his kingdom, and will "sit on thrones judging the twelve tribes of Israel" (Luke 22:28–30; cf. Matt. 19:28).[48] It is those who suffer who will receive the kingdom. Exactly the same argument is found in Wisdom 3:1–8 (RSV): the righteous who are tortured and killed on account of the law of God are judged to have been punished in the sight of men but "their hope is full of immortality"; they have been tested and found worthy of God; they are accepted by God "like a sacrificial burnt offering"; and they "will govern nations and rule over peoples, and the Lord will reign over them for ever."[49]

The "coming of the Son of Man," therefore, in Jesus' reforged vision, is fulfilled at two levels. It is the vindication and exaltation of the one who will take upon himself the role of the Son of Man who suffers.[50] The

---

[46] Wright makes the important point that the destruction of the temple within a generation of Jesus' death vindicated him as a prophet (Wright, *Victory*, 362).

[47] This is an image of standing before a ruler on his throne (cf. Dan. 1:5; Matt. 27:11) that fits the judgment-enthronement scene of Daniel's vision much better than the descent motif of the second coming.

[48] Ps. 122:5 is probably in the background. Cf. Hagner, *Matthew*, 565. Cf. Moule, "Son of Man," 278, for the link between this statement and Dan. 7. Luke 12:8–9 (cf. Matt. 10:32–33) may also belong in this context.

[49] Cf. Wis. 5:4–5.

[50] Cf. France, *Mark*, 500–501.

historical setting for this appears to be the transition from the old covenant, which had as its hub the Jerusalem temple, to the new covenant – the reorganization of spiritual life around the person of Jesus Christ, who "died for our sins in accordance with the Scriptures" (1 Cor. 15:3). What marks the transition most decisively in this apocalyptic narrative is the destruction of Jerusalem – the "day when the Son of Man is revealed" (Luke 17:30). This is the validation of the message of judgment that formed an inseparable part of the teaching of both John the Baptist and Jesus and later of the early church. It must also have underscored the significance of the particular prophecies about the destruction of the temple and the substitution of his own "body" in its place (John 2:19; cf. Matt. 26:61; 27:40; Mark 14:58; 15:29). The more positive thought attached to the motif of the *parousia* of the Son of Man is the achievement of a dominion that transcends the boundaries of Israel, brought about through the preaching of the good news about Jesus to all nations.

But the "coming of the Son of Man" is also, more concretely and more visibly, the vindication and establishment of the church in the world as a rebuttal to those who have sought to destroy it. Just as the "saints of the Most High," oppressed and worn down by the fourth beast, eventually received the kingdom (Dan. 7:18, 22, 27), so too the followers of Jesus, having been dragged before synagogues and rulers, accused, reviled, beaten, imprisoned, having lived through the turmoil of war and the hardships of flight from Judea, will eventually be established as the new people of God in the world.[51]

Heaven and earth will pass away . . .

Jesus adds: "Heaven and earth will pass away, but my words will not pass away" (Mark 13:31; cf. Luke 21:33; Matt. 24:35).

[51] Cf. Wright: "The 'coming of the son of man' is thus good first-century metaphorical language for two things: the defeat of the enemies of the true people of god, and the vindication of the true people themselves" (Wright, *Victory*, 362).

The point of the statement is, in the first place, rhetorical: it underlines the permanence of Jesus' words.[52] Regardless of what the phrase signifies exactly, the argument here does not directly equate it with the events that will come upon "this generation," and we are not bound to infer from this verse that Jesus linked the fulfillment of all these things with the dissolution of this present universe, whether literally or figuratively understood. Nevertheless, the idea of the heavens and the earth disappearing and being replaced by new heavens and a new earth is prominent in the Old Testament and its usage here is suggestive.

In the later chapters of Isaiah the creation of new heavens and a new earth is made the symbol of a far-reaching restoration of Israel and renewal of the worship of God. The event follows on from judgment upon a "rebellious people" (Isa. 65:2; cf. 66:24).[53] Jerusalem will become a place of rejoicing; "no more shall be heard in it the sound of weeping and the cry of distress" (65:19). Salvation will be extended to the Gentiles (51:4–6); some of them will be employed as priests and Levites in the house of the Lord (66:21); and all flesh will come to worship before the Lord (66:23).

If Jesus had this background in mind, then we should probably assume that he meant the disciples to interpret the coming events *in the light* of this resonant Old Testament vision. There is an unfulfilled residue in the utopian details, especially in the depiction of Jerusalem as a place of unalloyed joy and unhindered prosperity. This might be regarded as poetic enhancement, the characteristic hyperbole of apocalyptic language, or as pointing to a greater fulfillment still to come. But it is entirely reasonable, given the nature of biblical foresight, to see the

---

[52] Cf. Wright, *Victory*, 364–65; France, *Mark*, 540.

[53] Elsewhere the degradation of the heavens and the earth is a concomitant effect of judgment (Isa. 24:4–5; 18–21; Jer. 4:23; Joel 2:10, 30; 3:16; Hag. 2:6, 21; Sir. 16:18). Jeremiah 31:36 is especially interesting, though the force of the metaphor in this context runs counter to Jesus' argument.

fulfillment of this prophetic image in the execution of judgment on Israel, the outpouring of the Spirit, and the incorporation of Gentiles into the people of God. The passing away of heaven and earth, in that case, as Jesus makes use of the motif, does not signify the collapse of the known universe but is essentially a metaphor for this radical restructuring of divine purpose. So when he says that the law will remain in force until "heaven and earth pass away" (Matt. 5:18), he means until the final judgment on the old religious system has taken place and the renewed, Spirit-filled, multi-ethnic people of God has come into its own. We may recall Isaiah 66:22 here: the descendants of this renewed people will endure as long as the *new* heavens and *new* earth remain before the Lord. This is a "new creation" people – not in any ontological sense, or even primarily in anticipation of some future overhaul of the universe, but as the outcome of the promise made in Isaiah that in the aftermath of destruction God would make all things new.

Other texts

It has been possible so far to make a case for the historical contingency of the coming of the Son of Man because, interpreted against the background of Daniel's vision, Jesus' words can be understood to describe not a descent to earth but a more complex judgment-enthronement scenario in which the special prerogatives of the Jewish nation as God's chosen people (and also, ultimately, the power of Rome) are superseded in the acknowledgement of Christ's lordship among the Gentiles. Other statements in the Gospels, however, appear more clearly to describe an earthward coming, or a coming that has a direct impact on people on earth, and not simply the approach of the Son of Man to the throne of God. This more conventional understanding, if it is correct, would make it difficult to locate the fulfillment of these predictions in the inauguration of a supra-national people of God. But as we consider these texts, we run up against the same basic historical constraint: the close connection between the coming of the Son of Man and the situation that confronted the disciples in Judea.

In Luke 18:7–8, for example, Jesus promises that God will vindicate the elect, who cry to him day and night, but then asks, "Nevertheless, when the Son of Man comes, will he find faith on earth?" We have suggested already that the parable of the unrighteous judge, to which this saying is attached, presupposes the particular circumstances of the early Jewish church. Luke 17:30 lends further weight to this: the revelation of the Son of Man is set firmly in the context of the destruction of Jerusalem. God is the righteous judge who will assuredly give judgment "for the saints of the Most High" (cf. Dan. 7:22). If this is the correct historical setting for the parable, we are led to suppose that a leading concern of the Son of Man, "when he comes," will be the spiritual condition of these first disciples.[54] The "faith" that he seeks is specifically the faith that will keep them obedient during this difficult period.

A statement in Matthew 16:27 appears to connect the coming of the Son of Man with the final judgment: "the Son of Man is going to come with his angels in the glory of his Father, and then he will repay each person according to what he has done." The context for Jesus' comments, however, is not necessarily universal or final. The issue here is the price paid in the short-term for following him. Jesus reassures the disciples that, when the Son of Man comes, he will repay each of them for what he has done. Verse 28 quite explicitly has the life-time of the disciples in view: "some standing here will not taste death . . ." We should endeavor, therefore, to situate this "repayment" within this more limited context, interpreting it in terms of the eventual victory of the early church over the blasphemous and murderous forces opposing it and of the

---

[54] We should then perhaps translate *epi tēs gēs* as "in the land" rather than "on the earth." Cf. Jer. 42:15 LXX; Luke 4:25; 23:44; Acts 7:4; perhaps also Luke 12:49, 51; 21:23.

special status accorded those who endure these afflictions. At this point Mark has a similar saying: "whoever is ashamed of me and of my words in this adulterous and sinful generation, of him will the Son of Man also be ashamed when he comes in the glory of his Father with the holy angels" (Mark 8:38). Again the expectation about the coming of the Son of Man cannot be separated from Jesus' warning that *this generation* of Jews would experience the kingdom of God coming with power.

The "transfiguration" of Jesus that is recounted immediately after these warnings (Matt. 17:1–8; Mark 9:2–8; Luke 9:28–36) is commonly understood as a disclosure of his true underlying divinity or as a prefiguring of the resurrection. But we can probably make better sense of it within a narrative-eschatological framework as a visible representation of the promise that precedes it in all three Synoptic Gospels: "there are some standing here who will not taste death until they see the Son of Man coming in his kingdom" (Matt. 16:28).[55] The transfiguration would then reiterate in physical form the conviction that within a generation they would see what it means for the Son of Man to come on the clouds of heaven to receive the kingdom from the Ancient of Days. It is hardly coincidental, then, that on their way back down the mountain Jesus instructs the disciples not to tell anyone about the vision "until the Son of Man is raised from the dead" (Matt. 17:9; Mark 9:9). Peter's allusion to the event in 2 Peter 1:16–19 lends support to this understanding.[56] When he claims that the apostles were "eyewitnesses of his majesty"

---

[55] Cf. Witherington, *Jesus, Paul,* 38. Hagner thinks that the proper context for the transfiguration in Matthew is not the logion about the coming of the Son of Man but Jesus' earlier announcement that he must suffer and be put to death (Hagner, *Matthew*, 489). But the Son of Man who comes on the clouds of heaven already represents the suffering saints of the Most High (cf. Dan. 7:25–27); see also R. Bauckham, *Jude, 2 Peter* (Waco, TX: Word, 1983), 211–12.

[56] See Bauckham's evaluation of the view that this passage refers not to the transfiguration but to a resurrection appearance (Bauckham, *Jude, 2 Peter*, 210–11).

(1:16), it is to confirm the veracity of what they had said about "the power and coming (*parousian*) of our Lord Jesus Christ." The transfiguration is, therefore, in some sense an argument for the *parousia*: it is, after all, a leading concern of 2 Peter to demonstrate that the "promise of his coming" was not idle fancy (3:4; cf. 1:16). If this is the case, then the "honor and glory" that the "beloved Son" received from the Father prefigure the "glory" that the "Son of Man" will receive from the Ancient of Days (Dan. 7:14). So when Peter says in verse 19 that "we have a firmer hold on the prophetic word," his point may well be that Daniel's prophecy concerning the vindication of the "son of man" has been visibly backed up, confirmed, by the dramatic vision of Christ's glory on the mountain.[57]

Given this historical framework we must again reconsider the manner and orientation of the coming of the Son of Man in these passages. Daniel's vision, we should recall, was already set on earth, and the "coming" of the one like a "son of man" was an approach to the Ancient of Days to receive sovereignty and take his place at the right hand of the Father. It would be from this position, then, that he looks for faith on earth – to see whether any have had the strength to "survive" the tribulation and "stand before the Son of Man" (Luke 21:36). From this position, too, the Son of Man will repay those who have lost their lives (probably Jesus means this quite literally) for his sake. We will see in later chapters how prominently this particular hope featured in the early church's vision of the future.

Two verses in John's Gospel speak apparently of a coming back, but again the event is expected within the

---

[57] Bauckham rejects this interpretation on the grounds that *echein ti bebaion* ought to mean "to have a firm hold on something" (Bauckham, *Jude, 2 Peter*, 223). But the comparative still suggests that they have a *firmer* grasp of the prophetic word *because of what was revealed*. It is likely that Peter also has texts such as Exod. 4:22; Ps. 2:7; Isa. 42:1 in mind (see the arguments in Bauckham, *Jude, 2 Peter*, 207–209).

lifetime of the disciples. In John 14:3 Jesus says: "And if I go and prepare a place for you, I will come again (*palin erchomai*) and will take you to myself, that where I am you may be also." In 21:22 he says to Peter, "If it is my will that he remain until I come, what is that to you? You follow me!" These are better understood as metaphors for the participation of the disciples in the story of the "Son of Man."

The Coming of the Christ in Acts

Two passages in Acts speak of a future coming of the risen Christ. When Jesus is taken into heaven, two men appear suddenly, standing beside the disciples, dressed in "white apparel" (*en esthēsesi leukais*), and ask them, "Men of Galilee, why do you stand looking into heaven? This Jesus, who was taken up from you into heaven, will come in the same way as you saw him go into heaven" (1:10–11). There are strong parallels between this scene and Luke's account of the experience of the women at the tomb: "behold, two men (the same expression is used: *kai idou andres duo*) stood by them in dazzling apparel (*en esthēti astraptousēi*)." On this occasion a similar question is posed: "Why do you seek the living among the dead?" (Luke 24:4–5). Like the disciples, the women were looking for Jesus where he was not to be found, and the two men go on to remind them that the Son of Man had to "be crucified and on the third day rise" (24:7) – we might add, in accordance with the Scriptures (cf. 1 Cor. 15:3–4). There is no overt reference to the "Son of Man" in Acts 1:10–11, but it is easy to think that Daniel's vision is again in the background. The words of the two men to the disciples become then, in effect, an affirmation – a reminder – that the expectations regarding the Son of Man, who comes with the clouds of heaven to the throne of the Ancient of Days, will be fulfilled. There is some support for this line of thinking to be found in the second passage.

When a lame beggar is miraculously healed outside the temple, Peter takes the opportunity to address the excited crowd that gathered in Solomon's Portico. He makes the point first that the man had been healed by the same God who had raised Jesus from the dead, whom they had handed over to Pilate, the representative of Roman imperial power. He then explains that the suffering of the Christ had been "foretold by the mouth of all the prophets." They should therefore repent, so that "your sins may be blotted out (*exaleiphthēnai*), that times of respite may come from the face of the Lord, and he may send the Christ appointed for you, Jesus, whom heaven must receive until the time for a restoration of all things" (Acts 3:19–21, translation mine).

Rather than simply assuming that the sending of the Christ refers to a second coming to earth, we need first to explore the intertextual background. First, and of importance in view of our general thesis, Peter's argument recalls the words of Gabriel in response to Daniel's prayer of repentance (Dan. 9:3–19): 70 weeks are determined "for sin to be completed, and to seal up sins, and to blot out (*apaleipsai*) the iniquities" (9:24 Theod.). This will lead to an "everlasting righteousness" and, interestingly, to the "anointing" (*tou chrisai*) of the holy of holies. The hope of restoration, therefore, is set in the immediate context of the build-up to the destruction of the city and the sanctuary, and beyond that of the judgment that is given against the foreign oppressor and in favor of the Son of Man.

Secondly, the prophecy of Zechariah from Luke's birth narrative anticipates Peter's speech at a number of points.[58] Peter says, for example, that heaven must receive the Christ "until the time for a restoration (*apokatastaseōs*) of all things, that God spoke by the mouth of his holy prophets from of old" (3:21, translation mine).[59] Zechariah speaks of God redeeming his people, raising up a horn of salvation, "as he spoke by the mouth of his holy prophets from of old"

[58] Cf. R. C. Tannehill, *The Narrative Unity of Luke-Acts: A Literary Interpretation* (Minneapolis: Fortress Press, 1990), 55, n. 17.

[59] Note also the reference to the covenant with the fathers and with Abraham in both passages (Luke 1:72–73; Acts 3:25).

(Luke 1:70). The repetition of this phrase, which is found nowhere else in the Greek Bible, can hardly be accidental and gives strong grounds for thinking that these passages are mutually interpretive. Zechariah then goes on to define this salvation as a deliverance "from our enemies" so that Israel "might serve him without fear, in holiness and righteousness before him all our days" (1:71–75).

Thirdly, in verses 22–25 Peter provides an explanation of what was spoken by the prophets. He quotes from Deuteronomy 18:15 the affirmation that God will raise up a prophet for Israel like Moses. The context for this statement in Deuteronomy is the entry of the people of Israel into the land of Canaan, and it is likely that Peter sees an analogy here with the entry of a redeemed remnant of Israel into the restored kingdom. Attached to this, however, there is the severe warning (combining Deut. 18:19 and Lev. 23:29) that "every soul that does not listen to that prophet shall be destroyed from the people" (Acts 3:23). This is presumably a reference to the impending national crisis predicted both by John the Baptist and by Jesus – the ax of divine judgment already laid to the root of the tree. The "respite" (*anapsuxeōs*) that is promised (literally a breathing space[60]) strongly suggests an opportunity to recover from hardship – or deliverance from the oppressive circumstances of Roman rule, which is presumably also what the disciples were driving at when they asked Jesus if at this time he would "restore (*apokathistaneis*) the kingdom to Israel" (Acts 1:6).[61] The urgency of the thought is underlined by the

---

[60] In Exod. 8:11 LXX *anapsuxis* refers to a "respite" from the plagues; cf. *anapsuchō* in Ps. 38:14 LXX; 2 Macc. 13:11; 2 Tim. 1:16.

[61] Note also Mark 9:12 (cf. Matt. 17:11): Elijah comes first to "restore all things." The verb is frequently used in the Gospels for healing. *apokathistanō* is used in the LXX for the restoration of Israel (especially to the land): Jer. 15:19; 16:15; 23:8; 24:6; 27:19; Ezek. 16:55; Dan. 4:36; Hos. 11:11. Wall thinks that "all things" in Acts 3:21 includes creation (R. W. Wall, "The Acts of the Apostles," in L. E. Keck, et al. (eds.), *The New Interpreter's Bible*, X (Nashville: Abingdon Press, 2002), 82), but there is no reason to believe that the scope of the restoration is any wider than in 1:6.

fact that all of the prophets from Samuel onwards also proclaimed "these days." Whatever the "restoration of all things" consists of exactly, it is a matter of immediate concern to Peter's audience: *they* are "the sons of the prophets" and cannot escape the implications either of this warning of impending judgment or, more positively, of the promise that in the "seed" of Abraham all the families of the earth would be blessed (3:25).

The sending of the Christ, therefore, must be interpreted within the eschatological framework of the impending destruction of Jerusalem and the renewal of the people through the suffering of the Son of Man. Peter may have in mind the familiar apocalyptic notion of the coming of the Lord to deliver Israel from her enemies. But there is a more intriguing possibility. He had earlier spoken in some detail of how the Jews had delivered up and repudiated Jesus "in the presence of Pilate" (*kata prosōpon Pilatou*) when he was about to release him back to them, asking for a murderer to be granted to them instead of the "Author of life" (Acts 3:13–15). His assurance now is that if they repent, this sin will be blotted out and its effect reversed: the one whom they repudiated will be sent back to them "from the presence of the Lord" (*apo prosōpou tou kuriou*). The opportunity is still there to receive the Author of life, when the Son of Man comes in power, when he delivers them from their enemies.

Four

Life and Death in the Age to Come

Attached to the description of the Son of Man coming with power and much glory is another recurrent Old Testament motif – the gathering of the elect from the four corners of the earth (Mark 13:27; Matt. 24:31; cf. John 11:51–52). Again, this has traditionally been thought to describe an event that has not yet taken place. We have imagined Jesus descending on the clouds from heaven and sending out his angels to assemble the faithful from across the world. But this imaginative projection may go beyond the spare and allusive outline of Jesus' narrative.

The Gathering of the Elect

The Old Testament texts speak of the gathering of those Jews who have been scattered, especially as a consequence of divine judgment, and envisage for the most part a renewed worship of God in terms that can easily be applied to the circumstances of the church. On the day that the people return to the Lord, he will bring back the outcasts from "the uttermost parts of heaven" and will "circumcise your heart and the heart of your offspring" (Deut. 30:1–6; cf. Rom. 2:29). In Isaiah 27:13, where there is also reference to a "great trumpet," the scattered Jews "will come and worship the LORD on the holy mountain at Jerusalem." In a later vision a "sign" is set up among the nations, from whom survivors will be sent to declare the glory of God in the world and bring the scattered Jews back to the holy mountain Jerusalem "as an offering to the LORD" (66:20). With the Jews who are brought back from exile God will make an "everlasting covenant" (Jer. 32:37–40), quite different from the old arrangement under Moses. This will be a covenant of forgiveness, a law written upon the hearts of the people (Jer. 31:31–34). The gathering of those who had been scattered abroad "as the four winds of heaven" in Zechariah 2:6–13 has as its goal the dwelling of God with his people (2:10; cf. 2 Cor. 6:16) and the attachment of many nations to the people of God (2:11).[1]

It would not strain the sense of Jesus' words to suppose that this gathering of the elect is fulfilled, first, in the reversal of the effects of judgment and, secondly, in the establishment of a renewed people of God, a messianic community, embracing Gentiles, circumcised in the heart rather than in the flesh (cf. Rom. 2:28–29; 2 Cor. 3:5–18), who worship in the power of the Holy Spirit on Mount Zion, the "city of the living God, the heavenly Jerusalem" (Heb. 12:22). Ironically, it was the high priest Caiaphas who saw most clearly how Jesus' death might be the means by which "the children of God who are scattered abroad" would be gathered into one (John 11:52) – an event which marks not the end but the beginning of Christ's kingdom. Jesus' curious remark to Nathanael about seeing "the angels of God ascending and descending on the Son of Man" (John 1:51) should also be read here. The allusion, of course, is to Jacob's dream (Gen. 28:12). The details are difficult to explain, but the larger point seems clear. Jesus appropriates for the Son of Man the content of Jacob's dream, the reiteration of the promise to Abraham: the Son of Man will be at the head of a global people through whom all the families of the earth shall be blessed (Gen. 28:14).

---

[1] See also Ps. 50:3–5; Isa. 43:6; Ezek. 34:13. Cf. Acts 15:14–18: James speaks of how "first God visited to take from the nations a people for his name" (15:14).

The acknowledgement of Christ among the nations and the entry of Gentiles into the kingdom of God is an indication to these Jewish disciples that their "redemption is drawing near" (Luke 21:28). The exhortation to "straighten up and raise your heads" suggests that the disciples will have been disgraced and downtrodden (cf. Job 10:15; Zech. 2:4 LXX; Sir. 11:13; 20:11; note also Ps. 24:7–10). There is a lesson to be learned from the fig tree: when life appears to break out on the dead branches, it is a sign that summer is near. So, when the disciples see all these things happening, it will be a sign for them that "it is near, at the gates." Luke is unambiguous at this point: it is not the returning Christ but the reign of God which is near (Luke 21:31), which will also be the "redemption" of the downtrodden disciples.

In Mark and Matthew we are not told *who or what* is near (Mark 13:29; Matt. 24:33). Despite Luke's reading it is often assumed that the reference is to the Son of Man, who is about to come on the clouds of heaven.[2] This is not an unreasonable interpretation of the image and does not, in any case, have much of a bearing on the question of the direction of his coming. It would most naturally describe a figure standing at the door of a house, perhaps the temple, about to enter (cf. Jas. 5:9; 2 Kgs. 5:9 LXX; Job 31:9 LXX), which suits neither the traditional understanding of the second coming nor Daniel's vision of the Son of Man approaching the throne of God. We should probably suppose, then, that the phrase refers more generally to the two climactic events which mark the end of the period of judgment and suffering: the revelation of the Son of Man "coming on the clouds of heaven" and the gathering of the elect (Mark 13:26–27; Matt. 24:30–31). Jerusalem has been destroyed, its people killed or led captive among the nations. The disciples have fled. And this has brought them

---

[2] See, e.g., Hagner, *Matthew*, 715; Hooker, *Mark*, 321. France argues that Jesus is still answering the disciples' question about the temple: it is the destruction of the temple that is near (France, *Mark*, 538).

to the turning point of salvation history. This is the moment at which Daniel's prophetic vision is about to become a reality, when the Son of Man who suffered, and those who suffered with him, are vindicated among the nations. Only in this way can we make sense of Jesus' insistence that "all these things" will take place within the life-time of "this generation."[3]

Being Watchful

The concluding paragraphs of this composite discourse are dominated by the image of a master coming to his house at an unexpected time and the "reckoning" that will take place on his arrival. If we hold to the view that the coming of the Son of Man in Jesus' teaching still lies in our future, the warnings and parables about readiness found here will naturally be seen to have a universal frame of reference. Our reading of Jesus' prophecy to this point, however, compels us to take seriously the possibility that the "house" in these stories is not the world but Israel, and perhaps quite specifically the temple. Lamenting over Jerusalem, Jesus had earlier declared: "see, your house is left to you desolate" (Matt. 23:38); and in Matthew 10:6 he speaks of the "lost sheep of the house of Israel."[4] On this assumption the *coming* of the master (in the parable of the ten maidens and the bridegroom) is the *coming* of the Son of Man, broadly as we have understood it in the preceding

---

[3] Cf. Wright, *Victory*, 364: "When Jerusalem is destroyed, and Jesus' people escape from the ruin just in time, *that will be* YHWH becoming king, bringing about the liberation of his true covenant people, the true return from exile, the beginning of the new world order." Whether the exilic motifs are as clear as Wright thinks, however, is debatable (see, e.g., C. A. Evans, "Jesus and the Continuing Exile of Israel," in Newman, *Jesus and the Restoration of Israel*, 77–100). See also Nolland, *Luke*, 1009–10; G. B. Caird, *The Language and Imagery of the Bible* (London: Duckworth, 1980), 243–71.

[4] Note also Acts 2:36; 7:42. The terminology is widespread in the Old Testament: "son of man, you dwell in the midst of a rebellious house" (Ezek. 12:2).

sections: judgment on faithless Israel, vindication of the disciples, and the transfer of sovereignty to the resurrected Christ. We have become accustomed to reading these stories as illustrations of a universalized spiritual truth. We recover their intense urgency only if, through a conscious act of historical reimagination, we grasp the seriousness of the crisis that bore down upon the early Jewish church.[5]

The parable about the master away from home in Mark 13:34–37, for example, addresses the problem of the uncertain timing of "that day or that hour" (13:32), but Jesus has no doubt that the day will come during the lifetime of his contemporaries (13:30–31). The story of an absent householder occurs in several forms. In Mark's concise version the disciples appear to be given the role of the "doorkeeper," who must stay awake throughout the night because he does not know at what hour the "master of the house will come."[6] Matthew has two parables that elaborate upon this motif. In the first, the faithful servant is the disciple who takes proper care of the people of the house; the wicked servant is presumably the disciple who behaves no better than the scribes and the Pharisees (Matt. 24:45–51; cf. Luke 12:42–48). In the second, the parable of the talents (Matt. 25:14–30; cf. Luke 19:12–27), the wicked servant is the one who fails to invest the money entrusted to him because he believes his master to be a "hard man, reaping where you did not sow, and gathering where you scattered no seed" (Matt. 25:24).[7] In both stories the good servant is "set over much" – a reference to the promised

---

[5] In Luke 21:35 it is said that "that day" will surprise "all who dwell on the face of the whole earth," suggesting a universal disaster. However, there are instances where this terminology is used in the OT in connection with judgment on Israel (e.g., Ezek. 38:20; Zeph. 1:2–3) or otherwise in a hyperbolic manner (Isa. 23:17; Jer. 25:26). In Luke 21:23 Jesus says: "there will be great distress upon the earth and wrath against this people," which may suggest a narrower understanding of "earth."

[6] Note the story of the doorkeeper who fell asleep, allowing Rechab and Baanah into the house to kill Ishbosheth in 2 Sam. 4:5–7 LXX.

[7] Cf. Wright, *Victory*, 632–39.

enthronement of those who faithfully endure the hardships of this time of tribulation. The parable of the wise and foolish virgins (Matt. 25:1–12), whatever its exact thrust, belongs in the same category.

This reading, finally, makes good sense of the analogy with the days of Noah and of Lot – catastrophic judgment coming suddenly upon a complacent and oblivious people (Matt. 24:37–39; cf. Luke 17:26–29).[8] Of two men working in a field, one will be taken, the other left; of two women grinding flour, one will be taken, the other left; of two people in bed, one will be taken, the other left (Matt. 24:40–41; Luke 17:34–35). The context strongly suggests – contrary to popular apocalyptic expectation – that it is the one who is *left behind* who is the lucky one. These sayings are about the effects of judgment on the day when the Son of Man is revealed: men and women at the time of the flood were suddenly swept away (Matt. 24:38–39; Luke 17:26–27); fire and sulfur fell from heaven and destroyed the people of Sodom (Luke 17:28–30); a householder fails to prevent a thief breaking in (Matt. 24:43; cf. Luke 12:39). The message for the disciples is to be prepared, but the dramatic focus in each story is on those who suffer judgment; and when judgment comes in the form of military invasion, those who are taken are the victims, those who are left are the survivors.[9] The few who are saved – like Noah who "entered the ark" and Lot who "went out from Sodom" – are the believing Jews in Judea who will flee to the mountains when they see Jerusalem surrounded by armies and the "abomination of desolation" standing in the holy place (Mark 13:14–16; Luke 21:21; Matt. 24:16–18).

---

[8] Luke has these stories earlier, but 21:34–35 is a clear allusion to them. See Wright, *Victory*, 365–67.

[9] Cf. Wright, *Victory*, 366. In Joel 2:9; Jer. 49:9 LXX the thief is an image of the invading force.

The Sheep and Goats

Jesus' teaching on the Mount of Olives closes with an account of a judgment that will take place when "the Son of Man comes in his glory, and all the angels with him" (Matt. 25:31–46), in which the "righteous" are separated from the "cursed" as a shepherd separates the sheep from the goats. We must, at this point, again ask ourselves the question that has pestered us all along the road of this study: Does this passage form part of the world's or of Israel's story? Is this the final judgment of all humankind, as has usually been supposed? Or must it somehow be linked to the disaster that overcame Israel and the reconstitution of the people of God around the Son of Man? A number of observations suggest that the narrower interpretation is more appropriate.[10]

First, the image of the Lord coming "and all the holy ones with him" in Zechariah 14:5 appears in the context of "a day of the LORD," when God will fight against the nations which plundered Jerusalem. There is here the characteristic shift from the destruction of Jerusalem to the destruction of the nations by whose instrumentality Israel was judged. On that day "living waters shall flow out from Jerusalem" and "the LORD will be king over all the earth" (Zech. 14:8–9). If this verse forms part of the background to the description of the Son of Man coming with the angels, it tends to connect the verse with divine judgment upon the enemies of Israel.

Secondly, the judgment appears to presuppose the particular conditions that Jesus expected his disciples to face in the period leading up to the invasion of Judea. It is "the least of these my brothers" who suffer hunger and thirst, who are strangers, naked, weak, and imprisoned; and it is to these that the teaching is principally directed.

Thirdly, a closely related thought is found in Matthew

---

[10] On the various interpretations of "all the nations" that have been proposed see Hagner, *Matthew*, 742.

10:42: "whoever gives one of these little ones even a cup of cold water because he is a disciple, truly, I say to you, he will by no means lose his reward." This verse comes at the end of the instruction that Jesus gave his disciples when he sent them out to proclaim the imminence of the kingdom of God to the "lost sheep of the house of Israel" (Matt. 10:6–7). Much of that teaching has to do with the hostility and rejection that the disciples – the little ones, the least of these my brothers – would encounter; but the closing verses illustrate a general principle: "Whoever receives you receives me, and whoever receives me receives him who sent me" (Matt. 10:40). The parallel between this statement and the rationale given for the separation of the righteous and the wicked in the sheep and goats judgment scene strongly suggests that the same concrete historical circumstances are in view, except that the perspective is wider. It is not the Jews who are judged according to how they have treated the disciples but the nations.

Finally, other passages connecting the Son of Man, his angels, and judgment may also be understood as statements about the fate of first-century Israel. In his explanation of the parable of the weeds Jesus says that the "Son of Man will send his angels, and they will gather out of his kingdom all causes of sin and all law-breakers" (Matt. 13:41). The restriction of the judgment to "his kingdom" suggests that its scope is not universal; and from the point of view of Jesus' audience the phrase "the close of the age" can only have signified a concrete, historical judgment on Israel. Jesus promises the disciples in Matthew 16:27 that "the Son of Man is going to come with his angels in the glory of his Father, and then he will repay each person according to what he has done." He then assures them, in the next verse, that the coming of the Son of Man in his kingdom will happen within the lifetime of some of those standing there. In Mark 8:38 (cf. Luke 9:26), the saying about those of whom the Son of Man will be ashamed "when he comes in the glory of his Father with the holy angels" includes the unambiguous qualifying phrase "in this adulterous and sinful generation."

What we have then, quite specifically, is a judgment of the nations *on the basis of* how they treated the disciples of Jesus during the period of crisis that accompanied the judgment on Israel and the end of the age. How do we relate this to the wider scheme of judgment at the coming of the Son of Man? We have argued that this judgment is not final or universal but must be understood within the framework of the renewal of the people of God and the transfer of sovereignty to the Christ. But are we supposed to reduce this further to the point where, as this story suggests, the nations are judged solely with regard to how they have treated Jesus' disciples? Possibly. The fourth beast in Daniel's vision is widely destructive: "it shall devour the whole earth, and trample it down, and break it to pieces" (Dan. 7:23). But the beast is destroyed because the little horn that appeared on its head "made war with the saints and prevailed over them, until the Ancient of Days came, and judgment was given for the saints of the Most High, and the time came when the saints possessed the kingdom" (7:21–22). There is not a close literary connection between the story of the sheep and the goats and Daniel 7, but we do need to take seriously the fact that at the heart of these apocalyptic visions is the suffering of the people of God at the hands of their enemies. Just as the persecuted saints of the Most High *are* the symbolic figure of the Son of Man in Daniel's vision, so at a more mundane and realistic level the persecuted disciples, who are hungry, thirsty, naked, alienated, sick, imprisoned, *are* the Son of Man (Matt. 25:40, 45) who now sits in judgment.

The End of Their World

Following a discussion about the likelihood of rich people entering the kingdom of God, Peter makes the observation to Jesus that the disciples have left everything in order to follow him. In response Jesus assures him that they will receive a hundredfold "in this time" and "in the age (*aiōni*) to come the life of the age (*aiōnion*)" (Mark 10:29–30; Luke 18:29–30). This is not an elegant translation – we would usually expect something like "in the age to come *eternal* life" (ESV). But it draws attention to the fact that the word *aiōnios* is simply the adjective derived from *aiōn*, which means "age." In view of this, we need to ask two questions. First, how does this "age to come" relate to normal history? Secondly, what is this "life" that is *aiōnios*?

The word *aiōn* occurs most frequently in biblical Greek in such phrases as *eis ton aiōna* ("for the age"), *eis tous aiōnas* ("for the ages"), or more emphatically *eis ton aiōna tou aiōnos* ("for the age of the age"). The meaning of these expressions is simply "forever" – but "forever" conceived as an unending extension of some particular historical circumstance, not as "eternity," which carries with it the clear connotation of time beyond death or beyond history. To give a mundane example: in the law of Moses, if a Hebrew slave chose not to be freed after six years, his master would bore his ear with an awl, and he would serve him *eis ton aiōna* – not for eternity, but for life (Exod. 21:6 LXX). The adjective *aiōnios* is used in the same way: it describes something that will last throughout the age, from generation to generation. If, however, there is a sense that we are approaching a boundary between two ages, it is natural to take these expressions as descriptive of the "age to come."

Our reading of Jesus' apocalyptic discourse suggests that he believed that the "close of the age" (Matt. 24:3) was not far off and was bound up with the historical fate of Second Temple Judaism.[11] The writer to the Hebrews uses

---

[11] Sir. 39:28 speaks of a "time of completion" (*kairōi sunteleias*) when winds created for vengeance will "pour out their strength and calm the anger of their Maker" (RSV). *sunteleia* is used to define the end of a particular historical period (e.g., Dan. 11:13, 27). For *sunteleiai tōn aiōnōn* see also: Sir. 43:7 S; *As. Mos.* 12:4; *4 Ezra* 6:25; *2 Bar.* 54:21; 69:4; 83:7. Tobit envisages the rebuilding of an inferior temple which will last "until the times of the age are completed." At that point all Israel will return from captivity and Jerusalem and the temple will be rebuilt "with a glorious building for all generations forever" (Tob. 14:5 RSV).

essentially the same phrase with reference to Christ's appearance "at the end of the ages (*epi sunteleiai tōn aiōnōn*) to put away sin by the sacrifice of himself" (Heb. 9:26); Paul believed that "the end of the ages" (*ta telē tōn aiōnōn*) had come upon his generation (1 Cor. 10:11). The age to come would then be the age of the renewed people of God, centered around Christ, constituted by a new covenant, their life defined not by the law of God but by the Spirit of God. This is the *palingenesia* (Matt. 19:28), the regeneration or rebirth of Israel after the devastation of divine judgment.[12]

If this is correct, what would be the effect of fitting the other sayings into the same eschatological framework? The judgment "at the close of the age" (*en tēi sunteleiai tou aiōnos*) that is depicted in two parables in Matthew (Matt. 13:39–40, 49), when the wicked are separated from the righteous, would need to be understood not as judgment on the whole of humanity at the end of history but as a decisive, perhaps final, judgment on Israel within history. The "anxieties of this age" (*hai merimnai tou aiōnos*) that choke the seeds sown among thorns (Mark 4:19; cf. Matt. 13:22) are not universal concerns ("cares of the world" as the ESV has it) but the particular anxieties of living under Roman occupation, with all that that entailed. The "deceitfulness of riches" is included here because wealth created a false sense of security at a time when survival depended on radical trust in God. When Jesus says, regarding the interpretation of this parable, that the disciples have been given the "secret of the kingdom of God" (Mark 4:11; Matt. 13:11), he has in mind a kingdom that will come in defiance of Satan (understood as the demonic or as the power behind Roman imperialism), through "tribulation or persecution," and in the midst of the stress of the current political state of affairs. The "sons

---

12 Josephus uses *palingenesia* for the restoration of Israel after the exile (*Ant*. 11.3.9 §66); Philo uses it for the regeneration of humankind following the flood (Philo, *Mos*. 2.65).

of this age" are commended for their shrewdness (Luke 16:8); the disciples are advised to "make friends for yourselves by means of unrighteous wealth," so that when their own resources fail they may find hospitality in the "dwellings of the age." The risen Christ promises the disciples that he will be with them "all the days until the close of the age" (Matt. 28:20).[13] It would be a hard-hearted exegete who would deny that this remains a valid promise for the church today; nevertheless, it should be read in the first place as an immediate and highly pertinent assurance regarding the crisis in Judea and the emergence of the church into the Roman world. The one who has suffered and overcome death promises to be with those who will suffer for his sake during the turmoil of the coming years. In this way, we recover the narrative context, we reconnect Jesus' words with the experience of the disciples, the concrete circumstances that they faced, and the particular story of Israel.

If the "age to come" is the age that follows the collapse of Second Temple Judaism, what are we to understand by the phrase *zōē aiōnios*? Instinctively, we read this as a reference to "eternal life" with God in heaven, but as we work through this material, we find ourselves increasingly blown by the winds of interpretation in the direction of a more realistic and "worldly" understanding. When Jesus promises his followers that they will inherit the "life of the age,"[14] he must mean the life that will be experienced by the people of God following the climax at the end of the age, following the judgment on Israel, the life that will last throughout the age which is to come – and which has now come. It is the life in the Spirit that is given to the people of God following suffering, death, and resurrection (cf. Dan. 12:2). This is the basis for the very concrete image in John's Gospel of the dead coming from the tombs in the near

---

[13] Cf. Zech. 8:23; Jub. 1:17, 26.

[14] Matt. 19:29; Mark 10:30; Luke 18:30; cf. Matt. 19:16; 25:46; Mark 10:17; Luke 10:25; 18:18.

future in response to the voice of the "Son of Man" – "those who have done good to the resurrection of life, and those who have done evil to the resurrection of judgment" (John 5:28–29; cf. Matt.27:52–53). But inseparable from the national metaphor is a much more realistic and literal hope of resurrection for those who suffer and die, because Jesus is "the resurrection and the life," and anyone who believes in him, "though he die, yet shall he live" (John 11:25).

With Jesus in paradise

Jesus' promise to the repentant criminal that "today you will be with me in Paradise" (Luke 23:43) has usually been read as a statement about what happens after death. This may be the case: *paradeisos* means "garden," especially the garden of Eden, and Jesus may have used it as a metaphor for the presence of God (cf. 2 Cor. 12:4; Rev. 2:7). The word, however, occurs in a highly suggestive context in Isaiah 51:3 LXX: "And now I will comfort you, O Zion; and I have comforted all her desert places; and I will make her desert places as a garden (*paradeison*) of the LORD." The wider passage speaks of the salvation of Zion following divine judgment and resonates at a number of points with the crucifixion narrative, not least:

> The Lord God has opened my ear, and I was not rebellious; I turned not backward. I gave my back to those who strike, and my cheeks to those who pull out the beard; I hid not my face from disgrace and spitting. But the Lord God helps me; therefore I have not been disgraced; therefore I have set my face like a flint, and I know that I shall not be put to shame. He who vindicates me is near. (Isa. 50:5–8)

Arguably the real promise here has to do less with the fate of the individual than with the restoration of Israel – not through violence (all the more pertinent if the "criminal" is not a petty thief but a revolutionary who sought the liberation of Israel through armed resistance) but through the suffering of the Servant of the Lord and through national repentance. "Paradise" is then not so much a place to which the soul goes at death, temporarily or otherwise, but a *metaphor* for the salvation of Israel which is to be accomplished through Jesus' death and resurrection. The promise is an assurance to those who "pursue righteousness" (Isa. 51:1) that the God who made Abraham many (51:2) will indeed comfort Zion and transform her wilderness into a garden like Eden.

Images of Judgment

There is no question that there is a lot of "hellish" language in the Gospels. If some of those to whom Jesus spoke would experience the life of the age to come, others faced a dreadful alternative: death and destruction, the outer darkness, the *gehenna* of fire, and Hades.

The path that leads to destruction

The image of two ways, one leading to life and one leading to death, is found in Jeremiah 21:8. King Zedekiah has sent a messenger to Jeremiah, hoping to hear from him that the Lord will perform one of the wonderful deeds for which he was renowned and force the belligerent Nebuchadnezzar to withdraw (21:1–2). Jeremiah's response is not reassuring: far from repelling the Chaldeans, the Lord himself "will fight against you with outstretched hand and strong arm, in anger and in fury and in great wrath" (21:5). But Jeremiah does hold out a fragile hope:

> Thus says the Lord: Behold, I set before you the way of life and the way of death. He who stays in this city shall die by the sword, by famine, and by pestilence, but he who goes out and surrenders to the Chaldeans who are besieging you shall live and shall have his life as a prize of war. For I have set my face against this city for harm and not for good, declares the Lord: it shall be given into the hand of the king of Babylon, and he shall burn it with fire. (Jer. 21:8–10)

Jesus puts before the people an equally realistic choice: a wide gate and broad path leading to destruction, or a narrow gate and difficult way leading to life (Matt. 7:13–14; cf. Luke 13:23–24). We can ask whether the word used here for "destruction" (*apōleia*) connotes annihilation or conscious torment. But the thought is quite straightforward: if something is destroyed, while the process of destruction is likely to be painful, the result is that it ceases to exist. Isaiah prophesies regarding Edom: "Her princes shall be no more, for her kings and her princes and her great men shall be for destruction (*eis apōleian*)" (Isa. 34:12 LXX). The more important question is whether Jesus is thinking in personal or national terms. The word can refer to the "death" of individuals (e.g., Num. 20:3; Wis. 1:13; 18:7; 2 Macc. 13:6), but more commonly, and certainly more appropriately here if Jesus has Jeremiah 21:8 in mind, it is used for the destruction of a city or people: destruction will come upon Babylon (Isa. 47:11 LXX); Antiochus Epiphanes plotted the final destruction of the Jews, in this case by selling them into slavery (1 Macc. 3:42).

This reading of Jesus' words has to be seriously considered. It is far more likely that his audience would have heard the echoes from the Old Testament and reapplied the ancient stories to their own circumstances than that they would have found in these statements the nucleus of a systematic and universalized eschatology. When he warns them that they will perish (*apoleisthe*) if they do not repent, he means that they will be killed – like the Galileans butchered by Pilate, or the eighteen people in Siloam who were killed when a tower collapsed upon them (Luke 13:4–5).[15]

The darkness outside

In response to the "faith" of the centurion who sought healing for his paralyzed servant, Jesus warns the Jews that "many will come from east and west and recline at table with Abraham, Isaac, and Jacob in the kingdom of heaven,

[15] Cf. E. E. Ellis, "New Testament Teaching on Hell," in Brower and Elliott, *"The Reader Must Understand,"* 213: "On these analogies the punishment of the wicked will be a life-destroying act with a permanent and unrecallable effect."

while the sons of the kingdom will be thrown into the outer darkness. In that place there will be weeping and gnashing of teeth" (Matt. 8:11–12). The inclusion of Gentiles and the exclusion of Jews are events within the immediate eschatological horizon: they belong to the transition from the old age of Second Temple Judaism to the new age of the Spirit. Luke places the saying in the context of Jesus' journey towards Jerusalem (Luke 13:28–29). When someone asks him, "Lord, will those who are saved be few?" (13:23), this is not a general theological question about quotas for heaven: it is a question about Israel. Jesus tells them to strive to enter by the narrow door. Once the householder has shut the door, many will stand outside protesting that they ate and drank in his presence, that he taught in their streets; but he will tell these "workers of evil" to depart. They will be thrust out of the kingdom of God and will weep and gnash their teeth on the outside.

The invited guests who maltreated and killed the king's servants and refused to attend the banquet incur the wrath of the king: "he sent his troops and destroyed those murderers and burned their city" (Matt. 22:7). The chief priests and the Pharisees were well aware that stories such as this were told against them (Matt. 21:45); they cannot have failed to hear in it a barely disguised threat of judgment against a complacent and hypocritical nation (cf. Isa. 5:24–26). A man who came to the party without a wedding garment was quickly bound and thrown into the darkness outside, where "there will be weeping and gnashing of teeth" (22:13). This curious coda to the story is hard to explain, but the imagery of exclusion clearly presupposes the same eschatological context.

When the householder shuts the door, when the marriage of the king's son is celebrated, when the master returns (Matt. 24:45–51; 25:14–30; Luke 19:12–28), when the bridegroom comes to the marriage feast (Matt. 25:1–13), there will be those who will be excluded, who will find themselves in the darkness outside, where "there will be wailing and gnashing of teeth." What for Jesus' hearers was this decisive moment? In Luke's Gospel Jesus tells the story of the pounds "because he was near to Jerusalem, and because they supposed that the kingdom of God was to appear immediately" (Luke 19:11). There will be a delay: a nobleman will go away "into a far country to receive for himself a kingdom and then return." But the parable does not for that reason cease to be of interest to the people of Jerusalem. The enemies who do not want the returning king to rule over them are Jesus' enemies (19:27); their punishment will come when the city is destroyed. The feckless servant who does nothing with his money is the disciple who is afraid to do anything with what Jesus has entrusted to him (19:20–24).

The refrain "there will be wailing (*klauthmos*) and gnashing (*brugmos*) of teeth" is curious. "Wailing" in Jewish writings readily refers to the sound made by those who suffer judgment: "Woe, woe, your punishments have come; now shall be your wailings (*klauthmoi*)" (Micah 7:4 LXX; cf. Isa. 30:19; 65:19; Bar. 4:11). Significantly, this verse in Micah is followed by a passage that must have been in Jesus' mind when he told the disciples that he had not come to bring peace but division: "the son treats the father with contempt, the daughter rises up against her mother, the daughter-in-law against her mother-in-law; a man's enemies are the men of his own house" (Micah 7:6; cf. Matt. 10:34–36; Luke 12:51–53). The "gnashing of teeth," however, typically signifies hostility towards the righteous Jew: "The wicked plots against the righteous, and gnashes (*bruxei*) his teeth at him" (Ps. 36:12 LXX; cf. Pss. 34:15–16; 111:9–10 LXX; Sir. 51:3); the members of the Jewish council who listened to Stephen's speech were enraged at the end and "gnashed (*ebruxon*) their teeth against him" (Acts 7:54, translation mine).[16] It seems quite likely, therefore, that what Jesus saw taking place in this "outer darkness" was the wailing of Jews under the judgment of God, while the gnashing of teeth refers to their hostility towards the righteous. In any

[16] In Lam. 2:16 it is the enemies of exiled Judah who gnash their teeth at the daughter of Jerusalem; in Job 16:9 it is God who becomes Job's enemy and gnashes his teeth against him.

case, we appear still to be in the real world of national crisis, not in some final metaphysical state of hell.

The Gehenna of fire

The Valley of Hinnom lay to the south-west of Jerusalem. The location acquired notoriety in ancient Israel because at one time people – among them King Ahab – had burned their children as offerings to Molech at a place in the valley called Topheth (2 Kgs. 23:10; 2 Chr. 28:3). The practice is mentioned in Jeremiah 7:31 as an example of the evil that the "sons of Judah" had done in the sight of the Lord; and the judgment he pronounces as a consequence is appalling:

> Therefore, behold, the days are coming, declares the LORD, when it will no more be called Topheth, or the Valley of the Son of Hinnom, but the Valley of Slaughter; for they will bury in Topheth, because there is no room elsewhere. And the dead bodies of this people will be food for the birds of the air, and for the beasts of the earth, and none will frighten them away. And I will silence in the cities of Judah and in the streets of Jerusalem the voice of mirth and the voice of gladness, the voice of the bridegroom and the voice of the bride, for the land shall become a waste. (Jer. 7:32–34)

Jeremiah is sent out later with a "potter's earthenware flask" to pronounce the same verdict and to smash the flask as a sign that the Lord will "break this people and this city, as one breaks a potter's vessel, so that it can never be mended" (Jer. 19:10–11). So the Valley of Hinnom becomes a symbol of divine judgment on the "kings of Judah and inhabitants of Jerusalem" (Jer. 19:3) – but not of an abstract or spiritual judgment: "in this place I will . . . cause their people to fall by the sword before their enemies, and by the hand of those who seek their life" (19:7). The valley represents the stark and extreme horror of military defeat.[17]

---

[17] In 4 Ezra 2:27–29, Gehenna is what the nations do to Israel in the day of tribulation and anguish: "The nations shall envy you but they shall not be able to do anything against you, says the Lord. My hands will cover you, that your sons may not see Gehenna."

By the first century, the Valley of Hinnom (in Greek *geenna*, Gehenna), because of these associations, had become the city's refuse dump, where slow fires smoldered day and night. So when Jesus warns that a person whose eyes cause him to sin risks being thrown into the "*geenna* of fire" (Matt. 18:9; cf. 5:22, 29–30; Mark 9:43, 45, 47), these connotations come shockingly into view, like images flashed on a screen. This must have been heard as, in some way, a reiteration, a reapplication, of Jeremiah's prophecy: the consequence of Israel's sin at both an individual and a national level would be military defeat on a dreadful scale. He lambasts the Pharisees for making proselytes who become "twice as much a child of *geenna* as yourselves" (Matt. 23:15). "You serpents, you brood of vipers," he rebukes them, "how are you to escape being sentenced to *geenna*?" (Matt. 23:33). By persecuting the prophets and wise men and scribes that God had sent to them and by inculcating the same hardness of heart into their followers, they are bringing upon themselves a judgment that will – in very real terms – leave the dead burning in the Valley of Hinnom.

In Mark 9:48 Gehenna is further characterized by reference to the vision in Isaiah 66:24 of the dead who have rebelled against God: "their worm shall not die, their fire shall not be quenched, and they shall be an abhorrence to all flesh." Again it must be stressed that this is not an image of eternal torment or punishment: these are the bodies of the dead, and it is because they are dead and exposed for the world to gaze upon that they are an abhorrence.[18]

---

[18] Head questions the evidence for the existence of a "fiery rubbish dump" in the Valley of Hinnom and argues that Isa. 66:24 provides the significant background to Mark 9:42–48. He also argues that elsewhere in Jewish thought the link between Isa. 66:24 and the Hinnom judgment gives rise to images of eternal torment (P. M. Head, "The Duration of Divine Judgment in the New Testament," in Brower and Elliott, *"The Reader Must Understand,"* 223–24). But it is difficult to see how a description of corpses being consumed – even eternally consumed – by fire and maggots can be construed as an "*experience* of judgment" (emphasis added). Corpses do not "experience" anything.

The distinction that Jesus makes between those who kill the body only and the one "who can destroy both soul and body in *geenna*" (Matt. 10:28; cf. Luke 12:5) can be read against the same background. The saying occurs in the context of his warning to his disciples that, as they undertake their mission of proclaiming the kingdom throughout the towns and villages of Israel, they will face violent opposition. They have no need, however, to fear those who can kill the body because they will be acknowledged by the Son of Man before the Father – they will be vindicated (Matt. 10:32). But the judgment of Gehenna that God will bring upon the nation will mean death without any prospect of vindication – not only the body but the soul also will be destroyed.

The image in Isaiah 66:24 of a fire that will not be quenched (*sbesthēsetai*) is picked up by John the Baptist and incorporated into a metaphor that depicts the coming judgment as the separation of the wheat from the chaff on the threshing floor: the wheat will be gathered into the granary, but the chaff will be burned "with unquenchable (*asbestōi*) fire" (Matt. 3:12; cf. Luke 3:17). Closely related to this are two parables that Jesus tells – one about the harvest at the "close of the age," when the angels will gather the weeds and throw them into the "fiery furnace" (Matt. 13:37–42), the other about fishermen who sort out the good fish from the bad: "so it will be at the close of the age," Jesus concludes. "The angels will come out and separate the evil from the righteous and throw them into the fiery furnace. In that place there will be weeping and gnashing of teeth" (Matt. 13:47–50). In a similar way Jesus reuses John's image of the tree that does not bear good fruit and is cut down and burned (Matt. 7:19; cf. 3:10).[19] The apocalyptic framework that we are working with suggests quite naturally that these sayings refer to the impending judgment on Israel – in John's words, the "wrath to come." "Even now," he says, "the ax is laid to the root of the trees"

[19] The image is used in a rather different way in John 15:6.

(Matt. 3:7, 10; cf. Luke 3:7, 9). What is good will be preserved, what is worthless will be destroyed.

The fire of Gehenna also merges into the more abstract idea of the "fire of the age" (*to pur to aiōnion*: cf. Matt. 18:8), which has been prepared for the devil and his angels and into which those from the nations who neglect or mistreat Jesus' disciples depart (Matt. 25:41). This judgment is also described as a "punishment (*kolasin*) of the age" (25:46), but this adds nothing that is not already in the image of fire.

Hades

Numerous texts in the Greek Old Testament place "Hades," which is equivalent to the Hebrew "Sheol," in synonymous parallelism with "death." For example, Hezekiah writes after his recovery from illness: "Those in Hades will not praise you, nor will those who have died bless you, nor will those in Hades hope for your mercy" (Isa. 38:18 LXX).[20] For Capernaum, therefore, to be "brought down to Hades" means that its inhabitants will be killed when judgment comes upon Israel: they will go down to the place of the dead (Matt. 11:23; Luke 10:15; cf. Isa. 14:11; Bar. 3:19). To go down into Hades can be construed as punishment for the wicked (cf. Pss. 9:18; 48:15 LXX), but this does not imply the continuing active punishment of the wicked in Hades: death itself is the punishment.

When Jesus tells Peter that he will build his church on this "rock" and that "the gates of Hades (*pulai hadou*) will not prevail[21] against it" (Matt. 16:18, translation mine), he means only that death will not overcome the church. The expression "gates of Hades" is a Semitic idiom for death, or proximity to death. For example, Jews who feared that they would be trampled to death by Antiochus' elephants cried out to God, "imploring the Ruler over every power to

---

[20] Cf. Num. 16:33; Ps. 6:6; 17:6; 48:15; 54:16; 88:49; 114:3 LXX; Prov. 2:18; 7:27; Isa. 28:15.

[21] *katischuō* with the genitive is dynamic, meaning to "overpower" rather than "withstand" (cf. Jer. 15:18 LXX).

manifest himself and be merciful to them, as they stood now at the gates of death (*pulai hadou*)" (3 Macc. 5:51 RSV).[22]

Hades is not a place of torment.[23] Rather than eat the flesh of an unlawful sacrifice, the righteous scribe Eleazar tells Antiochus' officials to "send him to Hades" (2 Macc. 6:23), clearly not expecting to suffer punishment there. The exception to this is Jesus' story about the rich man and Lazarus (Luke 16:19–23), which deserves careful consideration. Ostensibly this rather curious parable, which appears to have some affinity with an Egyptian folktale known in the first century,[24] is about the failure of the wealthy to act justly towards the poor: it is naturally read as an attack on the Pharisees who were "lovers of money" (16:14). More often, though, it has been a bone of contention in the debate over the nature of hell: R. A. Peterson, for example, draws the conclusion that this parable teaches that the wicked will enter an "intermediate state after death" in which they will "endure torment and agony."[25] Certain observations, however, suggest that this sort of interpretation entirely misses the point of the story.

First, the image of one who must eat what falls from the table (as Lazarus does from the rich man's table) is used by the Syrophoenician woman to justify her boldness when she begs Jesus to cast a demon out of her daughter (Mark 7:28; cf. Matt. 15:27). It is likely that we are meant to view Lazarus in the same light, as one who is not merely wretchedly poor but spiritually disenfranchised.[26] Lazarus is a Jewish name, and apart from this intertextual echo there is no reason to think that he represents the Gentiles who will come into the kingdom in the place of the leaders

---

22 Cf. 3 Macc. 6:31; Job 38:17; Pss. 9:14; 106:18 LXX; Isa. 38:10; Wis. 16:13.

23 Cf. Nolland, *Luke*, 557.

24 See Nolland, *Luke*, 826–27.

25 E. W. Fudge and R. A. Peterson, *Two Views of Hell: A Biblical and Theological Dialogue* (Downers Grove: InterVarsity Press, 2000), 172.

26 Wright suggests that the story makes much the same point as the parable of the prodigal son: outcast, exiled Israel is welcomed by a loving father (Wright, *Victory*, 255–56).

of the people. He corresponds to the "poor and crippled and blind and lame" who are brought in from the streets and lanes of the city in Jesus' parable of the great banquet – not to those beyond the walls of the city who are compelled to come in later (Luke 14:16–24).

Secondly, when Lazarus dies, he is not buried but is carried by angels to Abraham's bosom; when the rich man dies, he is buried in the ground and finds himself, therefore, in Hades, the grave, the place of the dead. This does not seem an accidental distinction. To be transported by angels signifies an exceptional honor – this is not a story about what happens to people when they die. To be deposited in the bosom of Abraham may point to a more precise theological argument – that it is Lazarus, not the rulers of Israel, who represents the true descendants of Abraham (cf. Luke 3:8).

Thirdly, while the rich man's five brothers could certainly have found in Moses and the prophets exhortations to act justly and defend the poor, they would also have found that such statements were embedded in eschatological contexts. The point was not that social and economic injustice were morally wrong, but that if Israel did not repent of its sin, including injustice towards the poor, the nation would come under judgment.[27] In the same way, when Mary proclaimed that God "has filled the hungry with good things, and the rich he has sent empty away," she had in mind a day of judgment and salvation for Israel (Luke 1:53).

This leads us towards the conclusion that the Hades in which the rich man is tormented is not the conventional Hades of the Old Testament, which, as we have seen, is not a place of punishment. Nor is it the traditional "hell" of popular Christian belief. Rather it is an image of the destruction that would come upon the "wealthy" in Israel, who despite the riches and glories of their religious

---

[27] Cf. Isa. 3:14–15; 10:1–3; 29:19–20; 41:17–18; Ezek. 22:27–31; Amos 2:6–7; 4:1–2; 8:4–14.

heritage failed to understand that, in the words of the beatitude, the kingdom of God would be given to the poor (cf. Luke 6:20).

To understand the future that Jesus unveiled for the four disciples who came to him on the Mount of Olives we must make a quite radical adjustment of perspective. We must go back and stand with them, on Jewish soil, and take upon ourselves the burden of their fears and uncertainties. We must see Jerusalem and its resplendent temple looming massively across the Kidron valley – Wadi en-Nar, the "Valley of Fire." We must feel ourselves as a beleaguered and insecure people of God within the suffocating embrace of an all-mighty and godless empire. We must hear Jesus' anguish over the blindness and obstinacy of this people and his conviction that judgment had become inescapable, merely a matter of time.

If we look to the future from here, if we look through the telescope of Jesus' prophetic vision, the field of view is dominated by the frightening prospect of a holy city besieged, a temple in flames, a people slaughtered, beneath a dark and angry sky. The question that presses urgently upon us is this: What will become of the people of God? More precisely, what will be the fate of this renewed Israel gathered symbolically around Jesus of Nazareth, bound together by a new covenant in his blood? The answer is found supremely in the vision of one like a son of Man, raised from the dead, who comes with the clouds of heaven to receive "dominion and glory and a kingdom, that all peoples, nations, and languages should serve him." In that vision lies the assurance that neither the Christ nor the church would be finally crushed by the juggernaut of divine judgment rolling towards the Jewish nation; both would, in the end, acquire an unshakable spiritual authority in the world. When would this come about? Jesus is quite clear: within a generation.

Five

The Suffering of the Saints

What did Paul see when he looked to the future? The horizon of Jesus' prophetic imagination was dominated by the conflagration that he believed would, within a generation, consume the city. This was no cynical or frivolous apocalyptic speculation. The vision gained its urgency from his intense and very personal involvement with this "people of God" – the Pharisees in their stubborn inability to grasp the reality of the coming kingdom; the women of Jerusalem, whose children would suffer the turmoil of rebellion and the savagery of Roman retaliation (Luke 23:28–30); the disciples, who had hitched their wagon to this controversial teacher from Nazareth with little idea of the trouble that awaited them not much further down the road. Jesus looked to the future from a position of passionate, even despairing, engagement in the fate of Israel.

Paul, however, was an outsider, a Jew of the Diaspora, who, despite his pedigree as a Pharisee, his erstwhile zeal for the law, and his continuing concern for the salvation of his people, roamed far beyond the national and theological boundaries of Judaism. The horizon of the future inevitably looked very different from Antioch or Ephesus or Corinth. Whereas the fate of Jerusalem and its temple was central to Jesus' teaching about the future, it appears to have been at best a marginal concern in Paul's eschatology. We have the impression that his expectation regarding the *parousia* of Christ, though in places no less vivid and intense, is not so firmly tethered historically and geographically.

The practical and pastoral needs of a very different audience have also had an impact. For example, whereas Jesus' apocalyptic teaching included a clear indication that few of his disciples would live to see the *parousia* event (Matt. 16:28; Mark 9:1; Luke 9:27; cf. John 21:22), the death of believers at Thessalonica some twenty years later, perhaps as a direct result of persecution, appears to have constituted a serious setback to the community's hopes regarding the coming of Christ. The passage of time had exposed, if not inconsistencies and weaknesses in his apocalyptic gospel, then at least the potential for misunderstanding and abuse, which had to be corrected.

Significant literary differences also arise with the change of context. Unlike Jesus' discourse, which has the appearance of a unified and coherent narrative, Paul's eschatology emerges from conversations with disparate groups of believers. Although to some degree the other threads in the dialogue can be reconstructed, there are likely to be serious ambiguities and gaps in the line of thought. There will be the difficulty of deciding to what extent his teaching has been deflected from any normative eschatological storyline by the rhetorical and pastoral demands of the particular situation addressed. Matters are complicated further by the question of whether Paul's thinking about the *parousia* and related issues underwent any significant development or revision during the course of his apostolic career. For example, do we see him adjusting the scope or focus of his eschatology in response to the non-occurrence of the *parousia*, as has often been claimed?

As we move from Jesus to Paul, therefore, we have to keep in mind that we are not looking at the future from the same place – the landscape has changed, the horizon has shifted. The starting point is a pervasive impression that Paul expected some form of crisis to come upon the world, or at least upon the world of his churches. This crisis is interpreted in general terms as a manifestation of the "wrath of God." At the heart of it is the appearance of an enigmatic figure who is described in 2 Thessalonians 2:3–10 as a "man of lawlessness," which will be the subject of Chapter 6.

The Present Distress

When Paul wrote to the community of believers at Corinth around A.D. 55, he spoke clearly and urgently of a state of crisis. The church had sought advice concerning relations between men and women (1 Cor. 7:1). His response, in the first place, consisted of instructions on how best to manage the pressures of human sexuality and the peculiar tensions of Christian marriage, especially in cases where one partner was not a believer. Underlying this, however, we may detect a pressing awareness that these ordinary human commitments would have to be lived out under difficult and disruptive social conditions. It is this awareness, above all, that skews Paul's sexual ethic in this chapter, giving rise both to his personal preference for being unmarried and to his recommendation that everyone should "remain in the condition in which he was called" (1 Cor. 7:20). When the community finds itself flying through severe turbulence, it is not the time to go casually walking up and down the aisles of the plane. Passengers are advised to remain seated, with their seatbelts fastened – and in Paul's view, frankly, it would be much better if they did not have a husband or wife or children to worry about.[1]

The nature of this social turbulence, however, is left unclear. What is the crisis? He speaks in verse 26 of "the present distress" (*tēn enestōsan anagkēn*).[2] The phrase does not refer to some future apocalyptic tribulation that might, in

---

[1] Cf. Caird, *Language*, 270–71.

[2] Rather than "impending": in 1 Esd. 9:6 the phrase *dia ton enestōta cheimōna* means "because of the bad weather that prevailed" (RSV); also *tois enestōsin* ("in the present situation") in 3 Macc. 1:16. In Rom. 8:38 (cf. 1 Cor. 3:22) "things present (*enestōta*)" are contrasted with "things to come (*mellonta*)." The sense "impending" is not found elsewhere in the LXX or Greek New Testament.

the event, be postponed indefinitely – Paul appears to have in mind the situation that the church currently faced in Corinth. There is some reason to regard it, specifically, as a reference to the social and economic hardships imposed on the church by an unsympathetic, and perhaps at times violent, local community. The word *anagkē* is used in Maccabees for the forceful constraint and persecution of the Jews (e.g., 2 Macc. 6:7; 15:2; 4 Macc. 5:13, 37; 6:24; 8:14, 22, 24; 9:6); Jesus uses it in Luke 21:23 to refer to the "distress" that will be caused by the Roman invasion of Judea.[3] When Paul says in verse 28 that the married will have "afflictions in the flesh" (*thlipsin . . . tēi sarki*) and that he would spare them such suffering, it is unlikely that he intends by this the normal troubles of married life.[4] He must mean that he would spare them the exceptional pain that they would face under the present difficult circumstances.

There is little else in 1 Corinthians to help us sharpen this impression, and we may prefer to think that *anagkē* refers to a more impersonal form of adversity such as the "dislocation" caused by famines in Greece during the reign of Claudius.[5] But other churches had very quickly encountered quite virulent and frightening opposition from within their local communities.[6] The church at Thessalonica, founded four or five years earlier, is a clear example: "you . . . became imitators of the churches of God in Christ Jesus that are in

[3] See 1 Sam. 22:2; Tob. 4:9 with respect to economic constraints.

[4] Against A. L. Moore, *The Parousia in the New Testament* (Leiden: Brill, 1966), 116, n. 2.

[5] A famine occurred around A.D. 51 and may have coincided with Paul's stay in Corinth (A. C. Thiselton, *The First Epistle to the Corinthians* [Grand Rapids/Carlisle: Eerdmans/Paternoster, 2000], 492). Following B. Winter, Thiselton suggests that "famine could well provide *a concrete instantiation of the eschatological question mark which stands over against the supposed stability, security, or permanence of lifestyles available in mid-first-century Roman society*" (Thiselton, *First Corinthians*, 573, emphasis his).

[6] We read later that many of the Corinthians are "weak and ill, and some have died" (11:30), but this is attributed to sin within the community rather than to external causes. The potential for Jewish hostility towards the church at Corinth is illustrated by Acts 18:1–17. The civil authorities regarded the disputes between the Christians and the Jews as an intra-Jewish matter.

Judea. For you suffered the same things from your own countrymen as they did from the Jews" (1 Thess. 2:14; cf. 1:6; Acts 17:1–9).[7] The church at Philippi faced similar hostility (Phil. 1:29–30). It is important that we do not underestimate how distressing this sort of rejection could be; or how much it would have shaped the theological, and indeed eschatological, outlook of those who experienced it. There is a real correlation between the intensity of persecution at Thessalonica and the intensity of apocalyptic expectation indicated in Paul's Letters to the Thessalonians.[8]

Equally important for understanding the sense of crisis that Paul evokes in 1 Corinthians 7 is his own experience of opposition and hardship. Provoked by the arrogance and complacency of the Corinthians, he has already catalogued the abuse suffered by the apostles for Christ's sake: contempt, slander, humiliation, persecution; they live as though under a sentence of death, "a spectacle to the world, to angels and to men," "the scum of the world, the refuse of all things" (4:9, 13). Later in the Letter, in his argument about the resurrection, he alludes to a routine sense of vulnerability ("I die every day!") and, somewhat enigmatically, to an occasion when he "fought with beasts at Ephesus" (15:31–32). It was natural enough to make his own suffering a pattern for the church's experience (Phil. 1:29–30).

The Imitation of Christ

The imitation of Paul, however, is also an imitation of Christ: "you became imitators of us and of the Lord, for

---

[7] See M. Bockmuehl, "1 Thessalonians 2:14–16 and the Church in Jerusalem," *TynBul* 52.1 (2001), 20–24, for a discussion of Jewish persecution of Christians in Judea.

[8] T.D. Still characterizes the Thessalonians' affliction as "external (i.e., observable, verifiable), non-Christian opposition which took the forms of verbal harassment, social ostracism, political sanctions and perhaps even some sort of physical abuse, which on the rarest of occasions may have resulted in martyrdom" (T. D. Still, *Conflict at Thessalonica: A Pauline Church and its Neighbours* [Sheffield: Sheffield Academic Press, 1999], 217). He also catalogues at some length the reasons for the hostility (228–67).

you received the word in much affliction" (1 Thess. 1:6). What Paul suffered, and what the church also suffered, was in some sense only a continuation of – or reenactment of – what Christ suffered before them.[9] Just how seriously Paul took this becomes apparent when we look at Colossians 1:24. Writing from prison, he assures his readers that he is able to rejoice in his sufferings for their sake and then goes on to say, according to the ESV translation: "and in my flesh I am filling up what is lacking in Christ's afflictions for the sake of his body, that is, the church." This statement has caused all sorts of problems for interpreters because it seems to imply that Paul considered Christ's sufferings on behalf of his "body" to have been in some way insufficient. Various solutions have been proposed, perhaps the most popular being that Paul is thinking here not of the personal sufferings of Christ but of the "messianic birth pains" in which all believers potentially participate.[10] But a more straightforward explanation is available. Most translations bring the phrase "in my flesh" forward in the sentence so that it attaches to "I complete." In the Greek text, however, it comes immediately after the words "what is lacking in Christ's afflictions," which suggests that what Paul has in mind is the extent to which what he has suffered *in his own flesh* still falls short of what Christ suffered.[11] This is why he

---

[9] To speak of a "realistic" or "mystical" participation in Christ's sufferings on the basis of a "somatic union," as Proudfoot does (C. M. Proudfoot, "Imitation or Realistic Participation?" *Int* 17 [1963], 152, 160), seems unnecessary. But the analogy between the suffering of the Christ and the suffering of the believer is not a matter *only* of imitation: it must be understood within a narrative and eschatological framework.

[10] Cf. P. T. O'Brien, *Colossians, Philemon* (Waco, TX: Word, 1982), 78–79; Witherington, *Jesus, Paul*, 158–59.

[11] Proudfoot (Proudfoot, "Imitation," 157) allows that grammatically *en tē sarki mou* could modify *ta husterēmata* ("what is lacking in my own flesh of the sufferings of the Christ") but thinks that *antanōplēroō* points to the supply coming "from an opposite quarter to the deficiency" (quoting J. B. highfoot, *Saint Paul's Epistles to the Collosians and to Philemon* [New York: Macmillan and Company, 1927], 163). But the prefix is just as well explained by the thought of a transfer between Christ's sufferings for the sake of his body and Paul's analogous sufferings "for your sake" (A. C. Perriman, "The Pattern of Christ's Sufferings: Colossians 1:24 and Philippians 3:10–11," *TynBul* 42.1 [1991], 67, n. 16).

rejoices: he has deliberately taken Christ's sufferings as the model or pattern for his own and expects that pattern to be completed, sooner or later, through his death.[12] So when he speaks of himself elsewhere, for example, as a man "sentenced to death" (1 Cor. 4:9), as a prisoner in a Roman triumphal procession facing execution (2 Cor. 2:14), as "carrying in the body the death of Jesus" (2 Cor. 4:10), as "dying, and behold we live" (2 Cor. 6:9), the thought of death is not merely intended to underline the severity of his suffering. It is more than a metaphor here. Paul believed himself to be following an eschatologically defined trajectory through suffering – one already traveled by Christ the firstfruits – that in all likelihood would end in death at the hands of his enemies.[13]

Sometimes he wished that the trajectory would reach its end sooner rather than later. In two passages he writes about his personal preference to be with Christ (2 Cor. 5:8; Phil. 1:23). In both cases the desire arises not as a matter of personal piety but out of the experience of intense suffering. It is because he carries "in the body the death of Jesus," because the "outer nature is wasting away," because the "tent, which is our earthly home" is close to being destroyed (2 Cor. 4:10, 16; 5:1), that he would rather see the whole thing through and be at home with the Lord. It is because he shares the sufferings of Christ, because his life hangs in the balance (Phil. 1:19–21; cf. 3:10), that he would rather "depart and be with Christ."

We see the same hope of imitating Christ expressed in Philippians 3:10–11, but here he takes the argument a step further and allows a curious note of uncertainty to creep in. He has counted his entire Jewish heritage as loss because of the "surpassing worth of knowing Christ Jesus my Lord,"

---

[12] See Perriman, "Pattern," 62–68.

[13] See J. R. White, "'Baptized on Account of the Dead': The Meaning of 1 Corinthians 15:29 in its Context," *JBL* 116.3 (1997), 495–96. White thinks that the difficult statement in 1 Cor. 15:29 presupposes this background: the "dead," on account of whom people are baptized, are the apostles who are "dying all the time" (493–98).

in order to be "found in him" (3:8–9). But this "gain" is understood in a very narrow sense. The righteousness that he has from God is centered on, and directed towards, the Christ who suffered and died: it comes through faith in Christ and it is the basis, more or less, for the particular "knowledge" of Christ that Paul seeks. To know Christ is to "share his sufferings, becoming like him in his death" (cf. 2 Cor. 1:5), because in this way (and perhaps only in this way) Paul will also come to know the "power of his resurrection." But why does he then express doubt ("that if possible . . .") about whether he will "attain (*katantēsō*) the resurrection from the dead" (3:11)?

The question probably needs to be answered on at least two levels. In the first place, Paul's language suggests that he is invoking an essentially Jewish hope. In his defense before Agrippa in Acts 26 he told the king: "I stand here on trial because of my hope in the promise made by God to our fathers, to which our twelve tribes hope to attain (*katantēsai*), as they earnestly worship night and day" (26:6–7). He finds it ironic, to say the least, that he should be accused *by Jews* of having this hope. "Why is it thought incredible by any of you that God raises the dead?" (26:8). He has argued in a similar fashion earlier, telling the Roman governor Felix of the hope which he had in God, which his accusers themselves accepted, that "there will be a resurrection of both the just and the unjust" (Acts 24:15; cf. 23:6; 28:20). The resurrection that Paul is so anxious to attain, therefore, is not a matter of private interest only: it is bound up with a national hope of restoration (cf. Dan. 12:1–3) – even though he has denied himself the option of trusting in his birthright as a "Hebrew of Hebrews" (Phil. 3:5). This suggests that Paul's uncertainty arises because the hope of personal resurrection cannot be entirely separated from a real historical uncertainty about the fate of Israel. Quite how we are to develop this entanglement of the individual and the national hope is unclear, but at least we are reminded that it is the concrete destiny of "Israel" that is at stake.

But there are two other factors to consider that affect Paul more directly. The first is the possibility that he might actually be alive at the "*parousia* of the Lord" (cf. 1 Thess. 4:15) and so be denied the chance to die and be raised from the dead as Christ was. The second is the fear that he might be disqualified from winning the "prize," the "imperishable crown" (1 Cor. 9:24–27). The image of successfully finishing the race recurs in Paul's final Letter, written when he was "already being poured out as a drink offering" (2 Tim. 4:6) – the time of his departure had come.[14] His satisfaction comes not only from the general thought that he has fulfilled his calling as an apostle, but also from knowing that he has at last come to the point where he may complete the pattern of Christ's sufferings and receive the "crown of righteousness" (4:8).

The call for the endurance of the faithful

If Paul was acutely aware of his own participation in Christ's sufferings, he was equally conscious of the fact that he was not making this painful journey alone. Indeed, the prospect of suffering appears to have been an integral part of the original gospel that he preached: "you yourselves know that we are destined for this. For when we were with you, we kept telling you beforehand that we were to suffer affliction, just as it has come to pass, and just as you know" (1 Thess. 3:3–4; cf. 2:2). When Paul and Barnabas revisited the churches of Asia Minor, they reminded the disciples that "through many tribulations we must enter the kingdom of God" (Acts 14:22; cf. 2 Thess. 1:5). We find the same argument in 1 Peter. Urging his readers to stand firm in the face of demonically inspired persecution, he reminds them that "the same kinds of suffering are being experienced by your brotherhood throughout the world" (1 Pet. 5:8–9).

---

[14] The word for "departure" in 2 Tim. 4:6 is *analusis;* the verb *analuō* is used in Phil. 1:23 to express Paul's desire to depart and be with Christ. It is natural to associate this idea with the thought of a departure through suffering in order to be with the resurrected Christ.

Likewise, Paul tells the Philippians: "it has been granted to you that for the sake of Christ you should not only believe in him but also suffer for his sake, engaged in the same conflict (*agōna*) that you saw I had and now hear that I still have" (1:29–30).[15] They are to keep in mind the example of Christ, who "became obedient unto death, even death on a cross" (2:8). In the continuation of his argument in Philippians 3 he urges those who are "mature" (*teleioi*) to think the same way – to press on, as he does, "toward the goal for the prize of the upward call of God in Christ Jesus' (3:14). The "upward call (*tēs anō klēseōs*) of God" is the call to resurrection (*anastasis*), from the dead; it is the prize held out to those who will suffer.[16] It is also the transformation of the "body of our humiliation to be like the body of his glory" (3:21, translation mine).[17] Again, we must be careful not to lose sight of Paul's argument here: he is not dealing in remote theological generalities. The "body of our humiliation" (*to sōma tēs tapeinōseōs hēmōn*) is not simply the lowly, frail, mundane human body; it is the body of the person who does what Christ did – makes himself of no account, humbles himself (*etapeinōsen heauton*), and becomes obedient to the point of death (cf. 2:7–8). If this is the case, we should understand the expression "enemies of the cross of Christ" in verse 18 as the precise eschatological counterpart to the "mature" who seek the "goal for the prize of the upward call of God in Christ Jesus." They are those – presumably believers[18] – who are unwilling to

[15] For the eschatological background to Paul's "conflict" (*agæōna*) see 4 Macc. 9:23; 11:20; 13:15; 15:29; 16:16; 17:11; cf. Col. 2:1; 1 Thess. 2:2; 1 Tim. 6:12; 2 Tim. 4:7; Heb. 12:1.

[16] See Perriman, "Pattern," 76–77. Note 4 Macc. 17:11–12: "Truly the contest in which they were engaged was divine, for on that day virtue gave the awards and tested them for their endurance. The prize was immortality in endless life." Paul's argument in Phil. 3 is very similar.

[17] Cf. 1 Cor. 15:49, though here the immediate issue is not suffering but the more abstract question of the nature of the resurrection body; 2 Cor. 3:18; 4:4; and J. D. G. Dunn, *Romans* (Dallas: Word, 1988), 483–84.

[18] G. F. Hawthorne, *Philippians* (Waco, TX: Word, 1983), 163; G. D. Fee, *Paul's Letter to the Philippians* (Grand Rapids: Eerdmans, 1995), 374–75.

follow the path of suffering, whose god is self-indulgence and the security of material life. It is in this specific sense that they walk as *enemies of the cross of Christ*.

The realization that many will choose the security of a worldly lifestyle over the insecurity of imitating Christ reduces Paul to tears. The threat that persecution posed to these fragile communities was at all times a source of considerable anxiety for him – because the broad path was bound to lead to destruction, because he feared that in the end he might have run or labored in vain (cf. 1 Thess. 3:5; Phil. 2:16), but more fundamentally, we must assume, because the *survival* of the church of Jesus Christ was at stake.[19]

Heirs with Christ

The same eschatological scenario needs to be kept in view when we read Romans 8. Paul's argument in the first half of the chapter is that the answer to the problem of the "law of sin and death" is the "law of the Spirit of life" (8:2). So when a believer cries out in prayer or worship "Abba! Father!," this is evidence that she is a child of God, and therefore an "heir" (8:16–17). The same connection is made in Galatians 4:6–7: those who have been adopted as sons receive the Spirit of the Son and therefore become heirs. At this point in Romans 8, however, a crucial distinction is introduced and the argument changes direction: "heirs of God, on the one hand (*men*), heirs together with Christ, on the other (*de*), *if indeed* we suffer together (with him) in order that we may be glorified together (with him)" (8:17, translation mine). To be an "heir with Christ" appears not to be automatically entailed in being an "heir of God" – in being set free from the law of sin and death by the law of the Spirit of life. Rather, it is made conditional upon the

[19] See R. E. Rubenstein, *When Jesus Became God* (San Diego/New York/London: Harcourt, 1999), 18, on the threat posed to the church by systematic persecution under Decius and Valerian. He quotes Frend ("'Christians joined with their pagan neighbors in a rush to sacrifice' and 'the Christian church practically collapsed'"), though he reckons "practically collapsed" to be an overstatement.

experience of suffering, which in turn becomes the ground for being glorified with Christ.[20] The same distinction is found in Philippians 1:29–30: it has been granted to them *not only* to believe in Christ *but also* to suffer for his sake.

This line of thought is developed in the second half of Romans 8. Although the narrative apocalyptic framework is not immediately apparent here, we should resist the temptation to generalize Paul's argument. He is not looking out across the hazy expanses of the universal human, or even Christian, condition; he is looking down the dark and narrow gully of an impending eschatological crisis. He is not writing for those of us who live on the distant plains; he is writing for believers in Rome and in the Roman world who were about to venture nervously into that gully, down the twisting narrow path that leads to life. This is, of course, a contentious point to make and needs some support.

First, the suffering that Paul has in mind is certainly not, to quote Hamlet, "the heartache and the thousand natural shocks that flesh is heir to";[21] nor is it the believer's identification with Christ in his death.[22] When he lists, in verse 35, "tribulation, or distress, or persecution, or famine, or nakedness, or danger, or sword," these are not the normal hazards of existence; they are to be understood as the consequences of being the people of God *in this present time* (*tou nun kairou*). They echo Paul's accounts of his own suffering for the sake of Christ: "danger," "hunger," and "nakedness" are mentioned in 2 Corinthians 11:23–27, "distress" and "persecutions" in 2 Corinthians 12:10. They evoke Jesus' description of his "brothers," who will experience hunger, thirst, nakedness, sickness, and

---

[20] The argument also appears in Rom. 5:2–5. Moo deals with the problem posed by the close connection that Paul makes between glory and suffering by generalizing the afflictions to include "all the evil that the Christian experiences" (D. Moo, *The Epistle to the Romans* [Grand Rapids/Cambridge: Eerdmans, 1996], 303).

[21] Cf. Moo, *Romans*, 511–12, n. 16.

[22] Dunn, *Romans*, 456.

imprisonment (Matt. 25:35–36). But it is the quotation from Psalm 44 in verse 36 that most clearly defines this as the suffering that the church endures because it is faithful to its Lord: "For your sake we are being killed all the day long; we are regarded as sheep to be slaughtered." The psalmist complains that Israel has been made "the taunt of our neighbors, the derision and scorn of those around us . . . a byword among the nations, a laughingstock among the peoples" (44:13–14). The language of "groaning" in Romans 8:23 (*stenazō, stenagmos*) strongly suggests the experience of those who are oppressed by the enemies of God.[23]

Secondly, behind the image of the creation subjected to "futility" and a "bondage to corruption (*phthoras*)" (Rom. 8:20–21) is not primarily the thought that the whole created order was corrupted by Adam's sin, though this may be in the background, but the prophetic conceit in Isaiah 24 of the earth having been cursed because of the sin of its inhabitants (cf. Jer. 12:4, 11).[24] Isaiah 24:3 reads in the LXX: "the earth will be corrupted with corruption (*phthora phtharēsetai*) and the earth will be despoiled with spoiling." It is because judgment presently hangs over the world that the creation yearns to see the revelation of the sons of God and the beginning of a new creation.

Thirdly, the "image of his Son" (Rom. 8:29), to which those who suffer are conformed, also has a restricted, eschatological sense in this context. It is specifically the image of the one who suffered, died, and was raised from the dead; and to become *like him* – at least as far as the

---

[23] Cf. Judg. 2:18; Pss. 6:7; 11:6; 78:11–12; 101:21 LXX; 1 Macc. 1:26; 3 Macc. 1:18; 4:2; 4 Macc. 9:21; Acts 7:34. Cf. Moo, *Romans*, 519, n. 59. Paul's conviction that "everything works together for good" has an eschatological orientation (cf. Dunn, *Romans*, 480).

[24] Cf. S. Eastman, "Whose Apocalypse? The Identity of the Sons of God in Romans 8:19," *JBL* 121.2 (2002), 275: "Insofar as the wider creation is included in this experience of suffering, it is as a corollary of Jerusalem's suffering." J. A. Motyer, *The Prophecy of Isaiah* (Leicester: Inter-Varsity Press, 1999), 199, argues that the Noahic covenant is in view.

present argument is concerned – is to go through a comparable process. It is to "imitate" him. Jesus is the "firstborn," which means that he was the first to be raised "from the dead" (cf. Col. 1:18; Rev. 1:5). But God has "foreknown," "predestined," "called" others to follow the same path of suffering, with the same hope of being "vindicated" (*edikaiōsen*) and "glorified" – not metaphorically but literally. This is not quite the image of a new eschatological humanity that it is often taken to be.[25] It addresses the particular and immediate problem of those who found that this new life in the Spirit had impelled them into a situation of considerable insecurity and hardship. These are the "sons of God" whose revelation creation awaits with eager longing (8:19), who suffer in the present time (8:18), who wait for the redemption of their bodies (8:23); they are the "many brothers" among whom Jesus is the firstborn son (8:29) – in the language of Hebrews 12:23, the "assembly of the firstborn who are enrolled in heaven."[26]

Finally, the expression "more than conquerors" (*hupernikōmen*) in verse 37 has unmistakable eschatological overtones. Paul's emphatic compound form is not found elsewhere, but the root word *nikaō* ("to conquer") is widely used to denote the victory of the righteous or faithful over oppression and brutality. The writer of 4 Maccabees celebrates the deaths of Eleazar and the seven sons and their mother: "By their endurance they conquered (*nikēsantes*) the tyrant, and thus their native land was purified through them" (4 Macc. 1:11 RSV). In Revelation not only Christ (5:5) but also the persecuted church (12:11; 15:2; 21:7; cf. 2:7, 11, 26; 3:5, 12, 21) is said to have conquered the power of death.

There is a powerful eschatological argument running through these texts. What we need to grasp here is not

---

[25] E.g., Dunn, *Romans*, 484: "a new race of eschatological people in whom God's design from the beginning of creation is at last fulfilled."

[26] Cf. Wis. 3:7: "In the time of their visitation they will shine forth, and will run like sparks through the stubble."

simply that the New Testament church faced persecution but that it interpreted its afflictions within the scope of an apocalyptic narrative – and that this narrative has quite precise implications with regard to the *outcome* of these sufferings. Paul develops the theme of the imitation of Christ's sufferings largely for practical and pastoral reasons; but behind it is the thought that Christ's experience represents or anticipates or includes the experience of the group. The suffering servant is at one level an individual, at another the righteous within Israel; the Son of Man is a symbol for the oppressed saints of the Most High, the wise within the nation.[27]

This may also help to explain why Paul finds it significant that the Gentile believers in Thessalonica received from their neighbors the same treatment that the churches in Judea had received from the Jews (1 Thess. 2:14). It confirms that they too, though not Jews, have entered into the drama of Daniel 7 – in much the same way that speaking in tongues, for example, was confirmation that Gentiles had become members of the people of God (cf. Acts 10:45–47). Their "steadfastness and faith" in all their afflictions is "evidence of the righteous judgment of God, that you may be considered worthy of the kingdom of God"; their persecutors will be afflicted and they will find rest at the coming of the Son of Man (2 Thess. 1:4–10). Likewise, it has been granted to the "saints" at Philippi that they should suffer for the sake of Christ, but this is a sign (a "clear omen") that they will see the same outcome: their opponents will be destroyed as the fourth beast was destroyed, but they will be vindicated and will receive the kingdom (Phil. 1:28). They have come to share in the same eschatological "contest" (*agōn*) that Paul himself faces – and indeed which the Maccabean martyrs, the prototype of the oppressed saints of the Most High, faced before him (cf. 4 Macc. 9:23; 11:20; 15:29; 16:16; 17:11).

The experience of suffering is central to the apocalyptic

---

[27] On the theme of suffering in Judaism see Wright, *Victory*, 577–92; R. P. Martin, *James* (Waco, TX: Word, 1988), xciii–xcviii.

narrative told in the early church and cannot be marginalized in our reading simply because it is marginal to the modern interpretive tradition and, indeed, to the life of the Western church. If it seems at times that there is in the New Testament a disconcerting enthusiasm for the suffering of the church, resulting perhaps in an exaggerated expectation of persecution, we should recognize the extent to which this arises, on the one hand, from a desire to emulate Christ and, on the other, from the apocalyptically inspired conviction that the kingdom of God would be inaugurated through the suffering of the saints.

The End of the Age

It is clear, however, that Paul did not expect the period of crisis to last very long.[28] The time "has grown very short," he tells the Corinthians (1 Cor. 7:29); "the present form of this world is passing away" (7:31). For the remaining period he urges a detachment from the normal way of things: "From now on, let those who have wives live as though they had none, and those who mourn as though they were not mourning, and those who rejoice as though they were not rejoicing, and those who buy as though they had no goods, and those who deal with the world as though they had no dealings with it" (7:29–31).

These statements must imply a restricted outlook on the future.[29] There is a tendency for interpreters to universalize what Paul has to say about the immediate circumstances faced by the Corinthians, so that his teaching in this chapter

---

[28] Cf. D. E. H. Whiteley, *The Theology of St Paul* (Oxford: Basil Blackwell, 1972), 243; H. J. Schoeps, *Paul: The Theology of the Apostle in the Light of Jewish Religious History* (Philadelphia: Westminster Press, 1959), 101–102; H. Ridderbos, *Paul: An Outline of his Theology* (London: SPCK, 1975), 489–90; Wenham, *Paul*, 297–99.

[29] Against, e.g., Moore, *Parousia*; B. Witherington, "Transcending Imminence: The Gordian Knot of Pauline Eschatology," in Brower and Elliott, *"The Reader Must Understand,"* 173–74.

acquires more an existential than an eschatological character. Fee argues, for example, that his concern is "not with the *amount* of time they have left, but with the radical new perspective the 'foreshortened future' gives one with regard to the *present* age."[30] But Paul's whole argument presupposes an exceptional and limited period of distress, not the general open-ended conditions of the church's existence. His purpose is not to provide an ordinary Christian ethic but to advise the Corinthian believers on how to deal with the particular and extraordinary circumstances that they faced. The amount of time left is very much his concern – "distress" is unpleasant. It may be permissible, by way of an apologetic, to point to the existential validity and motivational value of the belief that the end, in whatever form, is nigh.[31] But our task is not to accommodate Paul to a much longer historical perspective (and indeed retrospective) but to *understand* him – to understand what *he* foresaw – and it is very doubtful that he construed matters in such a generalized and a-historical fashion.

It is likely that the phrase "the end of the ages" in 1 Corinthians 10:11 points to the same state of affairs. The passage is an argument against spiritual complacency. The people of Israel all participated in the saving events of the Exodus, yet many of them indulged in idolatry and immorality and as a result were "overthrown in the wilderness" (10:5). Paul takes this as paradigmatic for the church: the events were "written down for our instruction, on whom the end of the ages has come" (10:11). This may

---

[30] G. D. Fee, *The First Epistle to the Corinthians* (Grand Rapids: Eerdmans, 1987), 339.

[31] Cf. Dunn, *Romans*, 792–93. Witherington thinks that the language of imminence is designed to "inculcate a sort of moral earnestness in believers so that their eyes will remain fixed upon the goal, eagerly longing for the fulfilment of God's plan for human history" (Witherington, *Jesus, Paul*, 48). Frame quotes Bengel: "each several generation, at whatever period existing, occupies during that period the position of those who shall be alive at the Lord's coming" (J. E. Frame, *The Epistles of St. Paul to the Thessalonians* [Edinburgh: T&T Clark, 1912], 173).

only refer in general terms to the transition from the old to the new that has taken place in Christ, but the form of expression and the following emphasis on endurance (10:13) suggest that "the end of the ages" denotes a period that will pass within the lifetime of those who currently face such temptations.

A less ambiguous passage is Romans 13:11–12, where Paul underscores his ethical exhortations with an emphatic assertion of the imminence of salvation: "salvation is nearer to us now than when we first believed. The night is far gone, the day is at hand." It can be argued, of course, that he sets no outer limit to this imminence and that a delay of two thousand years or more is not technically in breach of the expectation expressed here.[32] Still, this is hardly a straightforward reading of the passage and we should endeavor to take seriously the much more limited and pressing timeframe that appears to be in view. What especially demands an explanation is the proximity to some decisive eschatological moment implied by the imagery of the approaching day and the explicit assertion that "salvation is nearer to us now than when we first believed" (13:11). The *nearness* of this "salvation," however it is to be understood, must be measured in relation to a period of no more than about twenty years.

Corresponding to such statements about the passing away of the current state of affairs are others which speak of the imminence of Christ's *parousia* and of the victory of God over evil. In 1 Thessalonians 4:15–17, for example, Paul appears to assume that he will be among the living "at the *parousia* of the Lord." It is arguable that he includes

---

[32] Cf. Dunn, *Romans*, 768. Moore maintains that Paul meant only that "every day brings the End one day nearer" (Moore, *Parousia*, 122). Witherington infers from the fact that Paul speaks of the day as having already arrived (*engiken*) that he cannot possibly have been thinking of the end of the world (Witherington, *Jesus, Paul*, 31–2). This is correct, but neither does he mean only that the eschatological age has somehow already begun. The night/day metaphor and the statement about the nearness of salvation make it clear that Paul believed that they were approaching a decisive eschatological transition.

himself simply because that was how things stood at that moment.[33] But the phrase "we who are alive, who are left" (*hēmeis hoi zōntes hoi perileipomenoi*), which occurs twice in this passage (15, 17; cf. 5:10), with its rather emphatic first-person pronoun, does not sound accidental. It is difficult to avoid the impression that Paul at this point, perhaps without having given the matter too much thought, expected the *parousia* to take place while he was still alive, and certainly within the lifetime of his readers.[34] Equally, the Thessalonians were surely led to believe that *within their lifetime* rest would be granted them and their persecutors punished "when the Lord Jesus is revealed from heaven" (2 Thess. 1:6–10). The same distinction between those who are dead and "we" who will be alive at the *parousia* appears in 1 Corinthians 15:51–52. The more theoretical nature of his argument about the resurrection in this passage, though, perhaps makes it more likely that this is simply a quirk of his rhetoric.[35]

Paul's assurance to the Roman believers in 16:20 ("the God of peace will speedily [*en tachei*] crush the accuser [*ton satanan*] under your feet," translation mine) betrays a similar sense of eschatological imminence. We are not far here from Jesus' story of the widow who pleads with the unjust judge to give her judgment against her "adversary" (*antidikos*): God will not delay long over his elect, he will vindicate them "speedily" (*en tachei*: Luke 18:2–8).[36] Lastly,

---

[33] See, e.g., Witherington, "Transcending Imminence," 174.

[34] Cf. E. Best, *The First and Second Epistles to the Thessalonians* (London: A & C Black, 1986), 194–96; F. F. Bruce, *1 and 2 Thessalonians* (Waco, TX: Word, 1982), 99. This may also be the case in 1 Cor. 15:51–53, but Paul's language here is less clear (R. F. Collins, *First Corinthians* [Collegeville, MN: The Liturgical Press, 1999], 581).

[35] Cf. Thiselton, *First Corinthians*, 1293–94.

[36] This certainly brings out the eschatological dimension, but the reference to Satan in Rom. 16:20 may have the false teachers of vv. 17–19 in view rather than external accusers of the brethren (see Moo, *Romans*, 932–33). Witherington thinks that Paul may be addressing a particular local problem of dissent, so that if *en tachei* is taken to mean "soon," the emphasis is nevertheless on "under *your* feet" ("Transcending Imminence," 180). His argument elsewhere that *en tachei* signifies how, not when, judgment will come is of little consolation to the abused widow (Witherington, *Jesus, Paul*, 31).

the Ephesians face an "evil day," a day of extreme spiritual conflict, when they will need the whole armor of God if they are to stand firm (Eph. 6:13). Although the argument appears somewhat generalized and may be given a wider application – it is commonly made the basis for a theology of spiritual warfare – the motivation is still fundamentally eschatological: the "evil day" is a Day of the Lord (cf. Jer. 17:17–18; Amos 5:18–20; 6:3), a day of unprecedented affliction (cf. Dan. 12:1). These are the evil days that Paul spoke of earlier (5:16), when the "wrath of God comes upon the sons of disobedience" (5:6). The terse assurance that "the Lord is near" in Philippians 4:5 may refer to the temporal nearness of the *parousia;* but the emphasis on prayer in verse 6 suggests that it may be intended to evoke the confidence expressed in the Psalms in particular that "the LORD is near" to the righteous who suffer and who cry out to him (cf. Pss. 33:19; 118:151; 144:18 LXX). This background seems more relevant than statements in the Prophets that the "day of the LORD" is near.[37]

On balance, therefore, I think that we are more honest in our judgment if we accept that Paul expected some decisive eschatological event or sequence of events to take place in the not too distant future, quite possibly within his own lifetime. Other statements in the New Testament add weight to this conclusion (cf. 1 Pet. 4:7; Heb. 10:25; Jas. 5:8; 1 John 2:18). We will give some thought later to the question of whether with the passage of time he leaned towards a more "realized" eschatology. Now we must ask what, in real terms, he expected to happen. What would have to be going on in the world for him to say, "Yes, that is what I was talking about"? One thing is clear: whatever the Day of the Lord might look like, it would have to be the sort of event that could plausibly be communicated to the church in Thessalonica, as Wright points out, by the Roman postal system (2 Thess. 2:1–2).[38]

---

[37] Cf. Joel 1:15; 2:1; 4:14; Obad. 1:15; Zeph. 1:7, 14; Isa. 13:6; Ezek. 30:3. Cf. Witherington, "Transcending Imminence," 172–73.

[38] Wright, "Jerusalem," 64.

A Day of Wrath

The essence of the Thessalonians' faith – and presumably, therefore, of Paul's preaching at Thessalonica – is summarized in 1 Thessalonians 1:9–10: they "turned to God from idols to serve the living and true God, and to wait for his Son from heaven, whom he raised from the dead, Jesus who delivers us from the wrath to come" (cf. 1 Cor. 1:7). The message appears quite simple: judgment was about to come upon the ancient world from which people could be rescued only by the appearing of Jesus from heaven.

The warning about "wrath" must be taken very realistically. This is not a post mortem or mythical judgment. It constitutes an event or state of affairs that would come upon a nation or upon the world, to be experienced in a very concrete and distressing manner. To speak of the "wrath of God" is to identify the divine purpose behind natural or military disasters or political oppression; the punishment of wrongdoing by governing authorities is a characteristic means by which the "wrath of God" is executed (Rom. 13:4). It is a mistake to think that the New Testament spiritualizes the more materialistic conception that is found in the Old (e.g., Ezek. 21:31; cf. 1 Macc. 1:64). When John the Baptist challenged the Pharisees and Sadducees who came to be baptized, "Who warned you to flee from the wrath to come?" (Matt. 3:7; cf. Luke 3:7), he had in mind just the sort of religious-political disaster that took place in A.D. 70. For Jesus, the "wrath" to come was the "great distress" (*anagkē megalē*) that the people of Israel would suffer during the Roman invasion (Luke 21:23). Paul must have been thinking along similar lines. Even when he speaks in the most general terms of the wrath of God, the background rumble of an impending historical crisis can still be heard. The wrath that comes upon the "sons of disobedience" (Eph. 5:6; cf. 2:3; Col. 3:6) is no less historical – and no less eschatological – in Paul's understanding than the wrath that will devastate Jerusalem or the wrath from which the Thessalonians will be rescued at the revelation of the Son from heaven.

Wrath upon Israel

Wrath comes first upon Israel. The sequence is made explicit in Romans 2:9: "tribulation and distress for every human being who does evil, the Jew first and also the Greek." There are two aspects to Paul's censure of Israel. On the one hand, the Jews have failed to achieve righteousness through the law (e.g., Rom. 9:31–32; 10:3–4). On the other, they have opposed what God has done to make righteousness available outside the law: they killed Jesus and the prophets before him and now "fill up the measure of their sins" by hindering the apostles from preaching the gospel to the Gentiles (1 Thess. 2:15–16). This second complaint is especially significant because it echoes Jesus' angry indictment of the scribes and Pharisees, who by their persecution of those sent to them "fill up the measure" of their fathers and so bring upon themselves the "judgment of Gehenna" (Matt. 23:29–39; cf. Luke 11:47–51). Whether or not this is evidence for a direct dependence on the synoptic traditions,[39] the argument is clearly the same: Paul believed that the consequence of the Jews' violent opposition to the preaching of the gospel would be some form of national disaster. They have become "vessels of wrath prepared for destruction" (Rom. 9:22).

Although we do not have the graphic portrayal of judgment on Jerusalem that we find in Jesus' discourse, there are nevertheless indications that Paul also thought of the wrath of God against Israel in concrete, historical terms. He concludes his catalogue of Jewish transgressions in 1 Thessalonians 2:15–16 with the statement that the wrath of God "has come (*ephthasen*) upon them to the end (*eis telos*)" (translation mine).[40] It is possible that he means only that the time-bomb of God's wrath has been primed in their midst but has not yet exploded. The argument that the past

---

[39] See Wenham, *Paul*, 319–21.

[40] Note *T. Levi* 6:11: "the wrath of the Lord came upon them to the uttermost"; and the arguments about its relation to this verse in the commentaries and Bockmuehl, "1 Thessalonians," 10; Witherington, *Jesus, Paul*, 103.

tense (aorist) of the verb is "prophetic," or "proleptic,"[41] would amount to much the same thing: it would still point to a day of wrath in the *foreseeable* future, judgment upon the generation of Jews that had killed the Lord Jesus and violently opposed the preaching of the gospel to the Gentiles. On the face of it, though, Paul seems to have had in mind an event that had already taken place – a first stage in a process, an escalation of conflict, which would culminate in the complete, and perhaps lasting, destruction of Jerusalem.[42]

Various suggestions have been made as to what this event might have been. It is usually reckoned that Paul wrote 1 Thessalonians while staying with Aquila and Priscilla in Corinth. We are told in Acts 18:2 that this couple had come to Corinth after the expulsion of the Jews from Rome in A.D. 49, quite possibly as a result of Jewish-Christian conflicts (cf. Suetonius, *Claud*. 25.4).[43] In the same year, fighting broke out in the temple at Passover after a Roman soldier had indecently exposed himself from the roof of the cloisters. According to Josephus, ten thousand Jews were killed, most of them trampled to death in the stampede to escape (*J.W.* 2.12.1 §224–227; *Ant*. 20.5.3 §105–112).[44] This was only the climax to a descent into chaos that had begun with the return of the Roman procurators in A.D. 44. A severe famine – easily read as a sign of impending judgment – occurred in Judea in

---

41 Cf. Frame, *Thessalonians*, 114. It is debatable whether 1 Thess. 2:13–16 is a prophetic passage of this nature.

42 In the context of judgment *eis telos* may mean "forever," "utterly." Ps. 88:47 LXX reads: "Until when, Lord? Will you turn away forever? Will your anger (*orgē*) burn as a fire?" (cf. Pss. 51:7; 73:1, 3, 11; 76:9; 78:5; 102:9 LXX).

43 See Wenham, *Paul*, 300, n. 18; Best, *Thessalonians*, 119–20; Bruce, *Thessalonians*, 49. Bockmuehl thinks an allusion to the Edict of Claudius in 1 Thess. 2:16 unlikely (Bockmuehl, "1 Thessalonians," 29).

44 Jewett thinks that the zealots who provoked the violence were actively anti-Christian (R. Jewett, "The Agitators and the Galatian Congregations," *NTS* 17 [1971], 198–212; see also Wenham, *Paul*, 301, n. 19).

A.D. 46–47 during the reign of Claudius (cf. Acts 11:27–30; Matt. 24:7; Mark 13:8; Luke 21:11); also in A.D. 46 a rebellion led by "a certain imposter named Theudas" was crushed by Rome (*Ant.* 20.5.1 §97; cf. Acts 5:36). Whether any of these events figured in Paul's thinking about the wrath of God is a matter for speculation, but to interpret such disasters as being fundamentally eschatological, as belonging to the end of the age, is fully consistent with Pauline and New Testament presuppositions.[45]

The focus in 1 Thessalonians 2:15–16 is on the Jews in Judea, which may lead us to suppose that the wrath is also centered on Judea. But to Paul's mind the Jews of the Diaspora were implicated in the national sin. In practical terms, any initiative from Judea to prevent the apostles speaking to the Gentiles would have found support in the synagogues scattered across the Roman world. But it is also important to note how Paul drew Jews of the Diaspora into the ambit of judgment on Jerusalem. He warned the Jews in Antioch of Pisidia to beware "lest what is said in the Prophets should come about: 'Look, you scoffers, be astounded and perish; for I am doing a work in your days, a work that you will not believe, even if one tells it to you'" (Acts 13:40–41). The quotation is from Habakkuk 1:5. It belongs to a vision in which the Chaldeans – "that bitter and hasty nation" – come in violence against Israel. If something like that were to happen again, it would not leave the Diaspora communities unscathed.

So when Paul writes in Romans 10:1 that "my heart's desire and prayer to God for them is that they may be saved," we should almost certainly understand this primarily in terms of deliverance from national and religious disaster. This conclusion is reinforced by a glance back at the preceding verses (9:27–33) in which he makes repeated reference to passages in Isaiah that speak of divine judgment upon the nation. If God has laid a "stone of stumbling" *in Zion* (9:33), we should think twice before

[45] Cf. Bockmuehl, "1 Thessalonians," 25–27.

removing it from that location: in Isaiah's prophecy it belongs to a warning to the "scoffers" who "rule this people in Jerusalem" that they will not escape death when the "overwhelming scourge passes through" (Isa. 28:14–19). It is difficult to know to what extent Paul shared Jesus' quite transparent premonition of the invasion of Judea and the destruction of the temple. It is likely, as we shall see, that the story of the man of lawlessness in 2 Thessalonians 2:3–7 overlaps with Jesus' apocalyptic discourse, but in Paul's narrative the man of lawlessness represents only the desecration of the temple, not its destruction.[46]

Wrath upon the nations

If judgment starts in Jerusalem, it certainly will not end there. Paul clearly believed that the fall-out from this event would affect the whole of the Roman world. The Gentile converts in Thessalonica were to expect a "Day of the Lord" that would take an immoral and idolatrous world by surprise, like a thief that comes in the night (1 Thess. 5:2–10). Again, we must stress the point that this was no vacuous spiritual exhortation: Paul was convinced that the community of believers in Thessalonica faced a very real and devastating manifestation of the wrath of God that would overturn the *pax et securitas* supposedly guaranteed by Roman imperial rule: "While people are saying, 'There is peace and security,' then sudden destruction will come upon them as labor pains come upon a pregnant woman, and they will not escape" (5:3; cf. 1:10).[47] His speech to the men of Athens in the Areopagus is more restrained but still manages to convey a sense of eschatological imminence: his audience must surely have understood him to mean that God, having for a long time overlooked their

[46] Dan. 9:26 LXX may suggest that the destruction of Jerusalem is implicit in the use of the typology by Paul and the tradition.

[47] Cf. Still, *Conflict*, 261–66; R. A. Horsley (ed.), *Paul and Empire: Religion and Power in Roman Imperial Society* (Harrisburg, PA: Trinity Press International, 1997), 162.

ignorance, now commands all men to repent *because the day on which he will judge the idolatrous pagan world is near* (Acts 17:30–31). In more general terms, Paul argues in Romans that all people who behave in an ungodly and unrighteous manner are storing up for themselves "wrath . . . on the day of wrath when God's righteous judgment will be revealed" (Rom. 2:5; cf. 2:8). All who live according to the passions of the flesh are liable to suffer the wrath of God (Eph. 2:3; Col. 3:6). In some sense, as with the judgment on Israel, this has already begun: the wrath of God *is being revealed* from heaven "against all ungodliness and unrighteousness of men" (Rom. 1:18). It will end in the overthrow of Rome as a power implacably hostile to the reconstituted people of God.

Judgment upon the nations appears to take on cosmic proportions in 2 Peter: "the heavens and earth that now exist are stored up for fire, being kept until the day of judgment and destruction of the ungodly"; "the heavens will pass away with a roar, and the heavenly bodies will be burned up and dissolved, and the earth and the works that are done on it will be exposed"; "the heavens will be set on fire and dissolved, and the heavenly bodies will melt as they burn!" (3:7, 10, 12). Doubts over authorship and the general impression that we are in more exotic apocalyptic territory have tended to marginalize this Letter, but we should not jump too quickly to the conclusion that the end envisaged here is the ultimate destruction of the physical universe.

In the first place, despite his use of Psalm 90:4 to account for the delay in Christ's coming and the argument about the Lord's forbearance (3:8–9), Peter still appears to believe that his readers – and those who scoff at their faith – will themselves experience the "day of God" (3:12; cf. 1:19; 3:14).[48] He certainly does not use the formula of Psalm 90:4, which makes a day equal to a thousand years, in order to suggest the possibility of an indefinite postponement. He may still have intended his language to be read literally,

---

[48] See Bauckham, *Jude, 2 Peter*, 310.

but we cannot take that view without also accepting that he believed that it was the *current generation* of scoffers who would be destroyed and the *current generation* of believers who would be rescued.

The judgment that is to come upon the world will be analogous to the flood and the destruction of Sodom and Gomorrah (2:4–10; 3:6). Both are examples of how a few righteous were rescued from a corrupt world or society – but, of course, in neither case at the expense of the whole cosmos. The particular point is made, however, that whereas once the world was destroyed by water, the judgment for which those who are now suffering affliction (cf. 2:9) wait will be one of *fire* (3:5–7). There is a reason for this. The climax of Peter's vision is the emergence of "new heavens and a new earth in which righteousness dwells" (3:13). The allusion to the final chapters of Isaiah cannot simply be noted and ignored: whatever is on the end of this line needs to be hauled to the surface. For Isaiah the creation of new heavens and a new earth, as we have seen already, was a sign of the renewal of Jerusalem (Isa. 65:17; cf. 66:22). What precedes this is judgment on the enemies of Israel who have trodden down the sanctuary (63:18). It is a judgment that will rend the heavens, that will make the mountains "melt" (*takēsontai*) – "as when fire kindles brushwood and the fire causes water to boil" (64:1–2); "the LORD will come in fire, and his chariots like the whirlwind, to render his anger in fury, and his rebuke with flames of fire" (66:15).

Other Old Testament texts resonate on the same frequency. In Isaiah 34 we have an account of a judgment against the nations, "a day of vengeance, a year of recompense for the cause of Zion" (34:8), when "All the host of heaven shall rot away" (34:4). The translation of this clause in the Vaticanus text of the Septuagint ("all the powers of the heavens will melt [*takēsontai*]") foreshadows the statement in 2 Peter 3:12 that the "heavenly bodies will melt (*tēketai*) as they burn."[49] Psalm 97 also appears to be in the background. The psalm opens

[49] See Bauckham, *Jude, 2 Peter*, 316, for the exegetical arguments.

with a declaration of the Lord's sovereignty over all the earth (97:1); fire goes before him and burns up his adversaries (97:3); the mountains melt (*etakēsan* in LXX) like wax (97:5); "He preserves the lives of his saints; he delivers them from the hand of the wicked" (97:10); "Light is sown for the righteous, and joy for the upright in heart" (97:11; cf. 2 Pet. 1:19).

A leading premise of this book has been that, generally speaking, when Old Testament quotations and allusions occur in the New Testament, they should be allowed to bring into focus the wider narrative or argumentative context from which they have been drawn. Peter means us to see the coming judgment upon the unrighteous as being analogous to the sort of judgment upon Israel's enemies that is foreseen by Isaiah or the psalmist. It is hard to believe that he would have gone to such lengths to evoke these earlier *historical* manifestations of divine judgment if what he had actually had in mind was something quite different. Of course, he may not have contextualized the Old Testament texts in this way – he may have read them quite literally. Or he may have understood them as prefiguring an infinitely greater cataclysm. But if we hold fast to another main premise of this book and assume that like the other authors of New Testament apocalyptic he sought to provide meaning and hope in the context of real and distressing historical circumstances, there appears no good reason not to interpret these texts in much the same way as we have interpreted Jesus and Paul. Peter believed that those who now opposed and reviled the church would suffer the chaos and destruction of divine judgment – just as Babylon had eventually been overthrown.

"The righteous shall live by faith"

The sequence "Jew first, then Greek" may simply reflect in quite general terms the salvation-historical priority of the Jews (cf. Rom. 2:9). But it may have a more exact temporal meaning in line with the Old Testament pattern: Israel is judged through the instrumentality of a foreign power, but this is followed by judgment upon the nations as a vindication of God's righteousness.

The key to understanding Paul's argument here may lie – perhaps surprisingly – in the quotation from Habakkuk 2:4 in Romans 1:17: "the one who is righteous because of faith shall live," or "the one who is righteous shall live by faith."[50] Habakkuk's statement occurs in the context of his "complaint" (Hab. 2:1) that God has failed to act against injustice. He has seen that God is about to rouse the Chaldeans to march against Israel, where justice has been perverted (1:4): "O LORD, you have ordained them as a judgment, and you, O Rock, have established them for reproof" (1:12). But for the prophet this presents a more troubling moral problem: how can God tolerate the greater wickedness of the Chaldeans, who bring such callous destruction upon other nations (1:13–17)? The vision that comes in response to this complaint is an assurance that "the arrogant man shall not abide" (2:5 RSV) and that in the end the victimized nations will "take up their taunt against him" (2:6a; cf. the "woes" of 2:6b–19). But the fulfillment of this vision will not appear immediately, and it is in respect of this delay that Habakkuk makes the statement that Paul quotes in Romans 1:17. In the face of turmoil and destruction the assurance is given that the arrogant oppressor will be defeated but "the righteous shall live by his faith" (Hab. 2:4). The exact meaning of this verse is unclear in both the Hebrew and Greek texts, but the positive statement would appear to be that "the righteous one *lives* by his faithfulness or steadfastness" – in other words, that the righteous will *survive* this period of violence through his or her persistent trust in God.

We have usually read the quotation in Paul in much more general terms. Douglas Moo, for example, notices the shift in meaning: "In Paul, the quotation functions to characterize how it is that one can attain right standing with God and so live eternally."[51] But this may be a mistake. The salvation mentioned in verse 16, made possible through the gospel, will be the means by which the

---

[50] The textual and exegetical difficulties presented by this quotation are numerous. See Moo, *Romans*, 76–77, for the textual variants.

[51] Moo, *Romans*, 77.

righteousness of God will be demonstrated – in the sense that the vision of Habakkuk 2 constitutes a vindication of the justice or righteousness of the God who allowed the Chaldeans to lay waste to Israel.[52] The one who shall "live" through the "wrath of God" (2:18) is the one who has faith or, more concretely, who is steadfast. It is important to note that the statement about the revelation of wrath is connected to the quotation by *gar* ("for"). There is no break in the argument here. Faith – persistent trust when God appears slow to intervene – is the means by which first the Jew, then the Greek, will survive the judgment that is coming upon the world.

Habakkuk 2:4 is quoted in two other places in the New Testament. Paul makes use of it in Galatians 3:11 in the course of his argument that God justifies the Gentiles by faith, but he does so in order to make the negative point that "no one is justified before God by the law." Since compliance in all respects of the law was an impossibility, the nation was bound to become subject to the curses set out in Deuteronomy 28:15–68, which included just the sort of military defeat that Habakkuk – and for that matter Jesus – foresaw: "The LORD will cause you to be defeated before your enemies . . . And you shall be a horror to all the kingdoms of the earth. And your dead body shall be food for all birds of the air and for the beasts of the earth, and there shall be no one to frighten them away" (28:25–26). The use of the verse in Hebrews 10:32–39 is even more to the point. The readers are exhorted to endure in the face of persecution until they receive what was promised (10:36). Habakkuk 2:3–4 then forms the basis for the expectation that God will come and defeat their enemies: if they are not those who shrink back to destruction but rather have faith, they will keep their souls (10:39).

---

[52] There is, therefore, no contradiction between the revelation of righteousness in v. 17 and the revelation of wrath in v. 18: the one is a demonstration of the other.

Where is the Promise of his Coming?

So we have a number of fragile communities of believers spread very thinly through the cities of the Roman world, filled with the Spirit of God but facing poverty, famine, bullying, ostracism, violence, and imprisonment, victimized by their neighbors, troubled in many instances by the casuistry of Judaizing missionaries, torn apart by party loyalties and disputes over charismatic experiences, increasingly under pressure to conform to local custom or accommodate their faith to the demands of the imperial cult, convinced for the most part that they were heading towards a massive shake-up of the social and political order, that a day of wrath, of chaos, of destruction, was at hand. The question, inevitably, was: How long would they have to put up with this? How long would they have to wait? "O LORD, how long shall I cry for help, and you will not hear?" (Hab. 1:2).

The writer to the Hebrews, as we have just seen, picks up this lament. He reminds his readers of the period following their "enlightenment" when they willingly put up with abuse and harassment, when they had compassion on those who had been imprisoned, when they joyfully accepted the plundering of their property (10:32–34). But it has gone on too long; doubts are creeping in; they are beginning to turn back from this difficult, narrow path. The whole Letter is an argument against giving up in the face of hardship and persecution, but here he quotes from Habakkuk 2:3–4: "For, 'Yet a little while, and the coming one will come and will not delay; but my righteous one shall live by faith, and if he shrinks back, my soul has no pleasure in him'" (Heb. 10:37–38). For James the problem is not so much the fearfulness of believers as the continuing injustice that his readers experience at the hands of the rich and powerful, the merchants, the landowners – those who have "laid up treasure in the last days" (Jas. 5:3). He urges the brethren patiently to endure the suffering, because the Lord will come, the judge is standing at the doors (Jas.

5:7–9). Finally, there will be those who ridicule the faith of these Christ-followers: "Where is the promise of his coming?" (2 Pet. 3:4). What is at stake here is not the truth or otherwise of a particular doctrine. The "promise of his coming" carried with it the vindication of *all* that they believed – their faith that Jesus was indeed King of kings and Lord of lords.

The early communities of Christ-followers had to live out their eschatology on the brink of a very uncertain future. What they had to sustain them was, on the one hand, a powerful sense of the presence of the risen Christ among them, especially as they worshipped, and on the other hand the stories that they told about how – and more importantly *when* – things would work out. One of the most puzzling of these stories – for the modern reader at least – concerned the coming of a figure of extreme "lawlessness" who would count equality with God a thing to be grasped.

Six

The Man of Lawlessness

If the first churches of the ancient Mediterranean world were taught by Paul and others that the coming of the Lord Jesus Christ would take place soon, within the horizon of their own lives, it is hardly surprising if they were sometimes persuaded that the train of salvation was already pulling into the eschatological terminus, that they should take down their luggage from the overhead racks and start elbowing their way to the doors. This is apparently what happened in Thessalonica. Paul deals with the outbreak of premature excitement by reminding them of the sequence of events that would take place before the Day of the Lord: a "mystery of lawlessness" is already at work in the world but is "restrained" in some way; there will be a "rebellion" and the restraint will be removed before the revelation of an arrogant and blasphemous "man of lawlessness" (2 Thess. 2:1–8; cf. 1 Thess. 5:1–2).

This notoriously difficult passage presents the reader with two basic problems. The first is one of interpretation: how are we to decipher the apocalyptic mysteries that appear in the text? What do these words and phrases mean? What strange entities and events, in the realm of history or of myth, are referred to here? The second is the broader, literary problem: how do we explain the *need* to decipher? Why is the passage so cryptic? What lies in the darkness beyond the text?

Two main reasons have commonly been put forward to explain why so much necessary information seems either to be missing from the text or to have been cunningly hidden behind the opaque terminology. There is the obvious point, first, that Paul is referring back to earlier, more extensive teaching: "Do you not remember that when I was still with you I told you this?" (2:5). It appears that what we have in 2 Thessalonians 2:3–7 is a highly compacted summary of a larger narrative, which would have been more or less comprehensible to anyone who knew the original teaching. This is certainly part of the explanation, but we still have to ask what this teaching was and why it has been reduced to these particular terms. Secondly, commentators have sometimes supposed that Paul chose to conceal the identity of the protagonists in this dangerous end-game in order to avoid incriminating himself or the recipients of the Letter should it fall into the wrong hands.[1] In general terms, such caution might have been a factor in the development of Jewish apocalyptic symbolism, but it is less clear that in the actual circumstances of Paul's correspondence with the Thessalonians, this was either a necessary or an appropriate expedient. We do not get the impression from the Letters or from Acts that he was at this stage reluctant to provoke political or religious hostility over matters of critical importance to his gospel; and he is quite open in this Letter about the massive implications of Christ's *parousia* for the world. If circumspection *was* a factor, we still cannot know exactly what Paul is saying here without somehow filling in the missing information. How are we to go about doing this?

It is difficult to find anything else in Paul's Letters that might cast useful light on these events – the key terms are unique to this passage. Attempts to find explanatory

---

[1] Frame cites the conjecture recorded by Augustine (*Civ.* 20.19) that Paul "was unwilling to use language more explicit lest he should incur the calumnious charge of wishing ill to the empire which it was hoped would be eternal" (Frame, *Thessalonians*, 260).

parallels in non-biblical sources have not been very successful either.[2] Allusions to Old Testament texts have commonly been noted, but not in any very coherent way: we tend to suppose merely that Paul has constructed his narrative in magpie fashion out of phrases and images pilfered from various Old Testament texts. This is where interpretation has consistently missed the point of Paul's account – by not taking seriously enough the intertextual indicators that are found in it.[3] The argument that we will put forward here is that Daniel's multilayered story of the crisis provoked by Antiochus Epiphanes, mediated in all likelihood by a tradition of interpretation that is largely invisible to us, provides the narrative background needed to make sense of the disjointed synopsis of 2 Thessalonians 2:3–7.

The tradition may well have included Jesus' apocalyptic discourse. His account of the judgment that will come upon Jerusalem certainly has the proportions and characteristics of the earlier calamity (cf. Matt. 24:15; Mark 13:14). David Wenham draws attention to three distinct motifs that appear in both texts: the call not to be shaken or misled (Mark 13:5–7; par. Matt. 24:4–6; Luke 21:8–9; 2 Thess. 2:2–3); an assault on the temple described in language drawn from Daniel's prophecy regarding Antiochus Epiphanes; and a warning about deceptive "signs and wonders."[4] The more extensive narrative and

---

[2] Wanamaker sees links with *Pss. Sol.* 17:11–22 (Wanamaker, *Thessalonians*, 245). For a summary of the relation of Paul to the Jewish Pseudepigrapha see L. J. Kreitzer, *Jesus and God in Paul's Eschatology* (Sheffield: JSOT Press, 1987), 171–73.

[3] The argument of Aus that Isa. 66 constitutes an interpretive background, though in the end unconvincing, is methodologically appropriate (Aus, "God's Plan," 537–53). Nicholl's recent attempt to develop the connection between 2 Thess. 2:3–7 and Daniel by identifying the archangel Michael as the restraining force should also be mentioned (C. Nicholl, "Michael, the Restrainer Removed [2 Thess. 2:6–7]," *JTS* 51.1 [2000], 27–53).

[4] D. Wenham, *Paul*, 317–19, and "Paul and the Synoptic Apocalypse," in R. T. France and D. Wenham (eds.), *Gospel Perspectives: Studies of History and Tradition in the Four Gospels*, II (Sheffield: JSOT Press, 1981), 345–75.

verbal correspondence, however, is with the Daniel texts; the typology which emerges here provides a better explanation of Paul's apocalyptic drama than the limited parallels found in the synoptic text. Most importantly, although Jesus makes reference to the "abomination of desolation," the central figure of the man of lawlessness is missing. The background text from Daniel is being used in different ways and for different purposes.

The Man of Lawlessness

The connection between the apocalyptic scenario of 2 Thessalonians 2:3–7 and the prophetic narratives in Daniel emerges most clearly in the description of the "man of lawlessness . . . who opposes and exalts himself against every so-called god or object of worship, so that he takes his seat in the temple of God, proclaiming himself to be God" (2 Thess. 2:3–4).[5] Paul appears to have drawn here chiefly on the description in Daniel of Antiochus IV, the self-styled *Theos Epiphanēs*, who "will be exalted against every god and will speak outrageous things against the God of gods" (Dan. 11:36 LXX; cf. 7:8, 25; 8:10, 23–24). The phraseology is perhaps not close enough to indicate a direct quotation, but a dependence of some sort on this prophetic type, mediated and adapted to whatever degree by Jewish and Christian tradition, seems unquestionable. Other Old Testament passages in which the kings of Babylon and Tyre are reproached for similar hubris and blasphemy (Isa. 14:13–14; Ezek. 28:2, 6, 9) may also have had some influence on the portrait but lack the same degree of narrative and contextual correspondence.[6] What this eclecticism suggests, however, is that the "man of

---

[5] The idea is perhaps not that he sits on the throne of God but that he seats himself alongside God, as another god, after the pluralistic pagan model. Cf. Ezek. 28:2.

[6] The phrase *huios anomias* occurs in Ps. 88:23 LXX to denote an opponent of David (cf. Aus, "God's Plan," 538, n. 11; Wanamaker, *Thessalonians*, 245).

lawlessness" is not simply the fulfillment of Daniel's prophecy but something new: the image is not interpreted but projected into the darkness of the future to make sense of new but analogous circumstances.

This typological background provides some guidance with regard to the general *significance* of Paul's man of lawlessness as an opponent of God and will prove invaluable in teasing out the meaning of the other elements in the narrative. Paul's man of lawlessness is a figure *like* Antiochus Epiphanes. So far, so good. But we still have only a typology, constructed from an earlier religious-political crisis and re-used by Paul, or by the tradition before him, with some measure of prophetic license.[7] It does not tell us to what concrete historical circumstance, actual or foreseen, Paul believed the typology referred. The "man of lawlessness" would take his seat in the temple of God and proclaim himself to be God or a god. But where or what was this temple? And if we could have asked Paul who this lawless person actually was, or would be, what sort of answer might he have given?

The temple

The scene of Antiochus' transgression was the temple in Jerusalem. Should we suppose that in Paul's mind the "man of lawlessness" would follow this bogeyman of Jewish nightmares into the same physical structure and take his seat there?[8] Or does he mean the temple in a metaphorical sense – as being the church, perhaps, or a heavenly temple,[9] or more abstractly the place of God's dwelling in the minds of men?[10]

---

[7] There is no need to suppose that the author of the tradition cited in 2 Thess. 2:3–7 was unaware of the original reference to Antiochus (as, e.g., Nicholl, "Michael," 40).

[8] Cf. J. Munck, *Paul and the Salvation of Mankind* (London: SCM Press, 1959), 131, 285; Wanamaker, *Thessalonians*, 246; Nicholl, "Michael," 36, n. 32.

[9] Cf. Frame, *Thessalonians*, 257.

[10] Cf. Bruce, *Thessalonians*, 169.

On the whole, the objections to taking the temple in a literal sense are not overwhelming. J. E. Frame thinks that a heathen ruler would set up a statue of himself rather than actually "sit" in the temple, but there is no reason why the temple should not be literal and the sitting figurative, anticipating the proclamation that "he himself is a god."[11] It could be argued from 2 Corinthians 6:14–18 that the effect of believers being "mis-yoked" with unbelievers is that "lawlessness" in the shape of Belial and the worship of idols is introduced into the "temple of God," which is the church. But here "temple," without the definite article in Greek, is a metaphor for the community of believers: "we are a temple of the living God" (6:16). In 2 Thessalonians 2:4 "*the* temple of God" is an object in an apocalyptic narrative. There may be some connection between the two texts: Paul may have seen lawlessness widely at work in the world while still expecting the "man of lawlessness" to make his appearance in Jerusalem.[12] But the rhetorical setting is different enough to suggest that the definite article with "temple" in the narrative context of 2 Thessalonians 2:3–4 points to a rather different meaning.

It is interesting here to consider the use of the article with "temple" in 1 Corinthians 3:17: "If any one destroys *the* temple of God (*ton naon tou theou*), God will destroy him. For *the* temple of God is holy (*ho . . . naos tou theou hagios estin*), which you are" (translation mine). This temple which is destroyed is clearly part of a metaphor that is applied to the community: "Do you not know that you are *a* temple of God?" (3:16). But a narrative element has been introduced which suggests that Paul may have in mind *the*

---

[11] Frame, *Thessalonians*, 257; cf. Bruce, *Thessalonians*, 169.

[12] This admittedly raises the question of whether or in what sense we might regard such a prophecy about the temple as having been fulfilled (cf. Wanamaker, *Thessalonians*, 248). On the matter of the man of lawlessness we may ask whether the interpretation of biblical prophecy permits us to view the already remarkable conjunction of the destruction of the temple and Nero's hubris as a fulfillment of 2 Thess. 2:3–4.

actual temple in Jerusalem and the possibility of its destruction: if a nation destroys (Paul has *phtheirei*) the temple of God, as the Babylonians did and as Rome would soon do, then God would destroy that nation. The *larger* metaphor that is applied to the more localized circumstances of the church in Corinth is then the *story* of how God will defeat the eschatological figure (Nebuchadnezzar, Antiochus, the Roman emperor, the man of lawlessness) who defiles or lays waste to the place of his dwelling in the world. This has no direct bearing on how we understand the reference to the temple in 2 Thessalonians 2:4, but according to Daniel 9:26 LXX (the Hebrew text is rather ambiguous) at the time of the Antiochene crisis "a kingdom of nations shall destroy (*phtherei*) the city and the holy place (*to hagion*)." If this formed part of the overall typology that Paul is using here (1 Cor. 3:17 is perhaps evidence that he was aware of this statement), then we may suppose that the temple in which the man of lawlessness sits is also the temple which is destroyed. Here we have perhaps the strongest positive argument in favor of the literal interpretation: according to the typology it is the place of worship of a people *under judgment* that is desolated. This must be the Jerusalem temple.

The identity of the man of lawlessness

To equate the man of lawlessness with the little horn of Daniel 7 – 12 does not tell us who this portentous figure would actually be. Paul's account of the appearance of the man of lawlessness is prophetic and his identity was (presumably) unknown to him. It does not constitute an *interpretation* of the statement to identify the man of lawlessness with any particular historical figure. The text, however, does establish certain parameters for interpretation deriving from the typological use of the Antiochene crisis. It is improbable, for example, that the man of lawlessness was expected to emerge from among the people of God, whether Israel or the church. The Antiochene crisis, as interpreted by Daniel, involved, fundamentally, the intrusion of a hostile and idolatrous *pagan* presence into the heart of Israel's worship. In Jesus' apocalyptic narrative, the "abomination of desolation" signified in some way the offence of an analogous Roman presence in the holy of holies. Although it could be argued that "lawlessness" implies rejection of the law and so must have its origins within the covenant,[13] in the antitheses of 2 Corinthians 6:14–16 "lawlessness" (*anomia*) is aligned with Beliar, the unbeliever, and idolatry. The virulent antipathy of Antiochus towards the Jewish law is recorded in the Maccabean writings (cf. 1 Macc. 1:41–57; 4 Macc. 4:24); Eleazar complains about the "abominable and lawless (*anomōn*) Gentiles" (3 Macc. 6:9 RSV). There appears to be no reason, therefore, why Paul should not have described a pagan figure as a "man of lawlessness." But the intrusion of lawlessness from outside prompted a response of lawlessness from within. Many of the people – "every one who forsook the law" – cooperated with the inspectors who were sent by Antiochus to enforce the abandonment of traditional practices: "they did evil in the land; they drove Israel into hiding in every place of refuge they had" (1 Macc. 1:52–53 RSV; cf. 2 Macc. 8:17).

It seems likely, then, that for Paul's readers the typological background pointed to the emergence of a pagan ruler who would seek to usurp the place of the God of Israel – not least by establishing some sort of idolatrous presence in the Jerusalem temple – and oppress those who regarded themselves as his elect. They might have expected the role to be filled by a local ruler, a client king – Antiochus was only a regional power, constrained by Egypt and answerable to Rome. Or they might have concluded that a prominent Roman figure was the more likely candidate – someone like Caligula, who had angered the Jews in A.D. 40 by threatening to erect his own statue, bearing the name Zeus Epiphanios Neos Gaios, in the

---

[13] Cf. Best, *Thessalonians*, 284.

temple (*Ant.* 18.8.1–9 §257–309).[14] In any case, it would not be a sudden development: the "mystery of lawlessness" was already at work – a steady, demoralizing increase in Gentile hostility towards the people of God and a corresponding internal collapse that Jesus himself had predicted: "many will fall away and betray one another and hate one another. And many false prophets will arise and lead many astray. And because lawlessness (*anomian*) will be increased, the love of many will grow cold" (Matt. 24:10–12). The impact that lawlessness had on Israel during the Maccabean crisis would be repeated – within the compass of Jesus' future, then within the broader horizon of Paul's expanded, but no less real and no less disturbing, eschatology.

The association of Beliar (the Greek form of "Belial") with "lawlessness" in 2 Corinthians 6:14–16 may provide a further clue to the identity of the man of lawlessness.[15] The name "Belial" derives from a Hebrew word meaning "worthlessness." Two points are worth mentioning with regard to the use of this word in the Old Testament. The first is that it is commonly translated in the Septuagint by words connoting "lawless behavior."[16] Secondly, as part of an oracle against Nineveh, the prophet Nahum speaks of a prominent figure who plots evil against the Lord and counsels "worthlessness" (1:11; cf. 1:15). This network of

---

[14] Harrison suggests that in Paul's view Caligula had become "the historical precursor to the destruction of the Jerusalem Temple and ultimately to the eschaton itself" (J. R. Harrison, "Paul and the Imperial Gospel at Thessaloniki," *JSNT* 25.1 [2002], 84). See also Ehrman, *Jesus*, 117; C. L. Mearns, "Early Eschatological Development in Paul: The Evidence of I and II Thessalonians," *NTS* 27.2 (1981), 153.

[15] See Frame, *Thessalonians*, 253–54.

[16] "Sons of worthlessness" (*benê-belîya'al*) in Deut. 13:13 is translated *andres paranomoi* ("lawless men"); cf. Judg. 19:22; 20:13; 1 Sam. 1:16; 2:12; 2 Sam. 16:7; 20:1; 1 Kgs. 21:10, 13; Prov. 6:12; also *paranomeis* in Job 34:18. Deut. 15:9 has *anomēma* ("lawless action") for *belîya'al*, 2 Sam. 22:5 has *anomia* ("lawlessness"; cf. Ps. 18:4). 3 Kgdms. 20:13 A has *apostasia* for *belîya'al* (cf. Bruce, *Thessalonians*, 167–68, citing Nestle; and 182–83, on this point).

associations is admittedly somewhat tenuous in itself, but it does suggest that behind this man of lawlessness lurks the shadowy figure of Belial, who at least by the time of 2 Corinthians had become for Paul an egregious opponent of Christ. As far as 2 Thessalonians is concerned, there is not much more that can be said about this. The Ascension of Isaiah, however, "prophesies" that Beliar, the "king of this world" will take on human form as a "lawless king" and will "persecute the plant which the Twelve Apostles of the Beloved have planted" (4:2–3). This king is cryptically but unmistakably identified as Nero, "the slayer of his mother" (4:2). In retrospect at least (this part of the text is generally reckoned to date from the end of the first century A.D.),[17] Nero's impiety and antipathy towards Christians must have marked him as an extremely "lawless" figure in the eyes of the church.[18]

The Rebellion

The appearance of the "man of lawlessness" is preceded by an act of transgression which Paul describes as the *apostasia* which must come first (2:3). Taken on its own this term would probably signify an act of rebellion on the part of the Jews either against God (cf. Josh. 22:22; 3 Kgdms. 20:13 A; 2 Chr. 29:19; Jer. 2:19; Acts 21:21) or against Rome – Josephus describes the Jewish revolt of A.D. 66 as an *apostasia*.[19] The verb *apostateō* signifies religious or political rebellion in the Septuagint (Neh. 2:19; 6:6; 1 Macc. 11:14; 3:16; 2 Macc. 5:11). If we take the rebellion to be essentially religious, it is

[17] J. H. Charlesworth (ed.), *The Old Testament Pseudepigrapha*, I and II (London: Darton, Longman & Todd, 1985), 149.

[18] Cf. Whiteley, *Theology*, 236: "It is possible that 'wickedness . . . in human form' was an 'indeterminate quantity' for St. Paul when he wrote 2 *Thess.*, but that during his last days in Rome he ascribed to it the determinate value '*Nero*.'" Note the description of Nero in *Sib. Or*. 5:33–34: "he will return declaring himself equal to God."

[19] Cf. Jos. *Vita* 43; *J.W.* 7.82, 164; *Ag. Ap.* 1.135–36; *Ant.* 13.219. The Jews had also come close to rebellion when Caligula attempted to have his statue erected in the temple (*J.W.* 2.10.1–4 §184–198).

conceivable that Paul also has in mind a defection within the church – perhaps 1 Timothy 4:1 offers some support for this: "in later times some will depart (*apostōsontai*) from the faith." It is less likely that he is predicting either an exclusively Christian apostasy or, quoting F. F. Bruce, a "large-scale revolt against public order" – an assault against those ruling authorities which have been instituted by God (Rom. 13:1–2).[20] In view of the terminology and the general context, we should probably assume that Paul addresses these matters from a fundamentally Jewish perspective, according to which *apostasia* would presuppose a covenantal relationship to God.[21]

So far these are very general considerations. The Daniel texts, however, take us a step further in reconstructing the underlying "story" to which *hē apostasia* refers. The related verb *aphistēmi* is used in Daniel 11:31 and 12:11 LXX for the "removal" (*apostēsousi*) of the perpetual sacrifice by the forces of Antiochus.[22] This is the first of a series of events described in Daniel 11:31–39 which culminates in the account of Antiochus' blasphemy. In 1 Maccabees 2:15 the act of offering pagan sacrifice under duress at Modein, on the occasion which sparked the Maccabean revolt, is described specifically as an *apostasia*. This goes beyond the use of the verb to refer to the *removal* of the temple sacrifice, but conceivably *hē apostasia* in 2 Thessalonians 2:3 is an abbreviated reference not only to the removal of the sacrifice in Daniel 11:31 and 12:11 but also to the offering of an "abomination of desolation" which immediately follows it. There is some ground for thinking, therefore, that it is a repetition, or perhaps a *fulfillment*, of this archetypal departure from true worship that Paul has in mind when he says that the *apostasia* must come first. We should note that in Daniel's narrative there are those who "by their sins defile a covenant among a hard people"

---

[20] Bruce, *Thessalonians*, 167; cf. Frame, *Thessalonians*, 251.

[21] Cf. Best, *Thessalonians*, 282; Wanamaker, *Thessalonians*, 244.

[22] Dan. 9:26 LXX has *apostathēsetai chrisma*: "an anointing shall be removed."

(11:32 LXX). As with the emergence of lawlessness, the two aspects go hand in hand: the desecration of the temple by a foreign power, the forcible removal of the sacrifice, is accompanied by the willful acquiescence of a sinful people in the apostasy.[23]

According to Daniel's account, the intervention of Antiochus will bring about a division in Israel between those Jews who defile the covenant and the pious – the "wise of the nation," as the angel calls them, who "understand many things" (Dan. 11:32–33 LXX).[24] This separation comes to a climax on the "day of affliction," when many of those sleeping in the earth will rise up: some will face reproach and scattering and shame, but the wise will shine as the stars of heaven (12:1–3). This parallels the contrast that Paul makes in this chapter between those who are deceived by the satanic power of the "man of lawlessness," who do not love the truth but "believe what is false," and those who have been chosen as "firstfruits to be saved, through sanctification by the Spirit and belief in the truth" (2 Thess. 2:10–14).

The correspondence can be developed further. Paul's earlier description of the wicked as those "not knowing God" (*mē eidosin theon*: 2 Thess. 1:8) recalls – antithetically – the description of the "wise" as "a people knowing God" in the Hebrew and Theodotion texts of Daniel 11:32.[25] The relationship of the wicked to the "man of lawlessness" is also suggested by the description of the Jews who associate themselves with Antiochus and defile the covenant as "those who act lawlessly" (*hoi anomountes*) and the "lawless" (*anomoi*: Dan. 11:32; 12:10 Theod.). The wise in

---

[23] Cf. 1 Macc. 1:11; and the description of religious corruption at the time of Pompey's invasion of Palestine in 63 B.C. in *Pss. Sol.* 2; 17:11–20. Pompey is described as *ho anomos* (17:11). Cf. Wanamaker, *Thessalonians*, 245.

[24] Note the parallels with Isa. 52:13 – 53:12: e.g., Isa. 52:13 LXX: "my servant shall understand"; cf. 53:11. See Goldingay, *Daniel*, 284.

[25] LXX has *ho dēmos ho ginōskōn tauta*. It is at least arguable that 2 Thess. 1:8 refers to Jews, despite 1 Thess. 4:5.

Israel, on the other hand, will be "tested and sanctified" (Dan. 12:10 LXX); they will suffer death, captivity, and plunder (11:33), but through this they will purify themselves up until the time of the end (11:35). In the same way, Paul encourages the Thessalonians to remain steadfast and faithful in the midst of persecution "that you may be considered worthy of the kingdom of God, for which you are also suffering" (2 Thess. 1:4–5; cf. 1:11; 2:13–14; 1 Thess. 5:23). This kingdom, in Paul's mind, is precisely the "kingdom" which is given to the suffering saints in Daniel 7:21–22, 25–27.

The Restraining Force

In 2 Thessalonians 2:3–10 Paul speaks first of a rebellion that must take place, then describes at greater length the revelation of a "man of lawlessness," who in his hostility towards the God of Israel and contempt for the temple will resemble Antiochus Epiphanes. While the actual identity of this figure remains undisclosed and probably unknown, the "lawlessness" which he epitomizes is already at work. There is, however, an additional factor in this end-game, which, if anything, has proved even more intractable to interpretation. Paul appears to have believed that the full horror of lawlessness would not be revealed before the removal of an agent whose function is defined solely by the verb *katechō* (2:7).

This activity has usually been understood as some sort of restraint imposed upon the presence of lawlessness in the world; and since both the neuter and the masculine forms of the present participle are used (*to katechon*/*ho katechōn*), commentators have generally drawn the conclusion that the restraining force must be defined in both impersonal and personal terms – both as a power or institution and as an individual. But we should be careful not to jump to conclusions. In biblical usage *katechō* has three main areas of meaning: (i) to detain, hold back, hold captive, seize (e.g., Gen. 24:56; 39:20; Luke 4:42); (ii) to possess, especially in the sense of possessing an inheritance (e.g., Dan. 7:18, 22; 2 Cor. 6:10); (iii) to hold fast, as when, for example, Paul urges the Thessalonians to "hold fast what is good" (e.g., 1 Thess. 5:21). Although it would be quite reasonable to think of this agent as a restraining force, the verb does not have an explicit object and it is only an inference that Paul has in mind something or someone which holds back either the mystery or the man of lawlessness. All we are directly told is that the revelation of the man of lawlessness is somehow dependent on the removal of the one who does whatever is signified by *katechō*.

The grammatical and factual problems that the narrative poses have made it very difficult to reconstruct with any confidence the rhetorical context that would make sense of the *katechon/katechōn* combination. A wide range of ingenious and not implausible candidates for the role of the restraining force have been offered over the years. Some have seen behind this text the common eschatological motif of the binding of Satan and have taken the restraining force to be God, Christ, the Spirit, the angel of Revelation 20:2, or the archangel Michael.[26] Roger Aus has suggested that *katechō* corresponds to the Hebrew word translated "shut the womb" in Isaiah 66:9: God *delays* the eschatological fulfillment, the coming to birth of his purposes.[27] Oscar Cullmann popularized the view that Paul had in mind the Gentile mission.[28] Many have assigned the part to the civilizing influence of Rome and of Claudius in particular; or if not Rome and the emperor, then whatever principle of order is currently

---

[26] See Frame, *Thessalonians*, 260–62; Best, *Thessalonians*, 296–97; Ridderbos, *Paul*, 524–26; M. J. J. Menken, *2 Thessalonians* (London/New York: Routledge, 1994), 108–13. Nicholl has recently revisited the argument that the restrainer is the archangel Michael (Nicholl, "Michael").

[27] Aus, "God's Plan," 544–48.

[28] O. Cullmann, "Le Caractère Eschatologique du Devoir Missionnaire et de la Conscience Apostolique de S. Paul: Étude sur le *katechon* (*-ōn*) de II Thess.2.6–7," *RHPR* 16 (1936), 210–45; also Munck, *Salvation*, 36–42; Moore, *Parousia*, 112–14; Aus, "God's Plan," 540.

operative.[29] Lastly, it has sometimes been argued that the *katechōn* is a lesser *evil* power: a false prophet, perhaps, who has "seized" the church in Thessalonica;[30] a hostile "occupying power" in the world, who will eventually be displaced by the man of lawlessness;[31] or Satan himself, who will be cast out of heaven (cf. Rev. 12:9) only to inspire the greater wickedness of the man of lawlessness.[32] Wanamaker thinks that the *katechon* is Rome, conceived not as a benign restraint but as a power antagonistic to God which "holds sway" or "prevails," and that Paul may have believed that the removal of Claudius would clear the way for the greater evil of Nero.[33]

The obscurity of Paul's narrative makes it as difficult to reject these various explanations outright as to accept them. Indeed, the argument has been put forward, on the assumption that the Letter is pseudepigraphic, that the author of 2 Thessalonians never intended the *katechon*/*katechōn* to be identifiable and that the search for a referent is futile.[34] Nevertheless, our analysis to this point suggests that a different approach might be profitable. If, as we have argued, the rebellion and the man of lawlessness have their origins in Daniel 7 – 12, we are bound to ask whether the activity denoted by *katechō* does not also have its counter-

---

29 C. J. Ellicott, *Commentary on the Epistles of St. Paul to the Thessalonians* (Grand Rapids: Zondervan, 1957), 112; L. Morris, "Man of Lawlessness and Restraining Power," in G. F. Hawthorne, R. P. Martin and D. G. Reid, *Dictionary of Paul and his Letters* (Downers Grove/Leicester: InterVarsity Press, 1993), 593; L. Morris, *1 & 2 Thessalonians* (London: Tyndale, 1976), 129–30; D. J. Williams, *1 and 2 Thessalonians* (Peabody, MA: Hendrickson, 1995), 127.

30 C. H. Giblin, *The Threat to Faith: An Exegetical and Theological Re-Examination of 2 Thessalonians 2* (AnBib 31; Rome: Pontifical Biblical Institute, 1967), 166–242.

31 Best, *Thessalonians*, 301.

32 P. S. Dixon, "The Evil Restraint in 2 Thess. 2:6," *JETS* 33.4 (1990), 448. Dixon thinks that the *katechon* and the "mystery of lawlessness" are to be equated, but while the *katechon* is to be removed, lawlessness continues in the form of the "lawless one."

33 Wanamaker, *Thessalonians*, 253–57; cf. J. W. Elias, *1 & 2 Thessalonians* (Scottdale, PA: Herald Press, 1995), 282–85.

34 L. J. Lietaert Peerbolte, "The KATÉXON/KATÉXŌN of 2 Thess. 2:6–7," *NovT* 39.2 (1997), 138–50.

part in these "prophecies" of the Antiochene crisis. I think it can be shown that this literary background provides a quite straightforward explanation of Paul's meaning. In the end it will be the coherence of the reconstruction, as much as any particular point of exegesis, that will recommend this reading over others.

Daniel is told, according to the Hebrew text, that towards the end of the seventy weeks of years which have been determined for the people of Israel an "anointed one" (*māšîaḥ*) will be cut off (9:26). This is probably a reference, prophetic or otherwise, to the high priest Onias III, who was displaced on the accession of Antiochus in 175 B.C. and killed in 171 B.C.[35] Following this a leader[36] will come who will devastate the people, put an end to the sacrifice and offering, and put in its place a "desolating abomination" (9:27). Nothing in this allusive narrative directly suggests that the high priest, or the priesthood generally, constituted a hindrance or restraint to Antiochus,[37] but we have, nevertheless, the type of a significant individual who is got "out of the way" (*ek mesou genētai*),[38] to use Paul's expression, prior to the appearance of a man of extreme lawlessness.[39]

---

[35] See Goldingay, *Daniel*, 262; Collins, *Daniel*, 356. Note 4 Macc. 4:15–16.

[36] According to Goldingay, *Daniel*, 262, this is Jason, the high priest who succeeded Onias, but Antiochus seems the more likely referent.

[37] Onias is described as a pious high priest who hated wickedness (2 Macc. 3:1; cf. 15:12), who was noted for opposing the theft of temple funds by Heliodorus (2 Macc. 3:4–40).

[38] It is curious, but probably no more than coincidental, that the word *parakleiō* ("to shut out, exclude") is used in 2 Macc. 4:34 to refer to the murder of Onias.

[39] There is some lexicological support for this argument. In the Hebrew text of Dan. 9:26 the word used for the removal of the anointed one is *kārat*, which means "to cut off," corresponding to *exolethreuthēsetai* in the Theodotion translation. The word *kārat* occurs frequently in the Old Testament in the phrase "cut off from the midst of the people," which is sometimes translated in the LXX by such equivalents as *exolethreuō/olethreuō ek mesou* or *ekkoptō ek mesou* followed by a genitive noun denoting the people (e.g., Exod. 31:14; Num. 4:18; 19:20; Jer. 44:7 [51:7 LXX]; Ezek. 14:8; Micah 5:9, 13). So when Paul says that *ho katechōn* will eventually "become out of the midst" (*ek mesou genētai*), we may suspect that the phrase is a reminiscence of this idiom and alludes, albeit somewhat loosely, to the removal of the anointed one in Dan. 9:26.

The Greek translations at this point, however, speak not of an "anointed one" but of an "anointing" (*chrisma*) which, according to the Septuagint text, is "removed" (*apostathēsetai*; Theod. has "cut off") just before the city and the holy place are destroyed by a "kingdom of Gentiles." This anointing would naturally have been interpreted in relation to the person and activity of the high priest, but it also allows a more *impersonal* understanding of the sanctity of the temple and the commitment of God to Jerusalem to emerge. Moreover, the safety of the city is seen to be in some way dependent on the presence of this anointing. We must inevitably ask, then, whether this more impersonal idea – *chrisma* is a neuter noun – may account for *to katechon* in 2 Thessalonians 2:6. The neuter participle would denote the principle underlying the activity of the "anointed one" in this narrative. What the Thessalonians have come to know in the midst of their persecutions is the same "anointing" – understood not in abstract terms but as the power from God to play the part of one who suffers and is "cut off" in the build up to the revelation of extreme lawlessness. It may seem odd that Paul should highlight this impersonal aspect here, but this may only reflect the influence of the original typology on the formation of this particular apocalyptic narrative.

A later version of the same events (Dan. 11:30–39) suggests another possible precursor for the *katechōn*. Daniel is told that forces from Antiochus will remove the daily offering and set up the abomination that makes desolate. Some of the Jews will acquiesce in this violation of the covenant, but "a people who know their God shall be strong and take action" (11:32 Theod.). Among the people there will be some who are wise, who will enlighten the multitude, but "for some days they shall stumble by sword and flame, by captivity and plunder" (11:33). Immediately following this statement we have the account of the king's self-magnification and blasphemy. Here, then, we have a group which not only offers active resistance to the man of lawlessness but is also, in some manner, removed from the scene before the manifestation of one who "shall speak astonishing things against the God of gods" (11:36). A passage in 1 Maccabees describing the response of faithful Jews to the decree of Antiochus reinforces this line of thought and provides insight into the sort of historical memories that would have given urgency and poignancy to Paul's hurried retracing of the apocalyptic narrative: "But many in Israel stood firm and were resolved in their hearts not to eat unclean food. They chose to die rather than to be defiled by food or to profane the holy covenant; and they did die. And very great wrath came upon Israel" (1 Macc. 1:62–64 RSV).

A group such as this is an unlikely referent for the singular participle *ho katechōn*, and it may be preferable to see in this a reference to some figure who functions, either literally or metaphorically, as an anointed high priest analogous to Onias III – James the Just, perhaps, who was martyred in A.D. 62 (*Ant.* 20.9.1 §197; cf. Eusebius, *Hist. eccl.* 2.23.4–18). However, *ho katechōn* does not have to be understood as an oblique reference to an identifiable individual. It may also be read in an indeterminate sense to mean "he who holds fast" or "he who restrains," rather as *ho nikōn* in Revelation denotes not any particular individual (as Christ, for example, might be called "the Conqueror") but simply "he who conquers" (Rev. 2:11, 26; 3:5, 12, 21; 21:7; cf. 1 John 5:5).[40] The one who restrains the spread of lawlessness, then, is potentially any believer who will stand firm, being willing to die rather than, in the words of 1 Maccabees, "profane the holy covenant."

There is another possible interpretive connection between Daniel 11:30–39 and what Paul says about the *katechon*/*katechōn*. According to the Theodotion text of Daniel 11:35 some of those who understand will be weak "in order to refine them with fire and to choose, and in order to be revealed at the end of the time (*tou apokaluphthēnai heōs kairou peras*)."[41] This

---

[40] Cf. *ho emmenōn*/*ho hupomenōn* in Dan. 12:12 LXX/Theod.

[41] Theodotion has the construction *tou apokaluphthēnai*; the corresponding phrase in LXX is *eis to katharisthēnai*. The thought is lacking in the Hebrew text.

sounds remarkably like Paul's statement in 2 Thessalonians 2:6 that they now know the *katechon* (which we have tentatively identified with the "anointing" of those who oppose lawlessness) "in order for him to be revealed in his time" (*eis to apokaluphthēnai auton en tōi heautou kairōi*). The problem is the masculine pronoun *auton*, which cannot have *to katechon* as its antecedent and would appear, therefore, to refer to the man of lawlessness. In verses 3 and 8 it is the man of lawlessness who is revealed and it would be natural to read "in order for him to be revealed in his time" in verse 6 as a parallel statement.[42]

There are two ways in which we might deal with this – other than abandon it as a hopelessly contorted line of exegesis. It is possible that Paul, or the tradition which he is summarizing here, understood *tou apokaluphthēnai* in Daniel 11:35 to refer not to those who have understanding but to the king, whose monstrous effrontery is "revealed," so to speak, in the next verse. The verb has no express subject and unlike the preceding verbs is in the passive.

It is perhaps more plausible, however, to think that the masculine pronoun anticipates the change to *ho katechōn* in verse 7, bearing in mind that this is a very compact summary, one which expressly assumes prior information on the part of the reader. Paul's argument would be, then, that he who now suffers as a result of his steadfast opposition to the mystery of lawlessness will eventually be "manifested" – we might add "in glory" – by way of vindication.[43] This would provide us with another instance of the general suffering-vindication motif, but two texts in Paul appear to reproduce this line of thought rather more closely and give further support to the argument. In

---

[42] Cf. Wanamaker, *Thessalonians*, 254.

[43] It remains unclear whether *eis to apokaluphthēnai* attaches to *to katechon* (Best, *Thessalonians*, 291; Wanamaker, *Thessalonians*, 253–54; Nicholl, "Michael," 27–8) or *oidate* (Giblin, *Threat*, 206–7; Dixon, "Restraint," 447). The decision is not of great consequence to the present interpretation.

Romans 8:18–19 he writes: "For I consider that the sufferings of this present time are not worth comparing with the glory that is to be revealed to us. For the creation waits with eager longing for *the revealing of the sons of God*." Colossians 3:4 has *phaneroō* instead of *apokaluptō*, but we find the same association of the *parousia* of Christ with the "manifestation" of the faithful believer: "When Christ who is your life appears, then *you also will appear* (*phanerōthēsesthe*) with him in glory."[44]

If this is the right background, how, finally, should we understand the use of *katechō*? The reference to the resistance of the "wise" in Daniel brings into view the thought of "holding fast" to a truth or ideal. This sense of *katechō* is well enough attested in Paul. In his earlier Letter to the Thessalonians, for example, he had urged them to "hold fast what is good" (*to kalon katechete*: 1 Thess. 5:21; cf. 1 Cor. 11:2; 15:2).[45] There are indications in this closing paraenesis that he is especially mindful of their suffering. This is no facile moral exhortation, therefore, but an urgent eschatological stance by which they may hope to be kept "blameless at the *parousia* of our Lord Jesus Christ" (5:23). Such a "holding fast" would be entirely relevant to the circumstances described in 2 Thessalonians 2:3–7. What Paul may have in mind, then, is not some power that currently *restrains* the presence of lawlessness in the world but the *faithful perseverance* of the church – perhaps epitomized in the figure of James the Just – in the face of the persecution that *results from* the presence of lawlessness. It also anticipates the encouragement in 2:15 to "stand firm and hold to the traditions."

The typology, however, also gives us the option of maintaining the traditional idea of someone (or something) who "restrains." The object of this restraint may be the

---

[44] It may be this underlying assumption that the one who suffers will be "revealed" (rather than the more abstract "anointing") which accounts for the premature masculine pronoun in v. 6.

[45] In 1 Cor. 15:2 the verb appears to be used, as here, without an object. Cf. also Luke 8:15; Heb. 3:6, 14; 10:23; and perhaps Neh. 3:4 LXX.

outbreak of lawlessness, but the contextual argument suggests that it is the rebellion which is held back by the activity of those who remain faithful to the covenant, whether this is the covenant with Moses or the new covenant in Christ. Specifically, according to the Hebrew text of Daniel 11:33, the "people knowing their God" are "strong" (the Greek texts have *katischuō*) and "give understanding to many," which, I would suggest, has been interpreted by Paul as the practical means by which the spread of lawlessness is hindered. This understanding makes better sense of the passage since the rebellion is effectively made the prior condition for the manifestation of the man of lawlessness.

The Daniel Typology

This analysis has been complex, but it has brought us, I think, to a reasonably coherent conclusion. What we have are two parallel apocalyptic narratives, the one seemingly constructed according to the pattern of the other. The removal of the sacrifice, the defiling of the covenant, the alliance of the faithless with the Gentile invaders – these evocative motifs have been contracted by Paul, who has told the story already, into the single term *apostasia*. The obstinate and anointed resistance of the "wise" to Antiochus' assault on Judaism becomes a figure for the faithfulness of an embattled, Spirit-empowered, "anointed" church which seeks to remain "blameless at the *parousia* of our Lord Jesus Christ" (1 Thess. 5:23). This, Paul believes, is the force that for a while will delay the manifestation of extreme lawlessness.[46] The analogy suggests a quite prosaic mechanism for this restraint – the wise will give understanding to the many, they shall lead many to righteousness (cf. Dan. 12:3); they will be like salt

[46] It is not inconceivable that Paul thought of himself and the other apostles (Peter? James?) as embodying in an outstanding manner the function of the *katechōn*. Paul's frequent comments about his own suffering might be seen in this light.

in the world (cf. Matt. 5:13), slowing the process of religious decay. Eventually, though, those who stand out against the apostasy will be removed – by death, by captivity, by dispersion – and the way will be made clear for the horrifying revelation of a figure who will seek to usurp the throne of God. The narrative concludes with the overthrow of the blasphemer. In Daniel this is merely alluded to ("the hour of his end will come and there will be no deliverer for him": 11:45 LXX), but Paul describes in more concrete and graphic terms how the Lord Jesus will destroy the lawless one "with the breath of his mouth and . . . by the appearing of his *parousia*" (2 Thess. 2:8).

By bringing the full typology into focus we have elicited from Paul's apocalyptic narrative a significant realism.[47] The passage has become much less speculative and mythical, partly because it is seen to depend upon a coherent Old Testament narrative, but also because it is now much easier to imagine how these foreseen events might play out. Moreover, although the man of lawlessness remains a unique and puzzling figure in Paul, the spiritual dynamic of "restraint," which has appeared so cryptic, is now seen to connect with a prominent and persistent theme in the Letters – the exhortation to stand firm in the face of opposition with the ultimate assurance of attaining the kingdom of God. The events of the Jewish War still provide the most plausible historical setting for the realization of the Antiochus typology. It is natural to think of an *apostasia* in Judea, a recklessness that culminates in judgment, temporarily restrained by the faithfulness of the body of Jesus' disciples in Jerusalem. However, the shift in focus away from the fate of Jerusalem towards the manifestation of a man of lawlessness no doubt reflects a

---

[47] It is sometimes maintained that it is inappropriate to look for "a specific and definite historical reference" in a passage which otherwise "keeps to veiled and allusive language": e.g., Nicholl, "Michael," 31; cf. Frame, *Thessalonians*, 260; Ridderbos, *Paul*, 525; E. J. Richard, *First and Second Thessalonians* (Collegeville, MN: The Liturgical Press, 1995), 328.

concern for the churches in the Roman world. Since Paul says that the Thessalonians now "know what it is that holds back," he clearly believes that they too have become involved in the crisis. They are encouraged to identify themselves with the "wise," who are strong in the face of opposition, who "turn many to righteousness" (Dan. 12:3), who are purified through their suffering, and who eventually will receive the kingdom that is given to the saints of the Most High

Seven

The *Parousia* of the Lord

Paul's prediction concerning the emergence of extreme lawlessness in 2 Thessalonians has brought to the surface a narrative structure that has the power to absorb much of the earlier argument about an escalating state of crisis and the likelihood that the churches of the Greco-Roman world would face severe hardship. The people of God – including now the Gentiles who have been grafted into the olive tree of Israel – find themselves facing a period of affliction analogous to the extreme tribulation occasioned by Antiochus' arrogant and vicious impiety. The righteous will not be exempt from the suffering: they are inextricably bound up in the fate of the nation. But they have the unshakable hope of a judgment, not too far off, a Day of the Lord that will lead to the destruction of the beast and the vindication of the "holy ones of the Most High." As we move now from the *parousia* of the lawless one to the *parousia* of the Lord – from the crisis to the remedy, from suffering to salvation, from faith to vindication – one of the questions that we are bound to ask is whether Daniel's narrative has any further explanatory power.

Rescue and Retribution

The drama of Christ's *parousia*, or "coming," is presented most vividly and most coherently in the two Letters to the church at Thessalonica (1 Thess. 4:15–17; 2 Thess. 1:7–10;

2:8). Numerous other statements, however, scattered through the New Testament Letters, connect the general argumentation with this apocalyptic subtext. The coming or appearing of the Lord is the point of reference in a number of texts that encourage believers to remain faithful and irreproachable (1 Cor. 1:7–8; 1 Thess. 3:13; 5:23; 1 Tim. 6:14–15; 1 Pet. 1:13; 1 John 2:28), to live upright and godly lives in the world (Tit. 2:12–13); it marks a day of judgment (1 Cor. 4:5; 2 Tim. 4:1; 1 Pet. 1:7); the dead in Christ will be raised at his *parousia* (1 Cor. 15:23; cf. 1 Thess. 4:16); Paul hopes for approval of his work at the Lord's coming (1 Thess. 2:19; 2 Tim. 4:8). Similar hopes and expectations are attached to the thought of the coming "day of the Lord (Jesus Christ)" (1 Cor. 1:8; 5:5; 2 Cor. 1:14; 1 Thess. 5:2; 2 Tim. 1:8; 4:8; 2 Pet. 3:10). It is clear that a great deal hangs on this prospect.

The integrity of the community

In the first of the Thessalonian Letters Paul outlines a quite straightforward sequence of events (1 Thess. 4:15–17). The Lord will descend (*katabēsetai*) from heaven accompanied by "all his saints" (1 Thess. 3:13), an event signaled by "a cry of command (*en keleusmati*) . . . the voice of an archangel . . . the trumpet of God" (4:16). The dead are then raised and with the living are "caught up[1] together with them in the clouds to meet the Lord in the air." This compressed narrative, however, acquires much greater complexity and depth when we empty the box of Old Testament allusions out on to the table and begin to sort through it.

The image of the Lord descending from heaven has various Old Testament antecedents. In the earlier texts the purpose is typically to speak with Moses (Exod. 19:11, 20; 34:5; Num. 11:25; Deut. 31:15 LXX);[2] in the prophetic

---

[1] Cf. Elijah (Wis. 4:11). Also J. D. G. Dunn, *The Theology of Paul the Apostle* (Grand Rapids/Cambridge: Eerdmans, 1998), 300, n. 28.

[2] Note also Gen. 11:5. See Dupont's argument that the *parousia* in Paul is modeled on Exod. 19:10–18 LXX; Deut. 33:2 LXX (discussed in J. Plevnik, *Paul and the Parousia: An Exegetical and Theological Investigation* [Peabody, MA: Hendrickson, 1997], 9–10). 1 Enoch 1:1–4: on the "day of tribulation" God will come from his dwelling and march on Mount Sinai (cf. 1 Enoch 25:3).

writings it is to fight either against Israel's enemies or against faithlessness within Israel, which is the more relevant background here. When the Jews sought an alliance with Egypt against the Assyrians, Isaiah warned that the Lord of Hosts would "descend to wage war on Mount Zion": he "will hold a shield over Jerusalem, and will deliver and preserve and save"; and "in that day people will reject the idols of silver and gold which their hands made" (Isa. 31:4–7 LXX). In Micah, judgment against Samaria and Jerusalem begins when the Lord "proceeds from his place and will descend (*katabēsetai*) and will set foot upon the high places of the earth" (Micah 1:3 LXX). There is an important adjunct to this thought: the Lord does not "descend" arbitrarily or for no particular reason; he descends into the turmoil of history to deal with a situation that actually threatens either the security or the sanctity of his people. If Paul re-uses this prophetic idea, it is because he has in view not a remote end-time state of affairs but an actual (present or impending) situation that requires a similar intervention.

The three sounds that accompany the descent contribute to the picture of God taking decisive action. They do not make the *parousia* a public event necessarily, as Ben Witherington argues;[3] they make it a *prophesied* event – both in the sense that it is foreseen and in the sense that it has a type in Old Testament prophecy. The trumpet must owe something to the "great trumpet" of Isaiah 27:12–13, which is blown on the day when the lost sons of Israel are gathered (*sunagagete*) from the nations of the world to "worship the LORD on the holy mountain at Jerusalem."[4] This is reflected in the meeting of the living and the dead with the Lord in the air, which is presumably also the "being gathered together to him" (*episunagōgēs ep' auton*) to

[3] Witherington, *Jesus, Paul*, 157; cf. G. L. Green, *The Letters to the Thessalonians* (Grand Rapids/Leicester: Eerdmans/Inter-Varsity Press, 2002), 224.

[4] The trumpet can also signal disaster for Israel (Ezek. 33:3–4; Jer. 4:5, 19).

which Paul alludes in 2 Thessalonians 2:1. The link between the "great trumpet" and the gathering (*episunaxousin*) of the chosen was also seen in Jesus' discourse (Matt. 24:31; cf. Mark 13:27). In Zechariah 9:14, in a passage that also has the prophecy about Jerusalem's king coming to the city on an ass (9:9), it is said that a trumpet will be blown on the day when the Lord will go out to fight for Israel against Greece. The "cry of command" is more obscure but probably has similar connotations – the association may have shown up in Philo's comment that God "by one single word of command (*heni keleusmati*), could easily collect together men living on the very confines of the earth" (Philo, *Praem.* 117).[5] There are no "archangels" as such in the Old Testament, but Daniel 12:1 LXX provides an interesting point of reference. The verse speaks of Michael, the "great angel," who shall stand up on a "day of affliction such as has not been from when they came into existence until that day." In Jude 9 Michael is referred to as an "archangel."[6]

These details are not incidental; they have not been added merely for dramatic effect. Along with the wider setting of the eschatological descent of God to judge and defend, they characterize the *parousia* of the Lord as an event *for the purpose* of safeguarding the integrity of the suffering people of God (communities such as the church in Thessalonica) and of ensuring that *all* in Christ, including those who have died since they abandoned their idols and turned to the living God, will accompany the Lord "in clouds" in order to be acknowledged before God and vindicated in the world. In this way the validity of the initial hope is preserved: having taken the dangerous step

---

[5] Cf. Isa. 66:6. Possibly the same idea is found in John 5:25. The only other biblical use of *keleusma* is Prov. 30:27 LXX. Plevnik argues that Paul has in mind a cry of rebuke to the enemies of God (Plevnik, *Parousia*, 45–50).

[6] Cf. Whiteley, *Theology*, 243. In Jewish apocalyptic Michael is the chief of the archangels (1 Enoch 24:6). Also Nicholl, "Michael," 33–35 et passim.

of abandoning the worship of idols and committing themselves to a "living and true God," the Thessalonians had to "wait for his Son from heaven, whom he raised from the dead, Jesus who delivers us from the wrath to come" (1 Thess. 1:9–10). They faced considerable hardship, but they were assured of eventual gain because God would intervene to save them – just as in the past he had delivered Israel from her enemies.[7]

Respite from suffering

In the second Thessalonian letter the revelation of the Lord Jesus from heaven is described twice: it comes first as a response to the suffering of the church (2 Thess. 1:4–10), secondly in reaction to the specific threat posed by the revelation of the man of lawlessness (2:8–10). In both cases it is linked directly to the actual circumstances of the community in Thessalonica, not to some inconceivable event beyond the historical horizon of the early church.

In the first account the Lord Jesus is "revealed from heaven with his mighty angels in flaming fire (*en puri phlogos*)" (1:7–8). The Thessalonians will be rescued from their afflictions and avenged (1:7–8); their persecutors will "suffer the punishment of eternal destruction, away from the presence of the Lord and from the glory of his might" (1:9). The passage unmistakably evokes Old Testament texts that describe the descent of God to fight against his enemies. When Jerusalem is besieged by the "multitude of all the nations that fight against Ariel," she will be visited by the Lord of Hosts, in an instant, suddenly, "with thunder and with earthquake and great noise, with whirlwind and tempest, and the flame of a devouring fire (*phlox puros katesthiousa*)" (Isa. 29:6). Jerusalem will be comforted, but the Lord will manifest his indignation against his enemies when he comes "in fire, and his chariots like the whirlwind, to render his anger in fury, and

---

[7] Cf. 2 Sam. 22:18; Ezra 8:31; Neh. 9:28; Pss. 18:1, 17, 48; 31:15; Micah 4:10; cf. Luke 1:74; Matt. 6:13.

his rebuke with flames of fire (*en phlogi puros*)" (66:14–15). There are also echoes of Daniel's narrative about the "saints" who suffer but are made worthy of the kingdom, whose enemies – those not knowing God – are judged and destroyed when the Lord comes to be glorified in his saints (cf. Ps. 36:28 LXX). The two motifs have been stitched together: there will be judgment on those who afflict the church and with that respite from the suffering; but at the same time it is precisely through the suffering that the believers in Thessalonica will receive the kingdom that is given to the "one like a son of man." This is the sense in which they will "obtain the glory of our Lord Jesus Christ" (2 Thess. 2:14).

Does the phrase "eternal destruction (*olethron aiōnion*), away from the presence of the Lord" (2 Thess. 1:9) suggest unending conscious torment after death for those who do not obey the gospel?[8] Ben Sirach lists various means of divine vengeance against the wicked, including "the sword that punishes the ungodly with destruction" (Sir. 39:30 RSV), which makes "destruction" virtually synonymous with physical death, as is widely the case in Jewish writings.[9] The word is also commonly used for material ruin (Prov. 1:26–27; 21:7; Hos. 9:6; Jer. 31:32) and for the destruction of a city or nation or land (Obad. 1:12–13; Jer. 31:2–3, 8; 32:31; Ezek. 6:14; 14:16).

We come nearest to Paul's usage here in 4 Maccabees 10:15. The fourth of the seven brothers put to death by Antiochus proclaims to his torturers: "by the blessed death of my brothers, by the eternal destruction (*ton aiōnion . . . olethron*) of the tyrant, and by the everlasting life of the pious, I will not renounce our noble brotherhood" (RSV). The brothers are in no doubt that through their suffering they "shall have the prize of virtue and shall be with God" (9:8), but they defiantly warn the tyrant: "justice has laid up for you intense and eternal fire and tortures (*basanois*), and these throughout all time will never let

[8] See, e.g., I. H. Marshall, *1 and 2 Thessalonians* (Vancouver: Regent College Publishing, 2002), 178–79; Green, *Thessalonians*, 292.

[9] 3 Kgdms. 13:34; Jer. 28:55; Wis. 1:12, 14; 18:13; Sir. 39:30; 2 Macc. 6:12; 13:6; 3 Macc. 6:29–30, 34; *Pss. Sol.* 8:1.

you go" (12:12; cf. 9:9; 10:11; 13:15). The language of fire and torture, however, is not drawn from some prior conception of a "hell" to which Antiochus will be consigned. The point is that his brutality will be turned back on him. Antiochus is threatened with unending torture because he inflicted extreme torture on the Jews. There is, rhetorically at least, a powerful notion of *retaliation* at work in the judgment. We see the same thing in the Old Testament: "O daughter of Babylon, doomed to be destroyed, blessed shall he be who *repays you with what you have done to us*! Blessed shall he be who takes your little ones and dashes them against the rock!" (Ps. 137:8–9). The last verse strikes us as horribly vindictive, but the important point to note here is that judgment takes the form of an eye for an eye. The expectation is that the enemies of Babylon will do to it what Babylon did to Jerusalem: the city will be destroyed, its children thrown against the rocks (cf. Jer. 51:34–35).

This idea of "repayment" is quite explicit in 2 Thessalonians 1:6: "God considers it just to repay with affliction those who afflict you." This will take place on the day when "the Lord Jesus is revealed from heaven with his mighty angels in flaming fire" (1:7), but if we keep in mind both the literary background and the constraints of immediate historical relevance, we may well conclude that what Paul envisages here is a quite literal repayment: the society that persecutes the church will itself be the victim of aggression. Whether he would have regarded the eventual fall of Rome to the invading Goths and Huns in the fourth and fifth centuries A.D. as adequate fulfillment of this expectation is impossible to know; but he would surely have seen some justice in the fact that the city which sent an army to besiege and destroy Jerusalem was itself sacked by an invading force.[10]

---

[10] The Visigoth ruler Alaric finally entered Rome in A.D. 410, at his third attempt, and ransacked the city. Though devastating for Rome, this was a more civilized act of aggression than the invasion of Judea and destruction of Jerusalem. Augustine's *City of God* is an analysis of this event in response to claims that the sacking was a consequence of the abandonment of the ancient gods in favor of Christianity. Note also Rev. 18:6.

The argument that "destruction *from the presence of the Lord*" implies an awareness of separation and therefore continuing existence is not compelling.[11] The point here is that the judgment will take place *in the presence of the Lord* – "when he comes on that day to be glorified in his saints" (1:9–10). Destruction, therefore, inevitably entails separation from the face of the Lord.[12]

Defeat of the man of lawlessness

In the second account the *parousia* of the man of lawlessness "by the activity of Satan with all power and false signs and wonders" is immediately countered by the *parousia* of the Lord Jesus, who will "kill" (*anelei*) the lawless one "with the breath of his mouth" and destroy him "by the appearing of his *parousia*" (2 Thess. 2:8–9). There is a clear allusion here to Isaiah's description of the "rod" that will come from the "root of Jesse": "he will strike the earth/land with the word of his mouth and with the breath of his lips will slay (*anelei*) the godless one" (Isa. 11:4 LXX).[13] This occurs in a passage in which God assures Isaiah that although only a "remnant of Israel" will survive the devastation of divine judgment, the wrath against the nation will soon be ended and the burden of Assyrian oppression will be removed (10:20–27). Then a new king will emerge, upon whom the Spirit of the Lord will rest, who will bring peace and justice to Israel; he will "rule over the nations" and "gather the lost ones of Israel" (11:10–12). If Paul had this larger argument in view, it sets the destruction of the man of lawlessness in the context of a

---

[11] Best, *Thessalonians*, 262; Green, *Thessalonians*, 292.

[12] An analogy is found in 3 Kgdms. 13:34 (=1 Kgs. 13:34). Jeroboam's consecration of priests for the high places "became sin to the house of Jeroboam, even to its destruction (*olethron*) and its disappearance from the face (*apo prosōpou*) of the earth." There is clearly no suggestion here that the house of Jeroboam was "conscious" of having been destroyed from the face of the earth.

[13] The "godless one" is indeterminate: any "godless" person. Paul has taken it to denote a particular individual.

process that moves from divine judgment against Israel through the overthrow of Israel's oppressor[14] to the restoration of the people and the establishment of a messianic rule over the nations. For Paul, the oppressor and instrument of divine judgment must have been Rome; the messianic reign, the exaltation of the name of Jesus above all other names, was to be brought about through the preaching of the gospel to the Gentiles.

If the man of lawlessness may be conceived as a concrete historical figure, the means by which he is destroyed are, in the first place, somewhat abstract and intangible. The invocation of the prophecy in Isaiah 10 – 11 already makes this a rather indirect and symbolic statement. But we must surely also take account of the fact that, for all the violence of the imagery, he is defeated by the *breath* of Christ's mouth and the *appearing* (*epiphaneia*) of his *parousia*. The "breath of his mouth" would seem to signify a spoken truth – the gospel perhaps, or more exactly, in view of the description of the righteous judge in Isaiah 11:3–4, a word of judgment.[15] In Revelation 19:11–21, in what appears to be John's counterpart to the defeat of the man of lawlessness, the beast is overthrown by the "Word of God" and by the sword that issues from his mouth. This does not mean that there is nothing more than a clash of worldviews here – the defeat of the enemies of God would be no less "real" than the persecution of the church. We do not make sense of the symbolism by jettisoning all historical ballast and allowing it to float up into the realm of myth, where heavenly beings wield fantastical weapons. But equally, we need to recognize that the eventual overthrow of imperial Rome will be an event of specific eschatological significance.

The phrase "the appearing of his *parousia*" may only be pleonastic.[16] It is striking, however, that *epiphaneia* is used

---

[14] Note also Dan. 7:11 (Theod.): the fourth beast, which oppressed the saints, was "slain (*anēirethē*) and destroyed."

[15] Cf. *Pss. Sol.* 17:24.

[16] Cf. Witherington, *Jesus, Paul*, 161. Best is probably right to think that a reference to the "onset" of the *parousia* is too weak (Best, *Thessalonians*, 304).

frequently in the Maccabean writings to denote "manifestations" from heaven by which beleaguered Jews are encouraged or their enemies confounded. Sometimes the reference is to some sort of visionary spectacle: the sudden appearance of horsemen in the temple at a time of crisis, for example (2 Macc. 3:24–26; cf. 2:21; 5:2–4; 12:22; 3 Macc. 5:51). But on occasion the mere success of the Jews in battle or some other fortuitous turn of events is regarded as an *epiphaneia* of God's presence (2 Macc. 15:27; 3 Macc. 5:8). Connotations of this nature are fully germane to Paul's argument here. We should not take the insertion of *epiphaneia* to mean that he thought of Christ's *parousia* as unreal or imaginary (in 2 Tim. 1:10 the word is used of Christ's first appearance), but it may well be appropriate to pick up in Paul's use of the word these overtones of divine intervention through *mundane* historical circumstances at a time of national crisis.

Once the thought of the *parousia* of Christ is situated in the context of a conflict with Roman imperialism, it seems certain that other connotations would have been picked up by Paul's readers. The word was commonly used to denote the arrival of a ruler in a place. The *parousia* of Nero to Corinth and Patras, for example, was celebrated by the minting of coins that bore the Latin texts *Adventus Aug(usti) Cor(inthi)* and *Adventus Augusti*; an inscription of Hadrian from Tegea refers to "the sixty-ninth year of the first *parousia* of the god Hadrian," which F. F. Bruce thinks would have signaled in people's minds the inauguration of a new era.[17] The word which Paul uses for the "meeting" of believers with the Lord (*apantēsis*: 1 Thess. 4:17) derives from – or at least is closely associated with – the same ideological context. It is characteristically used with reference to what happens when people go out from a town or city to meet someone who is approaching. Luke describes how believers from Rome came out of the city as far as the Forum of Appius and Three Taverns to meet (*eis*

---

[17] Bruce, *Thessalonians*, 57; also Harrison, "Imperial Gospel," 83.

apantēsin) Paul's party (Acts 28:15). Cicero describes the response to Julius Caesar's tour of Italy in 49 B.C.: "Imagine what *apantēseis* are being made from the towns, what honors" (Cicero, *Att.* 8.16.2).[18] While *epiphaneia* has a home in Jewish apocalyptic, it is also a term redolent of imperial propaganda. An inscription on a statue of Claudius, for example, reads: "Tiberius Claudius Caesar Sebastos Germanicus god manifest (*theon epiphanē*), savior (*sōtēra*) of our people too."[19]

The *parousia* of Christ in the Roman world, then, was Christ coming to play the part in people's lives that the emperor and the imperial cult would otherwise have played: the *parousia* of the Son of Man supersedes the *parousia* of the man of lawlessness. The language is a direct challenge to the prevailing ideology – it both mimics and subverts – and if we disconnect the prophecy from its political context, we render it almost vacuous.[20] What these passages describe, by means of the highly charged rhetoric of Old Testament apocalyptic, is what needs to happen for this political-religious shift to come about. The opposition of Roman imperial ideology that Paul foresees, whether manifested in the hubris and ambition of particular historical figures or in the banal hostility of local institutions and communities, needs to be overcome – not through violence or militancy but through the word of the Lord and the willingness of believers to suffer for the sake of Christ. These "saints," who suffer as Christ suffered, will be vindicated, their afflictions will end, and they will come to share in the glory (cf. Col. 3:4; 2 Thess. 2:14) of the Son of

[18] Interestingly, Cicero, though writing in Latin, uses the Greek word: "quas fieri censes *apantēseis* ex oppidis, quos honores." Plevnik, following Dupont, doubts the relevance of the Hellenistic background for Paul's conception of the *parousia*, finding its origins instead in the Sinai theophany (Plevnik, *Parousia*, 7–10). Harrison maintains, however, that Paul's Gentile readers would naturally have interpreted the motif according to a "more familiar Hellenistic grid" (Harrison, "Imperial Gospel," 85).

[19] Harrison, "Imperial Gospel," 83, n. 50.

[20] Cf. Wright, *Resurrection*, 231–32.

Man to whom the kingdom is given. There is a level of realism to this prospect that should not be missed: the church that has remained true to Christ will be publicly acknowledged along with him when the transfer of sovereignty takes place.

The gathering to meet the Lord

Paul speaks, finally, of the resurrected dead and the living being "caught up (*harpagēsometha*[21]) together with them in the clouds to meet the Lord in the air"; as a result they will always be with the Lord (1 Thess. 4:16–17). 2 Thessalonians 2:1 makes reference to the same event.

Antiochus' campaign against Israel rather fizzles out at the end of Daniel 11: "the hour of his ending will come and there will be no deliverer for him" (LXX). At this point, however, a climax is reached in the story of Israel. According to the Septuagint text, the great angel Michael, who "stands over the sons of your people," will come near (12:1). There will be a period of affliction more severe than anything previously experienced by Israel; but at that time "all the people will be lifted up (*hupsōthēsetai*), whoever is found enrolled in the book," and "many of those sleeping in the earth will rise up, some to eternal life, some to reproach, some to scattering and to eternal shame" (12:2). Elsewhere in the Septuagint translation of Daniel *hupsōthēsetai* is used metaphorically (cf. 4:22; 8:4, 10, 25; 11:12, 36, 37) and we should probably understand it in the same sense here. In the Hebrew and Theodotion texts, however, the thought is of deliverance or salvation from the affliction. In any case, there is an apparent distinction between those who are "saved" or "lifted up" in the midst of an end-time crisis and the dead who are raised. If we take into account the overall importance of these chapters

[21] Given the eschatological context, *harpazō* may have the connotation of snatching someone from danger (cf. Acts 23:10; Jude 23; Rev. 12:5) and would therefore be close to the idea of Dan. 12:1 (MT and Theod.) that the elect are delivered from a time of great affliction. In Acts 8:39; 2 Cor. 12:2, 4, however, the thought of rescue is not present.

in Daniel for Paul's eschatology and the specific possibility that Michael is the archangel whose voice signals the *parousia* of the Lord in 1 Thessalonians 4:16, it seems likely that Paul's statement about the dead and the living at the *parousia* owes something to Daniel's prophecy about the deliverance of the righteous on the Day of the Lord.[22] The snatching up of the living is how, within the terms of the apocalyptic narrative, he conceptualizes the rescue of those who suffer from their afflictions.

According to 1 Thessalonians 3:13 Paul expects believers to have to stand "before our God and Father at the *parousia* of our Lord Jesus with all his holy ones (*pantōn tōn hagiōn autou*)." There has been much debate over whether these "holy ones" are angels or people. If Zechariah 14:5 is in the background, the thought is of Jesus coming in the place of God with the hosts of heaven to fight against the nations which have been gathered against Jerusalem. This is exactly the typology which emerges in 2 Thessalonians 1:6–7: those who afflict the church will be punished "when the Lord Jesus is revealed from heaven with his mighty angels." However, in the vision of Daniel 7 the "holy ones" are oppressed Israel, who receive the kingdom which in Daniel's vision was given to the human figure. Since the thought in 1 Thessalonians 3:13 is not of God's vengeance against those who oppress the church but of bringing the faithful into the presence of God, the vision of Daniel 7 constitutes the more likely background. Moreover, since the Son of Man figure is seen coming "upon the clouds of heaven," it would be natural to associate the "saints" who receive the kingdom with the same imagery. This would account for the clouds that apparently "transport" those

---

[22] If the "word of the Lord" derives in any way from the earthly Jesus, it is possible that 1 Thess. 4:16–17 is indicative of Jesus' own reflections upon Dan. 12:1–2, though the thought of the *descent* of the Son of Man goes beyond the less precise "coming" of the apocalyptic discourse. Isa. 26:18–19 may also be in the background. Note D. P. Bailey, "The Intertextual Relationship of Daniel 12:2 and Isaiah 26:19: Evidence from Qumran and the Greek Versions," *TynBul* 51.2 (2000), 305–308.

who have been caught up to meet the Lord.[23] The implication would then be that they are brought with Christ into the presence of God to receive their share in the kingdom that is given to the Son of Man.[24] Whereas for Daniel the one like a son of Man in some sense is, or represents, the saints of the Most High, Paul imagines that the saints will *accompany* the Christ.

The *parousia* of Christ, according to these narratives, has two basic consequences: on the one hand, the rescue and vindication of those who are afflicted; on the other, the destruction of their enemies. We have argued, moreover, that these outcomes are still to be located within the circumscribed horizon of a historically relevant eschatology: we must read them from where Paul stood, looking forward into *his* future. What we need to do now is connect these narrative themes with other material in Paul relating to the vindication of those who belong to Christ and the confession of Christ's sovereignty.

The Firstfruits to be Saved

As he comes to the end of his account of the defeat of the lawlessness that had ensconced itself at the heart of Israel's worship, Paul finds nevertheless that he has reason to give thanks. Many will be deceived by this satanic presence and will perish "because they refused to love the truth and so be saved" (2 Thess. 2:9–10) – the thousands of Jews who thought that they could deal with the crisis on their own terms, on the basis of their own *rightness*. Nevertheless, God has chosen the believers in Thessalonica to be "firstfruits (*aparchēn*) to be saved, through sanctification by the Spirit and belief in the truth" (2:13). The word "firstfruits"

---

[23] Note also Isa. 60:8: "who are these who fly as clouds," referring to the gathering of the lost of Israel.

[24] The same argument is perhaps to be found in 2 Cor. 4:14. Note also Rom. 14:10; Col. 1:22, 28. Dan. 7:13 LXX may be relevant here: the human figure comes to the Ancient of Days and "those approaching were near to him."

here is problematic. Although a number of manuscripts have *ap' archēs*, "from the beginning," the textual evidence is generally in favor of "firstfruits."[25] But what is the point of the metaphor?[26] Paul certainly appears to be saying more than that they were the first believers in Thessalonica (cf. 1 Cor. 16:15; Rom. 16:5). The phrase marks them out as a distinct group, contrasted with those who did not love the truth, who took pleasure in unrighteousness, and who therefore would not be saved. Moreover, they were set apart as firstfruits so that they might "obtain the glory of our Lord Jesus Christ" (2:14). We could easily read too much into this, but Paul's language here is compatible with a story that ascribes a distinct destiny to a group that suffers maltreatment during the transition to the age to come. It also anticipates the description in Revelation 14:4 of the 144,000 who have been "redeemed from mankind as *firstfruits* for God and the Lamb."

Before we consider other texts (in particular 1 Cor. 15:20–24), there are some general points that can be made in support of this argument. First, it fits the outline of Daniel's vision of the Son of Man: the kingdom is given to the "saints of the Most High," against whom the little horn had waged war. At the time of the great affliction, the people will be delivered and many of those sleeping in the earth will be raised – some to eternal life, others to reproach, scattering and shame (12:1–2). This is not a general resurrection of all the dead at the end of the world; it forms part of God's response to the specific crisis described in these chapters.[27] The same is true in the case of

---

25 Bruce, *Thessalonians*, 190; Green, *Thessalonians*, 326.

26 Marshall regards as the "decisive argument" against *aparchēn* the fact that "it does not make sense in the context; one cannot see of what greater harvest the readers can be said to be the firstfruits" (Marshall, *Thessalonians*, 207).

27 Cf. Wright, *Resurrection*, 113: "The prediction of resurrection is not an isolated piece of speculation about the ultimate fate of humans, or even Judaeans, in general, but a specific promise addressed to a specific situation." See also Wright, *New Testament*, 323, for the thought that resurrection is given specifically to those "who had died for the ancestral laws"; and 331: "Again and again we have seen that this belief is bound up with the struggle to maintain obedience to Israel's ancestral laws in the face of persecution."

the Maccabean martyrs, which at one level at least is what Daniel was talking about. So the second of the seven brothers says: "the King of the universe will raise us up to an everlasting renewal of life, because we have died for his laws" (2 Macc. 7:9 RSV). They are encouraged by their mother: "the Creator of the world . . . will in his mercy give life and breath back to you again, since you now forget yourselves for the sake of his laws" (2 Macc. 7:23 RSV). 4 Maccabees likens their cruel and protracted deaths to a divine contest in which the prize for their endurance was "immortality in endless life" (17:12 RSV). The limited scope of this resurrection is underlined by the hope expressed by the youngest son that their deaths would mark an end to Israel's afflictions (2 Macc. 7:38). They die for the sake of the continuation of the people of God; their personal resurrection is the "resurrection" of the nation.

So here is the pattern: at a time of eschatological crisis a small group will suffer because of their obedience to the God of Israel; their belief is that they do not suffer in vain, that God will vindicate them by raising them to life; but they also have the hope that through their faithfulness the wrath of God against Israel, the brunt of which they themselves have taken, will be brought to an end. The resurrection of the saints is the "resurrection" of the people of God.

Secondly, it takes seriously the consistent argument in the New Testament that the hope of life held out to the early church stood at the end of a path of suffering. We see this pattern in the Gospels. A young ruler comes to Jesus and asks what "good deed" he should do in order to have eternal life (Matt. 19:16; Mark 10:17; Luke 18:18). Jesus points him first to the commandments but then, in response to the man's claim that he has observed the Torah from his youth, puts to him a disconcerting challenge: "If you would be perfect, go, sell what you possess and give to the poor, and you will have treasure in heaven; and come, follow me" (Matt. 19:21). It seems that this is a step too far for the young man, who "went away sorrowful." We can easily miss the point of this story. The man risked not entering the kingdom of God not because he was wealthy, as though being wealthy were intrinsically sinful, but because he was reluctant to do what was necessary in order to follow Jesus *under those circumstances.* If he was not prepared to leave everything, he could not possibly take the narrow, dangerous path that Jesus had marked out for himself and his disciples. But if he did not follow, he could not enter the kingdom, he could not inherit eternal life.

The implication of this argument seems quite clear: in Jesus' terms, entry into the kingdom of heaven was contingent upon pursuing a way of life that would render people socially vulnerable. Sooner or later, it would bring them into conflict with religious and political forces that would resort to crucifixion in order to suppress the belief that God had made Jesus Lord (Matt. 10:38; Mark 8:34; Luke 9:23). When Peter reminds Jesus that the disciples have taken just that course, he assures them that "in the new world, when the Son of Man will sit on his glorious throne, you who have followed me will also sit on twelve thrones, judging the twelve tribes of Israel" (Matt. 19:28; cf. Luke 18:29–30; 22:30).[28] In other words, within the bounds of Israel's eschatological horizon they receive what was promised in Daniel's vision to the saints of the Most High – kingdom, glory, and dominion (Dan. 7:14, 18, 27).

Thirdly, it allows us to maintain a coherence of perspective and narrative in our reading of New Testament eschatology. If we must accept that crisis and judgment were matters of immediate historical relevance, we should not be surprised if the promise of survival, vindication, resurrection, new life, and participation in the kingdom, also proves to be contingent upon the same general historical circumstances.

Christ, parousia, and the end

Perhaps the most intriguing text to consider is 1 Cor-

---

[28] Mark 10:30 makes "eternal life" the reward for enduring persecution.

inthians 15:20–24. Having addressed in rather negative terms the argument of some that there is no resurrection of the dead, Paul goes on to make the positive assertion: "in fact Christ has been raised from the dead, the firstfruits of those who have fallen asleep" (15:20). The relationship between the one and the many that is implicit in this narrower use of the "firstfruits" metaphor needs explanation: just as death came by one man, so the resurrection of the dead comes through one man (15:21–22). So there is an order to things: "Christ the firstfruits, then those who belong to Christ at his coming, then the end . . ." (15:23–24, translation mine). The first two stages in the sequence are clear enough. Christ has been raised in advance of any collective resurrection: he is the beginning of the resurrection, the "firstborn from the dead" (Col. 1:18), the "firstborn among many brothers" (Rom. 8:29). Then, at the *parousia*, those believers who "have fallen asleep" – probably in Paul's estimation a relatively small number – will be raised in their turn. The difficulty lies with the last phrase, "then the end" (*eita to telos*). Does this refer to a third stage, a third phase of resurrection perhaps, occurring an indefinite period of time after the *parousia* of Christ?[29] Or should we conclude, with the majority of commentators, that these are only different moments in the same grand finale – in other words, that the *parousia is* the end?

It is often argued that *eita* ("then") has less a temporal than a logical function here, indicating only that the events of the "end" (the final defeat of death, the handing over of the kingdom) follow on as an inevitable and more or less immediate corollary to the *parousia*.[30] This is an attractive interpretation for those of an anti-chiliastic persuasion

---

[29] We cannot make *to telos* mean "the rest" here (cf. Thiselton, *First Corinthians*, 1230–31). Paul refers not to a third category of resurrection but to a moment in a sequence. The question is whether that moment coincides with the *parousia* or comes some time after it. Whether or not there is a third resurrection at "the end" is not within the purview of the argument, but it is not ruled out. The final defeat of death at this point may entail the corollary that a final resurrection of all the dead has taken place (cf. Rev. 20:12–15).

[30] E.g., Fee, *First Corinthians*, 753–54; Plevnik, *Parousia*, 126–27; R. F. Collins, *First Corinthians*, 552.

because it effectively precludes any sort of messianic interregnum on earth, at least as far as Paul is concerned. The matter is not to be settled, however, by appealing to the meaning of *eita* (in 1 Cor. 15:5–7 *epeita* and *eita* are used to denote a clear temporal sequence). The adverb cannot be merely interpretive in this context (it makes little sense grammatically or logically to substitute "therefore" or "in that case"); and if Paul believed that the handing over of the kingdom to the Father would take place at the *parousia*, the phrase becomes superfluous. He needed only to say: "then those of Christ at his *parousia*, when he delivers the kingdom." There is no reason to introduce a reference to the "end" into the argument at this point unless it constitutes a distinct and significant third moment some time after the *parousia* since the argument is not about when the end will come but whether and how the dead will be raised. In 1 and 2 Thessalonians the *parousia* of Christ is the moment when those who afflict the church are overthrown and destroyed. These must be counted among Christ's enemies, but there is no indication that *all* of his enemies or the *final* enemy, death, are defeated at this time. This strongly suggests that in Paul's mind a significant period of time would intervene between the *parousia* and the final dénouement, during which Christ's enemies are destroyed.[31] The resurrection at the *parousia* of those who have fallen asleep in Christ would constitute, therefore, a limited event within the eschatological horizon of the church in the Roman world: they are absorbed into the metaphor of Christ as firstfruits. What happens at the "end," then, is the resurrection of all humankind, believers and non-believers (the "resurrection of both the just and the unjust" that Paul mentions in Acts 24:15). It is important to note that neither here nor in 1 Thessalonians 4:15–17 is there any mention of the non-Christian dead at the time of the *parousia*.

---

[31] Cf. W. B. Wallis, "The Problem of an Intermediate Kingdom in I Corinthians 15:20–28," *JETS* 18.4 (1975), 230–33.

One important consideration in this argument is that there must be room in the eschatological timetable for the reign of believers with Christ. "Or do you not know that the saints will judge the world?" Paul asks the Corinthians (1 Cor. 6:2), and chides them for their presumption in supposing that they have already become kings (4:8). "If we have died with him," he writes to Timothy, "we will also live with him; if we endure, we will also reign with him" (2 Tim. 2:11–12). Revelation 20:4–6 appears to identify this "reign" as the thousand-year reign of those who come to life in the first resurrection (cf. Matt. 19:28; Luke 22:29–30; Rev. 3:21).[32] When is this going to happen? We will have more to say on this in the next section, but it must begin at the *parousia*, when the oppressor of the Son of Man is defeated, and last until that moment (the "end") when Christ transfers the kingdom to God the Father: from that point on the kingdom no longer belongs to those who suffered, who were oppressed by their enemies, because all suffering, including death, has been brought to an end. We should probably also connect the future reign of believers with Christ with the consistent thought in Paul that the inheritance of the kingdom of God by the saints is a future event (1 Cor. 6:9–10; Gal. 5:21; Eph. 1:14, 18; 5:5; Col. 1:12; 3:24; 2 Tim. 4:1, 18) – one which will take place at the *parousia* and the resurrection of those who belong to Christ (1 Cor. 15:50).

Other texts

The same line of thought runs through the second half of Romans 8, as we saw in Chapter 5. Those who suffer with Christ will be glorified with him (8:17). For those who are called for this specific purpose, the suffering can only work for good (8:28). Christ will not be the only one to suffer and be vindicated and glorified: others have been chosen to be "conformed (*summorphous*) to the image of his Son," so that he will be the "firstborn among many brothers" (8:29–30).

---

[32] Cf. Wallis, "Problem," 237–38.

Whatever hardship they face in the coming years – tribulation, distress, persecution, famine, peril, sword – nothing will separate them from the love of God.

The "prize of the upward call of God in Christ Jesus" in Philippians 3:14 is not the prospect of a general resurrection of the Christian dead but the specific hope held out to those who, in order to gain Christ, must share in the sufferings of Christ (Phil. 3:8–10, 14).[33] When Paul says that "Christ Jesus has made me his own," he means that his life has been claimed by the one who made himself nothing, humbled himself, became obedient to the point of a brutal and degrading death at the hands of his enemies (Phil. 2:7–8). But by the same token he has the hope of following the trajectory through death to resurrection and participation in the kingdom that will be transferred from Rome to the Son of Man. Whatever Paul meant exactly by the thought that "our citizenship is in heaven,"[34] it serves as the basis for his confidence that those who "stand firm . . . in the Lord," who do not worship the "belly," who do not choose to safeguard their physical well-being at the expense of following Christ, who allow themselves to be humiliated in the body, will eventually be changed "to be conformed (*summorphon*) to his glorious body" (3:20–21).

---

[33] I would both agree and disagree with N. T. Wright here when he maintains that the "upward call" is not to be interpreted "as a call which summons people to leave 'earth' for ever and live instead in 'heaven'" (Wright, *Resurrection*, 235). The verse certainly does not establish this sort of "escapist" eschatology as a paradigm for all Christians, but it is applied in a quite literal sense to the early church *insofar as* it conformed to the pattern of Christ's sufferings, in imitation of the persecuted saints of the Most High.

[34] Wright argues that the phrase does not mean that all believers will one day go to live in heaven but determines the "status and allegiance" that citizens have who must remain in the colonies (Wright, *Resurrection*, 230). This may be generally true, but I would question its relevance in this particular context: if there is a resurrection in advance of the general resurrection, those who suffer and are raised with Christ will reign with him "in heaven." It is in what we might call the "post-eschatological" context of the church that Wright's argument acquires its proper significance.

What we do not have here is a general argument about the transformation of the believer *apart from* sharing in his sufferings and "being conformed to (*summorphizomenos*) his death" – the link between *summorphizomenos* in verse 10 and *summorphon* in verse 21 makes this entirely clear.

Lastly, Paul writes to Timothy telling him that he endures everything – imprisonment, the prospect of execution – for the sake of those who have come to believe in Jesus Christ, and he quotes a trustworthy "saying" that must in some way have encapsulated a core wisdom for the church: "If we have died with him, we will also live with him; if we endure, we will also reign with him; if we deny him, he also will deny us; if we are faithless, he remains faithful – for he cannot deny himself" (2 Tim. 2:11–13). Although the words "if we have died with him" are probably to be taken figuratively (cf. Rom. 6:8), the saying nevertheless reinforces the eschatological corollary: those who endure suffering will reign with Christ.

This may help us to explain why Paul had to correct a misunderstanding on the part of the Thessalonians about the fate of those who fall asleep before the *parousia* (1 Thess. 4:13–18).[35] Our argument has been that he understood the "wrath to come" (1 Thess. 1:10) not as a final judgment but as an event or process within history – a judgment upon the world that opposed the preaching of Christ's lordship and persecuted those who confessed his name. The deliverance that would take place at the *parousia* of the Lord, then, would also be an event within history: the church would not be finally overcome by the world, nor would it be swept away in the destruction that was to come. Let us suppose that the Thessalonians understood this and entertained the hope – perhaps less clearly formulated than it is in this Letter – of consciously participating in the "coming of the Son of Man" and sharing in his kingdom. They may also have known about

---

[35] See also Best, *Thessalonians*, 180–84; S. Kim, "The Jesus Tradition in 1 Thess 4.13–5.11," *NTS* 48.2 (2002), 230.

a resurrection of the dead *at the end of all things*, but this would have been little consolation under the immediate circumstances: those who had recently died would be raised in the general resurrection of the dead but they would still miss out on the *parousia*.[36] Paul addresses the problem by introducing the idea of an advance resurrection of "the dead in Christ," drawing on Daniel 12:2, corresponding to the "first resurrection" of the martyrs in Revelation 20:4–6, so that the dead and the living together would participate in the fulfillment of the vision regarding the Son of Man.

The puzzling statement in 1 Peter 4:6 about preaching the gospel to the dead may address the same basic problem. If Peter believed that the judgment of the present world (4:7, 17–18) and the manifestation of the chief Shepherd (5:4) were at hand, he would naturally have thought of the *parousia* primarily as an event to be experienced by the living: it was something worth being alive for. That assumption raises the question, however: What was the point of people believing in the gospel but dying before its consummation? What use was vindication to them? The answer is that God will be judge not of the living only but also of the dead (4:5): those who have fallen asleep in Christ, though "judged in the flesh like men," will be raised and will "live in the spirit like God" (RSV).

In conclusion: in Paul's thinking, the *parousia* of Christ would be an event primarily for the sake of those who were called to suffer as the good news about Jesus was proclaimed and lived out across the Greco-Roman world. It would make no difference whether they were alive or dead at the moment when the hostility was finally overcome and Christ could be openly acknowledged as Lord in the world. Either way, those who shared in his sufferings – the firstfruits to be saved – would share in his life and rule at

---

[36] The possibility of theological prejudice against the dead is illustrated by 4 Ezra 13:24: "Understand therefore that those who are left are more blessed than those who have died."

the right hand of God. The dead would be raised and the living would undergo the necessary transformation because flesh and blood cannot inherit a kingdom that is given to the resurrected Son of Man, the perishable cannot inherit the imperishable (1 Cor. 15:50–52). Of course, the participation of the living in this is problematic if we wish to preserve the contemporary historical relevance of this hope. But if the *parousia* is a *story* about the rescue and vindication of the church by which Paul and others gave shape to a very uncertain future, the "snatching up" and transformation of the living may simply be a natural extension of the narrative logic, aided perhaps by the distinction in Daniel 12:1–3 between those who are raised and those who are delivered. Paul could not see how things would actually turn out, he could not see what was on the other side of the door, but he was compelled by the Spirit and by the developing apocalyptic tradition to tell a story about the eventual victory of Christ and the real participation of those who suffered in that victory. God would not turn a deaf ear to those who cried out for judgment against their persecutors.

The Defeat of Christ's Enemies

Paul's account in 1 Corinthians 15:24–28 of the events leading up to the "end," when he "delivers the kingdom to God the Father after destroying every rule and every authority and power," draws principally on Psalm 110 (109 LXX). In verse 27 he also alludes to Psalm 8:6 (8:7 LXX), but this functions only really as a gloss on the text of this key "messianic" psalm, underlining the fact that *all* Christ's enemies, including death, must ultimately be subjected to him. Psalm 110, which was clearly of great significance both for Jesus' self-understanding (Mark 12:35–37; Matt. 22:43–45; Luke 20:41–44) and for the early church's understanding of what the risen Christ had become,[37]

[37] Fee, *First Corinthians*, 754–55, n. 43.

speaks of the reign of the anointed king who has been invited to sit at the right hand of God. This is a reign "in the midst of your enemies" (110:2), in the "splendors of the saints" (109:3 LXX). It will last until the enemies of the king – the rulers of the nations – have been subjugated.

There are two aspects to this motif: the invitation to sit *now* at the right hand of God and the promise that *at some point in the future* the king's enemies will be defeated. Essentially the same distinction is found in Psalm 2:7–9: the king is today "begotten" as a son of God, but the defeat of the kings of the earth who plot "against the Lord and against his anointed" is a future event. In the New Testament, the first aspect is understood to have been realized in the ascension. In his sermon on the day of Pentecost Peter tells the bemused crowd that Jesus was raised from the dead and exalted as Lord at the right hand of God (Acts 2:32–36; cf. Mark 16:19). It is a sign of honor and glory, perhaps especially the honor achieved through obedience in the face of suffering (cf. Matt. 20:21–23; Heb. 1:3; 10:12; 12:2). Seated at the right hand of God, Christ has poured out *his* Spirit on the disciples – the Spirit of a son who knows God as "father," who faithfully pursues the implications of that knowledge, who is prepared to be the servant who suffers in the confidence that the Father will act quickly to vindicate those who trust in him. At the right hand of God, Christ intercedes for those who must now suffer persecution for his sake (Rom. 8:34; cf. Heb. 7:25; 8:1), ministers in the heavenly sanctuary (Heb. 8:1–2), and waits to appear in glory – in other words, to be vindicated publicly in the world (Col. 3:1–4). But while he is already confessed as "Lord" by those who believe in him, the defeat of his enemies remains a future prospect, for which he must "wait" (Heb. 10:13). We may suppose that the importance of Psalm 110 for the early church lay at least as much in the hope expressed that the enemies of the king would be defeated as in the confirmation of Christ's position at the right hand of God.

It is clear both from Jesus' apocalyptic discourse and

from 2 Thessalonians 2:3–10 that the *parousia* of Christ will mark the climax to a period of oppression and affliction when, in the symbolic language of Daniel 7, the overweening horn of the fourth beast will make war against the saints (Dan. 7:21, 25). During this period there will be no victory for believers other than the victory of faith over persecution, which is an imitation of Christ's suffering and which carries with it the hope of sharing with him in glory. In Ephesians 6:10–17 Paul sets out the strategy by which communities of disciples will overcome the devil and the spiritual forces of evil in the heavenly places (6:11–12). If they are to survive the "evil day" that is approaching (6:13), they will need to equip themselves with certain fundamental moral and spiritual attributes: truth, righteousness, the gospel of peace, faith. There are two important things to note about Paul's argument here. First, these qualities will have a *protective* function. The church will sooner or later face considerable hostility; they will be accused of blasphemy, atheism, immorality; they will be harassed and persecuted by their opponents. These attributes are the means by which they will stand against the one who inspires such virulent opposition, the accuser, the devil, the genius behind the imperial cult, who – to use Peter's vivid metaphor – "prowls around like a roaring lion, seeking someone to devour" (1 Pet. 5:8). Secondly, there is nothing esoteric or mysterious about the components of this armor: they will be preserved not by the dark arts of spiritual warfare but by speaking the truth, by acting righteously, by preaching a message of peace, and by trusting in God. The only offensive weapon they are permitted to carry is the "sword of the Spirit, which is the word of God" (6:17). Peter's strategy is the same: put away malice, deceit, hypocrisy, envy, slander; abstain from passions of the flesh; be subject to human institutions; live honorably, love the brotherhood, fear God; be willing to suffer for the sake of what is good (1 Pet. 2:1–20). "For to this you have been called, because Christ also suffered for you, leaving you an example, so that you might follow in his steps" (1 Pet. 2:21).

If they stand, if they do not give up, the *parousia* will be the moment of "salvation" (cf. Rom. 13:11) when the church is rescued from the wrath of God, those who persecute the church come under judgment, and the lawlessness that threatened to wreak havoc at the heart of the people of God is destroyed. It is significant that Psalm 110 depicts the subjection of the king's enemies as a judgment of the nations, which is the theologically necessary response both to the defeat of Israel and the persecution of the saints. Then the kingdom will be given to the "holy people of the Most High," and "all the powers will be subjected to them and they will obey them" (Dan. 7:27 LXX). At this point at least we begin to see the concrete fulfillment of the second aspect of Psalm 110:1.

Not now and not yet

Occasionally the subjection of all things to Christ appears to be spoken of as a present reality, as having already taken place. On closer inspection, however, these texts are found either to be rather restricted in their scope or to prefigure what remains at that point a future outcome. It appears, in fact, that the New Testament is rather less confused about the relation between the present and the future than the commonly invoked eschatological principle of "now and not yet" suggests. The overriding enemy will be defeated and the kingdom given to the Son of Man at the *parousia*.

When the seventy return to Jesus from their mission trip, they are exultant: "even the demons are subject (*hupotassetai*) to us in your name!" (Luke 10:17; cf. 10:20). What we see here, however, as with Jesus' exorcisms, is likely to be an *anticipation* of the defeat of Satan, the adversary and oppressor of the people of God. "I saw Satan fall like lightning from heaven," Jesus replies. This apocalyptic fragment depicts a future event that must have something to do with the coming of the Son of Man (cf. Dan. 7:27) and the fall of imperial Rome (cf. Rev. 12:7–10; 20:1–3; Rom. 16:20).[38]

---

[38] Cf. Nolland, *Luke*, 563–64; Evans, "Defeating Satan," 168–69.

Philippians 2:9 is a confession that the exalted Christ has received "the name that is above every name," yet the prospect that "every knee should bow . . . and every tongue confess that Jesus Christ is Lord" (2:10) belongs to the future. The program derived from Psalm 110 recurs: the belief that Christ has been raised by God to a place of highest honor, but a deferment of real sovereignty to some point in the future. In Romans we find the passionate affirmation that no force, supernatural or otherwise, can separate the believer from Christ (8:38–39), but this certainly does not mean that hostility towards the people of God has been eradicated. Similarly, in 1 Peter 3:22 "angels, authorities, and powers" are said to be subject to Christ who is at the right hand of God. Whatever exactly may be meant by these statements, they clearly do not translate into immunity from opposition, spiritual or otherwise, for those in Christ (cf. 1 Pet. 4:12). The writer to the Hebrews makes the paradox explicit when he asserts that God has "subjected (*hupetaxen*) the world to come" (that is, the world following the *parousia*) not to angels but to the Son of Man, leaving nothing outside his control (Heb. 2:5–8), but admits that they do not yet see all things in subjection to him (2:8–9). What they see at that moment is Jesus promoted to the right hand of God, "crowned with glory and honor because of the suffering of death." Incidentally, the "world to come" in verse 5 is *tēn oikoumenēn tēn mellousan* – simply the inhabited world as it would be once the present imperial régime and the satanic power behind it have been overthrown.

Finally, we should give some thought to the common view that Ephesians and Colossians present a more realized form of eschatology than the other Letters attributed to Paul. Here Christ is not only seated at the right hand of God, but all things appear already to have been put under (*hupetaxen*) his feet (Eph. 1:20–22); the "rulers and authorities" have been disarmed (Col. 2:15); the believer has already been raised with Christ (Col. 2:12; 3:1), transferred to the kingdom of the Son (Col. 1:13). At the same time, however, there are several statements that point to the influence of the basic eschatological schema that we have found elsewhere: the age to come has not yet arrived (Eph. 1:21); the wrath of God is coming upon the present world (Eph. 5:6; Col. 3:6); the spiritual forces of darkness that dominate this age have not yet been defeated and can be expected to oppose the believer "in the evil day" (Eph. 6:13); Christ will appear (Col. 3:4) and those who believe in him will "share in the inheritance of the saints in light" and be glorified with him (Col. 1:12; 3:4).[39]

What distinguishes these Letters from those with a stronger apocalyptic content may not be the forlorn fading of the futurist hope but the absence in the case of these churches of any *immediate* threat of persecution.[40] What defined the corporate spiritual experience of these believers was not suffering, the birth pains of the new age – not yet at least – but the abundance of spiritual blessings in the heavenly places (Eph. 1:3), the "unsearchable riches of Christ" (Eph. 3:8), the "fullness of God" (Eph. 3:19), the "treasures of wisdom and knowledge" (Col. 2:3), being "filled in him, who is the head of all rule and authority" (Col. 2:10), and so on. Being relatively at peace with the local community, these churches were in a position to experience *in advance* the goodness of the age that was to come – before the *parousia*, before the victory over the forces of evil and lawlessness that threatened to overwhelm the church. It is *as though* they have already been raised up with Christ, made to sit with him at the right hand of God, so that "in the coming ages he might show the immeasurable riches of his grace in kindness toward us in Christ Jesus" (Eph. 2:6–7; Col. 3:1); it is *as though* they have already been transferred to the kingdom of the Son (Col. 1:13).

---

[39] Cf. T. D. Still, "Eschatology in Colossians: How Realized is It?" *NTS* 50.1 (2004).

[40] As, e.g., A. T. Lincoln, *Ephesians* (Dallas: Word, 1990), lxxxv.

Eight

The City Which is Sodom and Egypt

The visions in the book of Revelation were given to John so that he could show to the servants of God – specifically the "seven churches that are in Asia" (1:4) – "the things that must soon (*en tachei*) take place" (Rev. 1:1; cf. 22:6). Those who take heed of the words of the prophecy will be blessed because "the time is near" (1:3). For many Christians this book is a dark, nightmarish place, a breeding ground for monstrous dreams and fantasies – and they would rather not go there. John's opening words, however, communicate a sense of urgency that either is fictitious or must lead us to suppose that this is in fact a quite *realistic* book: he is writing to real communities of believers (even if the seven churches are symbolic) about real and imminent events. If we keep this in mind and hold to our principle of reading the Old Testament background as part of the argument, we will find a story emerging that has already become very familiar to us.

The story begins with a vision of Christ – the Son of Man figure who suffered, died, was raised, and has been exalted. He is "the faithful witness," who "freed us from our sins by his blood," who was "pierced" (Rev. 1:5, 7). He is the "firstborn of the dead," the "living one" who died but is alive forevermore (1:5, 18). He is the "ruler of kings on earth," to whom belongs "glory and dominion forever and ever," who is "coming with the clouds," who now stands in the midst of the seven golden lampstands "like a son of man" but adorned with the attributes of deity, from whose mouth issues a "sharp two-edged sword," who holds the "keys of Death and Hades" (1:5, 6, 7, 13–16, 18).

John, however, is in exile on Patmos, one of the Sporades islands off the coast of Asia Minor. He writes to believers whose experience is similar to his own: he shares with them in Jesus "the tribulation and the kingdom and the patient endurance" (1:9). It is a theme that runs through the letters to the seven churches in Revelation 2 – 3. In each case we have a community that is under stress or encountering persecution. Some have endured patiently, others have become complacent or have compromised their faith. In each case the exhortation is to remain faithful, to the point of death if necessary. The one who "conquers" will be rewarded in ways that anticipate later visions both of the victory over "Babylon the great" and of the inauguration of a new creation. He will eat of the tree of life (1:7; cf. 22:14); he will not be hurt by the second death (2:11; cf. 20:6); he will be given a new name that only he knows (2:17; cf. 19:12); he will rule over the nations with a rod of iron (2:26–27; cf. 19:15); his name will not be blotted from the book of life (3:5; cf. 20:12); he will be made a pillar in the temple of God in the new Jerusalem (3:12; cf. 21:2–3); and finally, he will be seated on the throne that Christ shares with his Father (3:21; 22:1).

This is a revelation, therefore, for the churches of Asia Minor, who through Christ have been made part of the priestly kingdom that Israel was meant to be (1:6; cf. Exod. 19:6), but who find, too, that they have been incorporated into that group of saints represented by the figure of the Son of Man. John's message, to this point at least, is very simple: those who endure patiently, who do not grow weary, who resist evil, who do not compromise in their teaching and practice by engaging in idolatry and immorality, who do not deny the name of Christ, will receive the kingdom, will come to reign with Christ, when their enemy is overthrown.

The Opening of the Scroll

The sequence of revelations in the body of John's vision begins with the opening of a scroll, which the Lamb takes from the one who is seated on the throne. When John first sees this scroll, he notices two curious things about it: it is "written within and on the back," and it is 'sealed with seven seals" (5:1). These descriptive details are important initial indicators regarding the significance of the scroll.

The first detail directs our attention to a similar scroll with "writing on the front and on the back," by which Ezekiel's prophetic ministry was initiated (Ezek. 2:9–10). The contextual parallels with the opening chapters of Ezekiel are numerous. John is apparently in exile on Patmos just as Ezekiel was "among the exiles by the Chebar canal" (Rev. 1:9; Ezek. 1:1). John saw a "door standing open in heaven" and was taken up in the Spirit to see the throne of God; Ezekiel writes: "the heavens were opened, and I saw visions of God" (Rev. 4:1–2; Ezek. 1:1). John's vision of the heavenly throne room has several details in common with Ezekiel's description of the throne of God, upon which is seated "a likeness with a human appearance" (Ezek. 1:26). For example, the "four living creatures" of Ezekiel's theophany reappear, in slightly modified form, as the "four living creatures" around the throne in John's vision (Rev. 4:6–8; Ezek. 1:5–12). Before the throne of God John sees a "sea of glass, like crystal"; in Ezekiel's vision the "expanse" between the throne of God and the four living creatures is "shining like awe-inspiring crystal" (Rev. 4:6; Ezek. 1:22). Some of these details have spilled back into John's earlier vision of Christ in the midst of the seven lampstands (1:12–20), at whose feet John fell as though dead (1:17; cf. Ezek. 1:28). This "one like a son of man" has a voice "like the roar of many waters," a simile drawn from the description of the noise of the living creatures' wings in Ezekiel (Rev. 1:15; Ezek. 1:24).

The content of Ezekiel's scroll is "words of lamentation and mourning and woe" (Ezek. 2:10). He is sent "to the people of Israel, to nations of rebels, who have rebelled against me. They and their fathers have transgressed against me to this very day" (2:3). Given the close parallels between the two contexts, therefore, we should reckon with the likelihood that the scroll which the Lamb receives from the throne of God will have something to do – either in its opening or in its contents – with the fate of Israel.

Two passages in the Old Testament, secondly, speak of the sealing up of the prophetic vision contained in a scroll or book. Isaiah says regarding the oracles of judgment against Jerusalem: "all these utterances will be to you as the words of a sealed (*esphragismenou*) book; if they give it to a person who can read, saying, 'Read these things,' he will say, 'I cannot read it, for it is sealed'" (Isa. 29:11 LXX). It is an image of the spiritual and moral obtuseness of the people of Jerusalem, which explains why in John's vision no one can be found to open the scroll (Rev. 5:3). The more important passage, however, is Daniel 12:4 (cf. 8:26): "And you, Daniel, hide the commands and seal (*sphragisai*) the book until the time of the end" (LXX). This is the "book of truth" that was revealed to Daniel by a figure "clothed in linen" on the banks of the river Tigris (Dan. 10:4–5, 21).[1] It contains a prophecy of the political events leading up to the Antiochene crisis, when the king of the north would remove the continual burnt offering from the temple, set up the "abomination that makes desolate" (11:31), and "exalt himself and magnify himself above every god, and . . . speak astonishing things against the God of gods" (11:36). The book was to be sealed up, therefore, until the time of the "shattering of the power of the holy people" (12:7) – a time of trouble "such as never has been since there was a nation till that time" (12:1).

There are good reasons for thinking, therefore, that the book (*biblion*) that John sees in the heavenly throne room is also – either directly or analogically – the book (*biblion*) that

---

[1] The book which is sealed may also be the book which contains the names of those who will be delivered from the affliction (Dan. 12:1).

Daniel is instructed to seal up "until the time of the end."[2] We may suppose, moreover, at least as a starting hypothesis, that the scroll will reveal something about a time of great tribulation for Israel when the wicked will be punished and the righteous delivered (cf. Dan. 12:1–3, 10).

Both these descriptive details strongly suggest, then, that the sequence of visions initiated by the opening of the seals must relate to the fate of Jerusalem. That will be the leading argument of this chapter. This possibility has not generally been considered by commentators: most have assumed that the book belongs to the end of the first century and has a thoroughly universal outlook. Can the supposition be further supported? In order to answer this we need to consider four questions. First, what are the Lamb's qualifications for opening the scroll? Secondly, what is the significance of the seven seals that must be opened before the contents of the scroll can be made known? Thirdly, what is announced or inaugurated by the series of seven trumpets that is introduced when the seventh seal is opened? Finally, what is the relation between the scroll given to the Lamb and the "little scroll" given to John by the angel in Revelation 10?

The Vision of the Lamb

The Lamb is introduced as "the Lion of the tribe of Judah, the Root of David" (Rev. 5:5). In Genesis 49:9 Judah is described by Jacob as "a lion's cub": "He stooped down; he crouched as a lion and as a lioness; who dares rouse him?" Attached to this metaphor are other statements about the future role of Judah: his hand shall be on the neck of his

---

[2] Bauckham argues that it is not the book of 12:4 that is in heaven but another book, to which the angel alludes in 12:9 (Bauckham, *Climax*, 251–53). This may be correct but it makes little difference to the interpretation whether we regard John's scroll as the scroll which is sealed in Dan. 12:4 (which includes the prophecy of deliverance and resurrection) or as a scroll containing further information about what will happen at the end of the period of three and a half times.

enemies; his brothers shall bow down before him; the "scepter shall not depart from Judah, nor the ruler's staff from between his feet"; and "to him shall be the obedience of the peoples" (Gen. 49:8, 10). The other title, "Root of David," derives from the description in Isaiah 11 of a Davidic ruler upon whom the Spirit of the Lord shall rest, who "shall strike the earth with the rod of his mouth, and with the breath of his lips . . . shall kill the wicked" (Isa. 11:4). In particular, Isaiah says that "In that day the root of Jesse, who shall stand as a signal for the peoples – of him shall the nations inquire, and his resting place shall be glorious" (11:10). Closely related to this is the further idea that at this time God "will assemble the banished of Israel, and gather the dispersed of Judah from the four corners of the earth" (11:12).

These allusions to the international scope of the Messiah's rule are rendered explicit in the song of the four living creatures and the twenty-four elders: "Worthy are you to take the scroll and to open its seals, for you were slain, and by your blood you ransomed people for God from every tribe and language and people and nation, and you have made them a kingdom and priests to our God, and they shall reign on the earth" (Rev. 5:9–10). The language is strongly reminiscent of Daniel's vision in the night, in which the "one like a son of man" is given "dominion and glory and a kingdom, that all peoples, nations, and languages should serve him" (Dan. 7:14). If this is correct, then we should probably also find some sort of correlation between this redeemed group, whom the Lamb has made "a kingdom and priests to our God," and the "people of the saints of the Most High" who receive the kingdom in Daniel 7:22, 27. These redeemed, moreover, "shall reign *on the earth*" (5:10): the reference is apparently, then, to the universal church, made up of believers from all nations.

The Seven Seals

The scroll is sealed with seven seals, which the Lamb must break before the contents of the scroll can be read. As each of the first four seals is opened a rider appears (6:2–8). The first, on a white horse, goes out "conquering, and to conquer." The second has a red horse; he is given a great sword and is permitted to take peace from the earth so that people should slay one another. The third rider, on a black horse, has a balance in his hand and is instructed, by a voice that comes from the midst of the four living creatures, to inflate the price of essential commodities – leading, presumably, to food shortages for the poor. Then, fourthly, Death appears, riding on a pale horse, with Hades following. They are given power over a quarter of the earth, "to kill with sword and with famine and with pestilence and by wild beasts of the earth."

Although Zechariah makes use of the symbolism of four riders on colored horses (Zech. 1:8–11; cf. 6:1–8), the more relevant background to the first four seals is found in a distinctive typology of judgment that appears both in Jeremiah 15:2 and in the Septuagint version of Ezekiel 5:12:

> Those who are for pestilence ("death" in LXX), to pestilence, and those who are for the sword, to the sword; those who are for famine, to famine, and those who are for captivity, to captivity. (Jer. 15:2)

> A fourth part of you will be destroyed by death, and a fourth part of you will be consumed by famine in the midst of you, and a fourth part of you I will scatter (them) to every wind, and a fourth part of you will fall by a sword (*en rhomphaiai*) round about you, and I will draw out a sword after them. (Ezek. 5:12 LXX)[3]

The correspondence is impressive, particularly if we notice on the one hand that, in Jeremiah 15:2 and in the Greek text of Ezekiel 5:12, "pestilence" is a translation of the Hebrew and Greek words for "death"; and on the other, that an inevitable concomitant of conquest in the ancient world

[3] In the Hebrew text pestilence and famine are combined in the first part of the judgment. The typology is also found in Matt. 24:6–8; Luke 21:9–11.

was the "scattering" of the defeated nation, their departure into exile and captivity.[4] Both these Old Testament texts have to do with judgment on Jerusalem: "Who will have pity on you, O Jerusalem, or who will grieve for you?" Jeremiah asks (Jer. 15:5). In Ezekiel judgment is attributed to the fact that Israel had defiled the sanctuary – "with all your detestable things and with all your abominations" (5:11). A later passage speaks of the "four disastrous acts of judgment, sword, famine, wild beasts, and pestilence," that God will send upon Jerusalem (Ezek. 14:21).[5] This is not quite the typology of the four riders, but it matches, with only one slight change of position, the concluding statement that Death and Hades were given power over a fourth of the "land" to kill "with sword (*en rhomphaiai*) and with famine and with pestilence and by wild beasts of the earth" (6:8).[6] The relevance of this for our understanding of the four seals is enhanced by the observation that in Ezekiel these "four disastrous acts of judgment" form part of the message given to the prophet after he has eaten the scroll.

The fifth seal

The opening of the fifth seal reveals "under the altar the souls of those who had been slain for the word of God and for the witness they had borne" (6:9). These martyrs, whose death is depicted as a sacrifice, cry out, "O Sovereign Lord, holy and true, how long before you will judge and avenge our blood on those who dwell on the earth?" (6:10). They are given white robes and told to wait until the number of those who are to be killed, as they had been, is completed. The identity of these "souls," however, is difficult to ascertain. They are not clearly identified as Christian martyrs – it is not said that their testimony is to Jesus, as is

---

4 See J. C. Poirier, "The First Rider: A Response to Michael Bachmann," *NTS* 45.2 (1999), 260.

5 Cf. Ezek. 33:27; Jer. 14:12.

6 That variation is permissible in the formula is evident from Jer. 15:2–3.

the case elsewhere (1:2, 9; 19:10; 20:4).[7] Conceivably, therefore, the vision should be repositioned in a Jewish context. Jesus himself provides a plausible historical framework for the judgment and vengeance for which these souls cry out:

> Therefore I send you prophets and wise men and scribes, some of whom you will kill and crucify, and some you will flog in your synagogues and persecute from town to town, so that on you may come all the righteous blood shed on earth, from the blood of innocent Abel to the blood of Zechariah the son of Barachiah, whom you murdered between the sanctuary and the altar. Truly, I say to you, all these things will come upon this generation. (Matt. 23:34–36)

These, then, would be the "souls" of those Jews throughout the ages who have suffered at the hands of sinful Israel. Possibly they are given white robes because they had not been able to wash their robes in the blood of the lamb (cf. 7:14), the reason being that these souls under the altar are those, from Abel to Zechariah, who died *before* Christ. They must wait for vindication until "the number of their fellow servants and their brothers should be complete" (6:11; cf. 16:5–7).

The sixth seal

The opening of the sixth seal elicits the same imagery of cosmic collapse that is associated with the destruction of Jerusalem in Jesus' apocalyptic discourse (cf. Mark 13:24–25; Matt. 24:29; Luke 21:25–26). This is the great day of the wrath of God and of the Lamb. There is certainly a universal dimension to the crisis: the imagery of verse 14, for example, is drawn from a prophecy against the nations in Isaiah 34:1–4. But still, we should read the details carefully. In an earlier chapter Isaiah speaks of a day when "the haughtiness of man shall be humbled, and the lofty

---

[7] See D. Aune, *Revelation* (Dallas: Word, 1997–98), 406; C. H. Giblin, "The Millennium (Rev 20.4–6) as Heaven," *NTS* 45.4 (1999), 558–59.

pride of men shall be brought low," when "people shall enter the caves of the rocks and the holes of the ground, from before the terror of the Lord, and from the splendor of his majesty, when he rises to terrify the earth" (2:17, 19; cf. 2:21). The scope of the catastrophe appears far-reaching, but the judgment is directed specifically against the "house of Jacob" on account of the people's idolatry and corruption (2:6; 3:1–5). Those who hide in the caves call upon the mountains and rocks to fall on them and hide them (Rev. 6:15). The source of the *topos* is Hosea 10:8, which again belongs to a prophecy of judgment on Israel's idolatry. Jesus makes use of the same imagery in Luke 23:30, where the reference is clearly to the Roman invasion of Judea. What terrifies the "kings of the earth and the great ones and the generals and the rich and the powerful, and everyone, slave and free" (Rev. 6:15), then, is not the prospect of their own immediate destruction but the scale of the catastrophe that is coming upon Israel.[8] The question that they ask – "the great day of their wrath has come, and who can stand?" (Rev. 6:17) – recalls Joel 2:11: "For the day of the LORD is great and very awesome; who can endure it?" But this is the day – a "day of darkness and gloom" (Joel 2:2) – when an army of divine judgment, like a devastating swarm of locusts, will march against Jerusalem.[9]

The sealing of the 144,000

At this point the opening of the seals is interrupted in response to the question uttered by the people of the earth: who can stand when the day of God's wrath comes upon Jerusalem? Four angels hold back the "four winds of the earth" to prevent them from blowing "on earth or sea or against any tree" (7:1). Frequently in the Old Testament the four winds of heaven are the force by which a people is scattered, or represent the distant places to which they are

[8] Cf. Lam.4:12; Ezek. 26:16; 27:35–36 with respect to Tyre.

[9] Cf. Mal. 3:2; Zeph.1:14–16.

scattered (e.g., Jer. 49:36; Dan. 11:4; Zech. 2:6). Moreover, the angels stand at the "four corners of the earth," a phrase which has similar connotations (cf. Isa. 11:12; Ezek. 7:2). However, in Daniel's vision in the night the "four winds of heaven were stirring up the great sea" from which the four beasts emerge (Dan. 7:2), and this is perhaps the more likely background to what John sees.[10] The angels restrain those forces which will stir up the agents of destruction.

Another angel ascends from the rising sun, carrying the "seal of the living God," and instructs the four angels, "Do not harm the earth or the sea or the trees, until we have sealed the servants of our God on their foreheads" (Rev. 7:2–3). The background to this protective measure is again to be found in Ezekiel. In a vision in which he is shown the appalling idolatry that is practiced in the temple, the prophet sees a "man clothed in linen, who had the writing case at his waist," who is directed by the Lord to go through Jerusalem and "put a mark upon the foreheads of the men who sigh and groan over all the abominations that are committed in it" (Ezek. 9:3–4; cf. 5:11–12). Then six other men are told to go through the city and, beginning at the sanctuary, to slay men and women, old and young; but they are to touch "no one on whom is the mark" (9:2, 5–6).

John does not witness the sealing of the saints. Instead he *hears* "the number of the sealed, 144,000, sealed from every tribe of the sons of Israel" (Rev. 7:4). The question that arises is: are these 144,000 – certainly a symbolic number – drawn from Israel, or do they represent in some way the whole church? Are they to be identified with the Jewish church in Judea, which is seen as a restoration of the Old Testament people of God (cf. Matt. 19:28; Luke 22:30; Jas. 1:1; 1 Pet. 1:1), living in the midst of a nation facing judgment? Or is the "Jewishness" of the 12,000 sealed from each of the tribes of Israel itself a symbolic quality,

[10] That these winds are "of the earth" may suggest a more demonic character; moreover, they blow not only on the sea but also on the earth and trees.

representing the universal people of God? The general argument at this point would suggest that this is the Jewish remnant in Judea, those who are appalled by Israel's abominations, who are to be protected from the devastating effects of divine judgment against Jerusalem.[11] We cannot fully understand the significance of this group, however, without taking into account both the vision of a "great multitude" (*ochlos polus*) that follows (7:9–16) and the later appearance of 144,000 with the Lamb on Mount Zion (14:1–5).

The great multitude

The relation between the 144,000 who are sealed and the "great multitude" is somewhat paradoxical. John *hears* the number of the sealed from the twelve tribes of Israel, but what he then *sees* is something quite different: a multinational crowd, which cannot be numbered, drawn "from every nation, from all tribes and peoples and languages."[12] Are these two distinct groups or is the "great multitude" a reinterpretation of an idealized Israel, rather as the Lamb that was slain is a reinterpretation of the Lion of Judah (5:5–6)?[13]

The "great multitude" is said to consist of those who have "come from the great tribulation (*tēs thlipseōs tēs megalēs*)" (7:14). Given the apparent relation between the scroll which the Lamb receives from God and the scroll which Daniel is told to seal (or which is sealed in heaven: Dan. 12:9), it seems likely that this "great tribulation" is (in some sense) the extreme crisis described in Daniel 12:1 – "a time of trouble, such as never has been since there was a nation till that time." Jesus alludes to this apocalyptic motif when he describes the "great affliction" (*thlipsis megalē*) that will come upon Jerusalem. This background may give

---

[11] Cf. Aune, *Revelation*, 441. Acts 21:20 mentions many ten thousands (*muriadēs*) of Jews in Jerusalem "who have believed."

[12] Cf. Aune, *Revelation*, 466.

[13] Cf. Bauckham, *Climax*, 215–16.

us some help in determining the link between these two groups. According to Daniel, during this period of distress there will be some among the people who are "wise" or "discerning," who will be refined through persecution (11:33, 35) but in the end will "shine like the brightness of the sky above" (12:3). These "wise" will also "turn many to righteousness" (12:3; cf. 11:33).[14] The link is perhaps a little tenuous, but it provides a coherent rationale for the juxtaposition of the two groups in John's vision. The 144,000 correspond to the "wise," who not only remain faithful during the "great tribulation" but also succeed in turning many others to righteousness. In the context of John's vision, these others are a "great multitude" from many nations.

It is doubtful that those who make up the "great multitude" are meant to be martyrs. On the one hand, they are surely too numerous. On the other, in contrast to the souls under the altar (6:9–11), it is not said that they have been slain for the word of God and their testimony; and it is their *own* robes that have been made white by the blood of the lamb: in other words, it is Christ's death, rather than their own, that has made them holy.[15] That they have "come from the great tribulation" probably means, then, that they are those who survive the period of judgment – in effect, the church. They are the innumerable descendants of Abraham (cf. Gen. 16:10), to whom it was promised that he would be the "father of a multitude of nations" (Gen. 17:4).

But are they in heaven or on earth? The idea in verse 15 that God will "shelter them" (*skēnōsei ep' autous*) is drawn from Ezekiel 37:27 LXX: "my dwelling place (*hē kataskēnōsis mou*) shall be among them." The following verse then reads: "Then the nations will know that I am the LORD who

---

[14] This is interpreted rather differently in the LXX.

[15] Bauckham (*Climax*, 226) considers the washing of the robes to be consonant with the theme of an eschatological war: after the shedding of blood clothing had to be washed and the army purified before participation in worship (Num. 31:19–20, 24; cf. 19:19; 1QM 14:2–3).

sanctifies Israel, when my sanctuary is in their midst forevermore." Israel is depicted as being itself the temple of God in the midst of the nations. John appears to have taken this image and transferred it to the church, presenting it as the great international multitude which serves as the dwelling place of God in the midst of the nations. Those who have come out of the great tribulation are now priests within this figurative temple (cf. 1 Pet. 2:9), serving God day and night. They are, in effect, the same "priests" who have been ransomed by the Lamb "from every tribe and language and people and nation" and who "shall reign on the earth" (Rev. 5:9–10).[16]

Verse 16 is a quotation of Isaiah 49:10. It belongs to a prophecy about the Servant of the Lord who not only will restore Israel but also will be given "as a light to the nations, that my salvation may reach to the end of the earth" (49:5–6). He will set free the prisoners and "those who are in darkness," and they "shall feed along the ways; on all bare heights shall be their pasture; they shall not hunger or thirst, neither scorching wind nor sun shall strike them, for he who has pity on them will lead them, and by springs of water will guide them" (49:9–10). This last clause is taken up in verse 17: the shepherd "will guide them to springs of living water (*zōēs pēgas udatōn*)." In John's Gospel Jesus tells the Samaritan woman that the water that he will give will become "a spring of water (*pēgē udatos*) welling up to eternal life" (John 4:14); and later the "living water" is expressly understood as the Spirit (John 7:38–39).

A passage in Jeremiah, which calls on the Lord "to save your people, the remnant of Israel" (Jer. 31:7), resonates with the same imagery. A "great multitude" (*ochlon polun*: Jer. 38:8 LXX) will be brought back from the north country and from the "farthest parts of the earth" (31:8). They will "walk by brooks of water" (31:9). The Lord will keep Israel "as a shepherd keeps his flock" (31:10). They shall "come

[16] Against Aune, *Revelation*, 440.

and sing aloud on the height of Zion" (31:12). They "shall hunger no more" (*ou peinasousin eti*: 38:12 LXX; cf. Rev. 7:16). God will "turn their mourning into joy"; he will "comfort them, and give them gladness for sorrow" (31:13). This, moreover, is a people who "survived the sword" and "found grace in the wilderness" (31:2).[17]

The vision, therefore, is of the restoration of scattered Israel to Zion, where God will dwell in their midst. This, however, is the "Israel" of the new covenant – a multinational entity filled with the Holy Spirit, the church in the age which has come.[18]

The 144,000 on Mount Zion

Before we attempt to determine the relation between the 144,000 who stand on Mount Zion (14:1–5) and the 144,000 who are sealed against destruction, we should consider how this group on Mount Zion relates to what precedes. The number in the second passage lacks the definite article, which is surprising if it is meant to refer back to the earlier occurrence. The omission should make us wary of assuming a simple equivalence between the two groups. It is more important to note that the Lamb appears on Mount Zion as one of a series of visionary creatures (the dragon, the beast from the sea, the beast from the land, and then the Lamb), just as in Daniel's vision in the night the human figure succeeds the four beasts. Whereas those who

[17] Other allusions reinforce this. In Ezek. 34 the shepherd, who is "my servant David," will tend the flock which has been rescued "from all places where they have been scattered on a day of clouds and thick darkness" (34:12; cf. 37:20–28). The statement in Rev. 7:17 that "God will wipe away every tear from their eyes" comes from Isaiah 25:8 in a context that speaks of the destruction of death (LXX has "death has grown strong and swallowed up"), which is spread like a veil over all the nations, and the removal of the "reproach of his people . . . from all the earth."

[18] Bauckham defines John's central conviction about the coming of God's kingdom on earth: "that the sacrificial death of the Lamb and the prophetic witness of his followers are God's strategy for winning all the nations of the world from the dominion of the beast to his own kingdom" (*Climax*, 336–37).

worship the beast from the sea are marked on the right hand or on the forehead with the "name of the beast or the number of its name" (13:16–17), the 144,000 have the Lamb's name or his Father's name "written on their foreheads." This quite clear contrast carries with it a further corollary: the 144,000 are those who were slain for not worshipping the beast (13:15). The significance of the number, therefore, is not that this group and the 144,000 from the twelve tribes of Israel are the same but that both groups have been sealed against the deleterious effects of a larger wickedness or calamity.[19]

The 144,000 seen on Mount Zion have been redeemed not from Israel alone but from the people (or "from the earth": 14:3) "as firstfruits for God and the Lamb" (14:4). It is often commented that this group has the characteristics of an eschatological army;[20] and it is arguable that they have more in common with the "armies of heaven" which accompany the Word of God in the final battle against the beast and the kings of the earth (19:11–16) than with the 144,000 from the twelve tribes of Israel. Like the armies of heaven, who follow the Word of God, these "virgins" follow the Lamb wherever he goes (14:4). Whereas the Word of God has "a name written that no one knows but himself" (19:12), the 144,000 sing a new song which they alone could learn (14:3). The image of "firstfruits" may suggest resurrection: they constitute, in effect, an extension of the "firstfruits" which is the resurrected Christ (1 Cor. 15:23). But they are, in any case, quite clearly those who have come to share in the "first resurrection" – those beheaded for their testimony to Jesus, who did not worship the blasphemous beast of Roman absolutism (Rev. 20:4–6).

---

[19] Aune lists a number of significant differences between the two groups but still concludes that the author intends to equate them (Aune, *Revelation*, 447–48).

[20] E.g., Bauckham, *Climax*, 229–32.

The Seven Trumpets

The opening of the first six seals has established the conditions for judgment on Israel: the four riders have been sent out into the land, ready to "kill with sword and with famine and with pestilence and by wild beasts of the earth"; unnatural portents in the heavens have presaged a catastrophic disaster; and the servants of God, who embody the fullness of restored Israel, have been sealed so that they will not be touched by the judgment. Then the seventh seal is opened. There is silence in heaven for about half an hour to allow the prayers of all the saints to be heard as they rise with the incense that burns on the golden altar before the throne of God. The golden censer is thrown down to the earth, generating "peals of thunder, rumblings, flashes of lightning, and an earthquake" (Rev. 8:5), and the seven angels who stand before God prepare to blow the seven trumpets that have been given to them.

The trumpet in the Old Testament frequently announces imminent judgment against Israel (cf. Isa. 58:1; Jer. 4:5, 19–21; 6:1, 17; Ezek. 33:3–6; Hos. 5:8; 8:1; Joel 2:1, 15).[21] As with the first four seals, the first four trumpets form a distinct grouping (8:7–12). In each case a heavenly phenomenon – something falling to earth, or the sun, moon and stars darkening – causes the pollution or destruction of a third of something in the earthly sphere.

We find ourselves here in a rather different imagistic environment, in which allusions to the plagues of Egypt predominate. The "hail and fire, mixed with blood," which burns up a third of the earth and of the trees and of the grass, recalls the seventh plague of hail and fire that

---

[21] In Jer. 51:27; Zech. 9:14 the trumpet announces war against Babylon. Seven priests blow seven trumpets (walking before the ark of the covenant) at the fall of Jericho (Josh. 6; cf. 1 Chr. 15:24; Neh. 12:41). Trumpets are blown to proclaim the accession of a king (cf. 1 Kgs. 1:34, 39; 2 Kgs. 9:13) and are associated especially with the kingship of God (cf. Pss. 47:5; 98:6; Zech. 9:14). John's seventh trumpet proclaims the "kingdom of our Lord and of his Christ" (11:15).

destroys "everything that was in the field in all the land of Egypt, both man and beast," as well as every plant and tree (Exod. 9:25). When a fiery mountain is thrown into the sea, a third of the sea is turned to blood, just as in the first plague the waters of the Nile are turned to blood (Exod. 7:20–21). The partial obliteration of the lights of heaven, which follows the blowing of the fourth trumpet, commonly accompanies divine judgment in the Old Testament (cf. Isa. 13:10; Joel 2:10; 3:15). Ezekiel 32:7 is especially significant in this regard because it forms part of an oracle against Pharaoh, king of Egypt: "When I blot you out, I will cover the heavens and make their stars dark; I will cover the sun with a cloud, and the moon shall not give its light." But in view of the earlier correspondences there may also be a reference to the ninth plague, when "there was pitch darkness in all the land of Egypt three days" (Exod. 10:22).

At first sight, this evocation of the plagues of Egypt suggests that what John has in view is God's judgment of the nations. We discover later, however, that the "great city" in which the "Lord was crucified" is "symbolically (*pneumatikōs*) . . . called Sodom and Egypt" (11:8).[22] If this city is Jerusalem (we will consider this disputed question in a moment), then it would be reasonable to think that it is still Israel that is the object of judgment here. The affliction of Egypt with plagues becomes a parable for the judgment of Israel. More direct support for this comes from the vision of the third trumpet, in which a star called "Wormwood" falls from heaven making a third of fresh waters bitter (8:11). The name derives from a vision of judgment on Israel found in Jeremiah: "Behold, I will feed this people with wormwood, and give them poisonous water to drink" (Jer. 9:15 RSV; cf. 23:15). The reason for the transfer of imagery is not difficult to find. Both Sodom and Egypt

---

[22] There may be an allusion to the destruction of Sodom by "sulfur and fire" in the fire that falls from heaven when the first trumpet is blown (Rev. 8:7; cf. Gen. 19:24). Cf. Joel 2:30.

were places subject to divine wrath from which the righteous (with the exception of Lot's wife) escaped unscathed.[23]

The "great mountain, burning with fire" that is cast into the sea and the "great star" which falls from heaven are not drawn from the plague narratives. It could be argued that both these objects are representative of Babylon and therefore, in John's apocalyptic symbology, of Rome. Babylon is depicted by Jeremiah as a "destroying mountain," which God will roll down from the crags and make into a "burnt mountain" (Jer. 51:25); and in Isaiah it is the "Day Star, son of Dawn," which is "fallen from heaven" (Isa. 14:12). The associations may well be correct, but we should note that these objects are the *instruments* by which judgment is executed upon the earth – just as "hail and fire, mixed with blood" are the means by which a third of the earth is burned up. There may be an anticipation of a later judgment on Rome, and it is certainly significant that the Day Star, having aspired to set his throne "above the stars of God," is instead "brought down to Sheol, to the far reaches of the pit" (Isa. 14:13, 15). But in the context of these trumpet visions "Babylon" is not the object of divine judgment but the means by which suffering is inflicted upon the earth. The star, as John informs us, is Wormwood, the source of extreme bitterness for Israel.

After the fourth trumpet John sees an eagle (*aetos*) flying "directly overhead," crying out, "Woe, woe, woe to those who dwell on the earth, at the blasts of the other trumpets that the three angels are about to blow!" (Rev. 8:13). The image may serve only to mark a transition and intensification in the sequence of trumpets, but a striking parallel in Hosea again suggests an orientation towards Israel: "set the trumpet to your lips! One like a vulture (LXX: *aetos*) is over the house of the Lord, because they have transgressed my covenant and rebelled against my law"

---

[23] The hail did not touch the people of Israel who were in the land of Goshen, or any of the servants of Pharaoh who feared the word of the Lord (Exod. 9:20, 26). Also 10:23.

(Hos. 8:1). The terminology is ambiguous both in Greek and Hebrew. If this is a vulture, then Israel is portrayed as a corpse (cf. Matt. 24:28; Luke 17:37); if an eagle, then Israel is perhaps the prey. In any case, there is good reason to think that John makes use of the image quite deliberately to evoke the motif of judgment on Israel on account of the nation's faithlessness and idolatry (cf. Hos. 8:4–6). Hosea's concern with idolatry may prove, in fact, to be significant when we come to the aftermath of the sixth trumpet (9:20).

The Exodus typology continues with the cloud of locusts that rises from the bottomless pit when the fifth trumpet is blown (9:1–12; cf. Exod. 10:12–20). More importantly, however, this is the army of locusts that Joel sees swarming against Israel: a trumpet is blown (9:1; cf. Joel 2:1), the air is darkened (9:2; cf. Joel 2:2), the locusts have the appearance of horses prepared for battle (9:7; cf. Joel 2:4), their teeth are like lion's teeth (9:8; cf. Joel 2:6).[24] By redirecting the imagery of the Egyptian plague through Joel's prophetic vision John adapts it to the circumstances of contemporary Israel.

The second woe, the sixth trumpet, sees the release of the "four angels who are bound at the great river Euphrates" (Rev. 9:14). These four angels, who command a massive force of horsemen, may represent a military threat to Rome on its eastern frontier from the Parthian empire, as is usually thought. But given the association of Rome with Babylon this is perhaps unlikely: "Babylon" was not under threat from forces amassed at the Euphrates. In the Old Testament, however, the river Euphrates constitutes the ideal northern boundary of Israel's territory (cf. Gen. 15:18; Exod. 23:31), from beyond which the archetypal invading army comes (e.g., Jer. 1:14–15).[25] There is also an obvious

---

[24] In John's vision the locusts are expressly told not to harm "the grass of the earth or any green growth or any tree" (Rev. 9:4; cf. Joel 1:9–20). Note, however, Jer. 51:27: judgment on Babylon is enacted by horses "like bristling locusts."

[25] Cf. G. B. Caird, *The Revelation of St. John the Divine* (London: A & C Black, 1984), 122. In Rev. 16:12, however, the drying up of the Euphrates has to do with the judgment on Rome.

association of the Euphrates with Babylon (cf. Jer. 51:63–64). It makes more sense, therefore, to see this as a military power deployed *against Israel* in a rerun of the Babylonian invasion. Habakkuk warns Israel that God is "raising up the Chaldeans [i.e., the Babylonians], that bitter and hasty nation, who march through the breadth of the earth, to seize dwellings not their own": "Their horses are swifter than leopards . . . their horsemen press proudly on. Their horsemen come from afar; they fly like an eagle swift to devour" (Hab. 1:6, 8). John says that the tails of the horses are like serpents, which may echo a passage in Jeremiah that speaks of the destructive agency of horses as part of God's judgment against Israel:

> "The snorting of their horses is heard from Dan; at the sound of the neighing of their stallions the whole land quakes. They come and devour the land and all that fills it, the city and those who dwell in it. For behold, I am sending among you serpents, adders that cannot be charmed, and they shall bite you," declares the LORD. My joy is gone; grief is upon me; my heart is sick within me. Behold, the cry of the daughter of my people from the length and breadth of the land: "Is the LORD not in Zion? Is her King not in her?" "Why have they provoked me to anger with their carved images and with their foreign idols?" (Jer. 8:16–19)

Whether or not John had this particular passage in mind when he envisioned the events associated with the sixth trumpet (the second woe), the reference here to Israel's idolatry is highly pertinent to our interpretation of this passage. For he goes on to say that "the rest of the people" (*hoi loipoi tōn anthrōpōn*: not "the rest of mankind" as in ESV), who escaped these plagues, "did not repent of the works of their hands nor give up worshipping demons and idols of gold and silver and bronze and stone and wood, which cannot see or hear or walk, nor did they repent of their murders or their sorceries or their sexual immorality or their thefts" (Rev. 9:20–21). This sounds like an attack on paganism, and it could well be. But we should not overlook the extent to which the Old Testament prophets blame the great catastrophes of divine judgment both on Israel's immorality and on her persistent idolatry: "Will you steal, murder, commit adultery, swear falsely, make offerings to Baal, and go after other gods that you have not known?" (Jer. 7:9). As we have seen, several of the texts from which John has drawn his language and imagery of judgment contain just these accusations (cf. Isa. 2:6–8, 20–21; Jer. 8:2; 9:14–15; 15:4; Ezek. 5:11; Hos. 8:1–5; 10:5–8).[26]

The Little Scroll

Nothing of what has been depicted so far has disclosed the *contents* of the scroll given to the Lamb in the throne room scene of Revelation 5. All that has occurred is that the seven seals have been broken and, at the breaking of the last seal, a sequence of seven trumpet blasts has been initiated, the last of which has not yet taken place. The scroll itself, which is of central symbolic importance for John's vision, has presumably remained unread in the throne room.

At this point, however, a "mighty angel" descends from heaven, festooned with the symbolism of divine disclosure, carrying in his hand a "little scroll," which is expressly said to be "open" (Rev. 10:1–2). There are good reasons, mostly of a literary nature, for thinking that this is the same scroll that was given to the Lamb.[27] For example, Ezekiel receives from the throne of God a scroll which combines details both from the scroll given to the Lamb and from the "little scroll" given to John: the scroll has writing on both sides and the prophet is told that he will find it sweet to eat. Similarly, Daniel is told to *seal* the scroll that relates what is to "happen to your people in the latter days" (Dan. 10:14) by an angel who has a strong affinity with the angel who descends from heaven to deliver the "little scroll" to John: both stand above water, both raise a hand to heaven and

---

[26] See also Deut. 32:16–17; Micah 5:1–14; Ezek. 43:7–9.

[27] See Bauckham, *Climax*, 243–57.

swear "by him who lives forever" (Dan. 12:6–7; Rev. 10:5–6; also Dan. 10:5–6; Rev. 10:1–3). If a real semantic distinction is attached to the diminutive form (*biblaridion*: "little scroll") used in chapter 10, it may only reflect the transference of the scroll from the heavenly realm to the earthly; or it may suggest that what the prophet receives here is only part of the contents of the original scroll. There are also good reasons for thinking that this is the angel who was said to have been sent to John by God in Revelation 1:1 and that the scroll, therefore, contains the "revelation of Jesus Christ" that is announced here.[28]

John takes the scroll and eats it, finding that it is sweet as honey in his mouth but bitter to his stomach, as the angel had warned. He is then told that he must again prophesy against (*epi*) "peoples and nations and languages and kings" (Rev. 10:10–11).

The measuring of the temple

The seventh trumpet will initiate the fulfillment of the "mystery of God . . . just as he announced to his servants the prophets" (Rev. 10:7), which must mark a climax to the sequence of visions associated with the opening of the scroll. Before this can take place, however, John is given a measuring rod and instructed to "measure the temple of God and the altar and those who worship there"; the outer courts and the rest of the city, however, will be given over to Gentile domination for a period of forty-two months (11:1–2).

This mention of the period of forty-two months, which is also the 1,260 days given to the two witnesses in which to prophesy (11:3), reminds us of the association of John's scroll with the scroll or book that Daniel is told to seal up until the time of the end (Dan. 12:4; cf. 12:9).[29] The duration

---

28 Cf. Bauckham, *Climax*, 254–55. Bauckham notes a further possible connection between the scroll and the *apokalupsis* of 1:1: the verbs *kaluptō* and *kataluptō* are used in Dan. 12:4 and 12:9 LXX for the concealing of the "ordinances" of the sealed scroll.

29 On the significance of these numbers see Bauckham, *Climax*, 400–404.

of the time of the end will be three and a half times (Dan. 12:7), which is equivalent to the period of 1,290 days from the time when "the regular burnt offering is taken away and the abomination that makes desolate is set up" (Dan. 12:11). John has connected this, however, with a conversation between two angelic figures related in Daniel 8:13–14, according to which during this same period the sanctuary and host will be given over "to be trampled underfoot" (cf. Zech. 12:3 LXX; Luke 21:24). Thus John is given the unsealed scroll at the beginning of the period of the "shattering of the power of the holy people" (Dan. 12:7) – in other words, at the beginning of the period of judgment upon Jerusalem.

The notion of measuring the temple is familiar from Old Testament prophecy concerning the restoration of Jerusalem. In the twenty-fifth year of the exile in Babylon, Ezekiel is taken in "visions of God" to the land of Israel and set down opposite "a structure like a city" (Ezek. 40:1–2). Standing in the gateway is a man with "a linen cord and a measuring reed," who instructs Ezekiel: "Declare all that you see to the house of Israel" (40:4). The lengthy and detailed process of surveying the temple concludes with the coming of the glory of the Lord to fill the temple again and the promise of God that "I will dwell in the midst of the people of Israel forever" (Ezek. 43:2–7).[30] A similar assurance is found in Zechariah: "And I will be to her a wall of fire all around, declares the LORD, and I will be the glory in her midst" (Zech. 2:5). This background strongly suggests that John's measuring of the temple serves the same purpose: it is a sign, on the one hand, that God will keep safe the temple building and the "priests" who worship there, even though the outer court will be given over to the Gentiles and, on the other hand, that the glory of the Lord will continue to dwell there.[31] The difficulty is to know

[30] The purpose of the detailed survey of the temple, however, is that the prophet might "describe to the house of Israel the temple, that they may be ashamed of their iniquities" (Ezek. 43:10).

[31] The fact that John does not actually measure the temple may indicate that these verses serve primarily to evoke the biblical background. The vision is left incomplete because its purpose is adequately fulfilled once the reader is reminded of the Old Testament visions and their argument about the glory of God.

whether, as John understood it, this was the literal temple in Jerusalem prior to its destruction or a symbolic temple – and, if the latter, a temple symbolic of what?

The general thesis that we are developing here is that the visions connected with the seals and the trumpets relate to judgment on the actual city of Jerusalem. John's measuring of the temple naturally falls into this framework. Jesus' use of the same motif in his apocalyptic discourse gives support to this argument: "Jerusalem will be trampled underfoot by the Gentiles, until the times of the Gentiles are fulfilled" (Luke 21:24). Moreover, nothing in the text suggests that the temple is a heavenly substitute for the defunct literal temple, as it is in Ezekiel's vision. Whereas Ezekiel is taken on a visionary journey to a "very high mountain" in Israel, on which stood the renewed temple, no such prelude is necessary in John's vision: the instruction to rise and measure the temple seems to presuppose that the "temple" is in existence. If the temple had already been destroyed, we would expect some explanation of where this purely visionary temple came from. This does not mean, however, that the vision relates only to the literal city: John is not saying that the invading Gentile power will not have access to the literal house of God, or that those worshipping there will be unharmed.[32] The point cannot be demonstrated definitively, but the meaning seems more likely to be that although Jerusalem itself will be destroyed by the Romans, the true worshippers of God (i.e., faithful Israel) will be preserved and God will continue to dwell in their midst. Within the symbolic structures of Revelation and of New Testament thought generally, it is much easier to interpret the protection of the worshippers in the temple symbolically than the trampling of the holy city by the nations.[33]

---

[32] The symbolism presupposes the *prophecy* of judgment (cf. Luke 21:24), not the actual event of the temple's destruction.

[33] The measuring of the temple, therefore, corresponds functionally to the sealing of the 144,000. Both episodes interrupt their respective series of seven at the same point: the 144,000 are sealed before the seventh seal is opened, the temple is measured before the seventh trumpet is blown.

The two witnesses

Although the precise identity of the two "witnesses" who are given authority to prophesy probably cannot be determined (and perhaps is not meant to be determined), some boundaries can be set to their interpretation. The context is either that of Israel prior to A.D. 70 or of Jewish Christianity. This episode connects directly with the measuring of the temple: the prophetic activity of the two witnesses takes place in the "great city that symbolically is called Sodom and Egypt, where their Lord was crucified" (Rev. 11:8), which is also the "holy city" of 11:2.[34] The period of time in which the nations will trample over the holy city (42 months) is the same as the time allotted for their testimony (1,260 days). We are also, according to the terms of our analysis, still in the period of the second woe against Jerusalem (9:13 – 11:13).

The allusion to Sodom and Egypt indicates that the city is facing divine judgment. The sackcloth in which the prophets are dressed (Rev. 11:3) is a sign of mourning for the wickedness of Jerusalem and the prospect of judgment (cf. Isa. 22:12; 32:11; Jer. 4:8; 6:26; Joel 1:8, 13; Amos 8:1). The power that they have to consume their enemies with fire from their mouths appears to be an apocalyptic intensification of Jeremiah 5:14: "Because you have spoken this word, behold, I am making my words in your mouth a fire, and this people wood, and the fire shall consume them." This statement precedes a warning that God will bring a nation (Babylon) against Israel, which will destroy the land. The theme of judgment also emerges in the allusions to Elijah and Moses (11:6). The three-year drought (three-and-a-half years according to Luke 4:25 and Jas. 5:17) during the ministry of Elijah was punishment for Ahab's idolatry (1 Kgs. 17:1). Elijah called down fire from

---

[34] Note also the tradition that prophets must die in Jerusalem (cf. Luke 13:33; Aune, *Revelation*, 620–21), though since these are symbolic prophets, it could still be argued that the "city" is only symbolically Jerusalem.

heaven upon the men sent from King Ahaziah of Israel because he had sought an oracle from "Baal-zebub, the god of Ekron" (2 Kgs. 1:10–12). Moses brought plagues upon Egypt, but in the context of this passage Egypt is Jerusalem, from which Jewish Christians will flee into the wilderness (cf. Rev. 12:6, 14).

The two witnesses are said to be "the two olive trees and the two lampstands that stand before the Lord of the earth" (Rev. 11:4). The allusion to Zechariah 4 is unmistakable, but the particular significance of the imagery is anything but clear. In brief, Zechariah has a vision of a gold lampstand, surmounted by seven lamps, with an olive tree on either side (4:2–3).[35] The two olive trees appear to represent Zerubbabel and Joshua, the high priest. Zechariah is told that Zerubbabel will rebuild the temple and that there will be unity between this "Branch" and the high priest at his side (3:8; 4:6–10; 6:11–13). In the vision the lampstand, which has seven lamps upon it, appears to represent the temple (cf. the "menorah" in the tabernacle: Exod. 25:31–35; 26:35) and the Spirit of God (cf. 4:6), who anoints the two olive trees (4:12).

The difficulty now lies in the fact that the two witnesses are identified both with the two olive trees and with *two* lampstands. What John appears to have done is to conflate the olive trees and the lampstands into a single function. If we recall also that the seven golden lampstands around the "one like son of man" in the opening vision are the seven churches (Rev. 1:12–13, 20), it may not be too great an inferential leap to think that the combined prophetic function of these two witnesses is allocated to a portion of the whole church and perhaps specifically, given the general context, to the Jewish church. The agreement of two witnesses is, of course, a familiar biblical legal

---

[35] In Zech. 1 – 4 there is a strong expression of commitment to Jerusalem. Zech. 4 must be understood against this background. Note also the joining of the nations to the Lord (2:11); and in Zech. 3 the renewal of the priesthood.

requirement (Num. 35:30; Deut. 17:6; 19:15).[36] They are, therefore, the church, or that outspoken part of the church, that testifies against the sinfulness of Israel and remains faithful to the point of death. They would correspond in some manner to the restraining force of 2 Thessalonians 2:3–7.

And just as the one who restrains in Paul's narrative is eventually forced "out of the way," so at the end of the period of 1,260 days the two witnesses are killed by the beast that ascends from the "bottomless pit" (11:7). This is perhaps a little difficult to explain if the city is Jerusalem and the beast Rome – an incongruity that has led some interpreters to conclude that the beast in fact represents Jewish opposition to the Christian community.[37] However, the beast "will make war" against the two witnesses, just as the little horn, Antiochus, in Daniel's vision made war against the saints of the Most High (Dan. 7:21). The typology would seem to imply that this is pagan aggression against the righteous within Israel. They remain unburied, and there is much rejoicing over their demise. But after three and a half days "a breath of life from God entered them," and in full view of their enemies they were taken up into heaven – in other words, they are vindicated (11:11–12). At the same time a great earthquake destroyed a tenth of the city, and seven thousand people were killed. The remainder "were terrified and gave glory to the God of heaven" (11:13).[38]

---

[36] Cf. Bauckham, *Climax*, 274.

[37] E.g., R. Van De Water, "Reconsidering the Beast from the Sea (Rev. 13.1)," *NTS* 46.2 (2000), 252–53.

[38] The repentance implicit in this phrase (cf. 14:7; 16:9) is difficult to situate historically. If the city is Jerusalem, neither the scale of the destruction nor the extent of the repentance fits the circumstances of A.D. 70. Aune suggests that it corresponds to the salvation of all Israel mentioned by Paul in Rom. 11:25–26 (*Revelation*, 629). Possibly it is Rome that is punished by God in this earthquake (cf. Ezek. 38:14–23, esp. 19–20; cf. Isa. 29:5–7). Bauckham understands the "great city" to signify the pagan world. The witness of the martyrs achieves what judgment fails to achieve – the conversion of the nations (*Climax*, 278–83).

With the seventh trumpet comes a decisive proclamation by "loud voices in heaven": "The kingdom of the world has become the kingdom of our Lord and of his Christ, and he shall reign forever and ever" (11:15). This is the fulfillment of "the mystery of God . . . just as he announced to his servants the prophets" (10:7). John may have Daniel's vision in mind at this point, but there is probably a more immediate allusion. The reference to the kingdom "of our Lord and of his Christ" recalls what is said in Psalm 2:2 about the rulers of the earth taking counsel "against the Lord and against his anointed."[39] The psalm has considerable thematic significance for John's vision because it is an affirmation of the rule of Israel's king over the nations: "Ask of me, and I will make the nations your heritage, and the ends of the earth your possession. You shall break them with a rod of iron and dash them in pieces like a potter's vessel" (Ps. 2:8–9). We are approaching a watershed in the book at which visions of judgment on Jerusalem give way to visions of judgment on the enemy of God's people. The faithful witness of the righteous has proved decisive for establishing the kingdom of the Christ, and they are rewarded for it (11:18). But the seventh trumpet is also an anticipation of a victory over "those who destroy the land" that has not yet been envisioned. This will be the theme of the next chapter.

---

[39] "The nations raged" (11:18) perhaps echoes *ephruaxan ethnē* in Ps. 2:1 LXX.

Nine

The Fall of Babylon the Great

With the last of the seven trumpets having been blown, John is shown a vivid allegorical drama (Rev. 12:1 – 13:18). The first part of the drama takes place in heaven. A woman is about to give birth but is threatened by a "great red dragon."[1] A male child is born and is quickly taken up to the throne of God to escape the clutches of the dragon; the woman flees into the wilderness to a place of security prepared by God. There is a battle in heaven and the dragon and his angels are defeated and thrown down to earth. The dragon immediately sets off in pursuit of the woman but is prevented from catching her and in anger goes "to make war on the rest of her offspring" (12:17). A beast arises from the sea, apparently at the dragon's behest – a composite creature, like a leopard, with the feet of a bear and a lion's mouth. It receives authority from the dragon, which it is allowed to exercise for a period of forty-two months. It blasphemes against God and makes war on the saints but is worshipped by all those whose names are not written in the book of life. Finally, a second beast appears, this time from the earth. It "exercises all the authority of the first beast in its presence" (13:12), deceiving the inhabitants of the earth by miraculous signs and compelling them to worship the first beast.

---

[1] Probably the woman and the dragon appear as constellations (*sēmeia*): Caird, *Revelation*, 148–49.

Notoriously, it causes all people to be marked on the right hand or on the forehead with the "name of the beast or the number of its name," which permits them to buy and sell.

What does it all mean? The identity of the woman is problematic. The male child born to her is certainly the Messiah, but the "birth" is probably not the literal birth of Jesus. The quotation from Psalm 2:9 ("who is to rule all the nations with a rod of iron"), the context for which is the accession of the king as "son of God" (cf. Ps. 2:7), points rather to the resurrection as the moment of the Messiah's "birth."[2] Paul says that Jesus was "designated Son of God in power according to the Spirit of holiness by his resurrection from the dead" (Rom. 1:4).

The imagistic background for the woman's flight into the wilderness is found in the exodus from Egypt. This is signaled very clearly by the statement that the woman was given "the two wings of the great eagle" (12:14), which recalls Exodus 19:4: "You have seen what I did to the Egyptians, and how I bore you on eagles' wings and brought you to myself." Given this, the flood of water, which the dragon pours from its mouth in an attempt to stop the woman but which is swallowed up by the earth (12:15–16), may correspond to the Red Sea, which failed to stop the Israelites from escaping into the desert. The feeding of the woman in the wilderness (12:6, 14), similarly, may allude to the miraculous feeding of Israel in the desert.[3] As mother of the Messiah the woman must in some way be identified with Israel (cf. Isa. 66:7–9). She cannot be the whole nation since her preservation in the wilderness can hardly be reconciled with the idea of judgment on Israel. It is difficult to be certain, but she is perhaps best identified with that faithful remnant within Israel – in effect, the Jewish Christian community in Judea – which fled into the desert (literally or symbolically) prior to the

---

[2] Cf. Caird, *Revelation*, 149–50.

[3] The verb used here for "nourished" (*trephō*) is used in Deut. 32:18 LXX with reference to God's provision for Israel in the wilderness.

destruction of Jerusalem, as Jesus had instructed it to do.[4]

Although ostensibly the dragon is defeated by Michael and his angels, a second and more realistic explanation is given by the voice that is then heard from heaven. The kingdom of God and the authority of his anointed one, and the corresponding overthrow of the accuser of the brethren, are achieved "by the blood of the Lamb and by the word of their testimony" (12:11). John sees in the faithful witness of the persecuted church a contributory factor in the establishment of the authority of Christ in the pagan world and the defeat of those forces within paganism which sought to suppress the church. In effect, in the terms of Daniel's vision, this is the "coming" of the Son of Man to receive authority and the execution of judgment on the fourth beast. The expulsion of Satan from heaven, however, means an intensification of evil on earth (12:12), especially for the rest of the woman's children (12:17).

The Beast from the Sea and the Beast from the Land

The two beasts that emerge as instruments of the dragon's hostility towards the rest of the woman's children are extremely enigmatic creatures. We can be fairly certain, however, that they represent Roman rule over the ancient world in some way. It has sometimes been held that the beasts and Babylon are to be identified with Jerusalem and Jewish hostility towards the church.[5] The most compelling argument against this view arising from this study is the shift in the source of the biblical language. If the preceding visions drew upon texts that describe judgment on recalcitrant Israel, we find now that John begins to shop for his imagery in a different aisle – Old Testament texts that speak of judgment on Israel's enemies, the instruments of God's wrath.

---

[4] Caird says that the agony of her labor is the "suffering endured by the loyal people of God as they waited for their anointed king" (*Revelation*, 149).

[5] Cf. Wright, "Jerusalem," 71; Water, "Beast," 245–61.

The first beast combines features from all four beasts of Daniel's vision and, like them, comes from the sea. This suggests that its function is similar but that it exceeds them in power and political influence. Like the fourth beast it speaks blasphemous words against God (Rev. 13:5–6; cf. Dan. 7:25), makes war on the saints (11:7; Dan. 7:21), and is permitted to exercise authority for a period of three-and-a-half years (13:5; Dan. 7:25). It has "ten horns and seven heads, with ten diadems on its horns and blasphemous names on its heads" (Rev. 13:1), which identifies it with the "scarlet beast" upon which the "great prostitute," Babylon, is seated (17:3). It is also probably the same as the beast which ascends from the abyss and makes war against the two witnesses (11:7). The second beast, which is perhaps to be identified with Roman provincial power in Asia Minor or with the imperial priesthood,[6] has no connection with Daniel's vision. It serves two ancillary functions: it deceives the people of the earth into worshipping the image of the first beast, causing those who refuse to worship it to be killed; and it restricts participation in commercial transactions to those who bear on the right hand or on the forehead the mark of "the name of the beast or the number of its name." Whether this is meant to signify or reflect a real historical practice is difficult to say, but it certainly points to the close integration of social and cultic life.

We are later given an explanation of the first beast (17:7–18). John is informed by one of the seven angels that the seven heads are the "seven mountains on which the woman is seated" (17:9), an unmistakable reference to the seven hills of Rome. But the heads are also seven kings, "five of whom have fallen, one is, the other has not yet come, and when he does come he must remain only a little while" (17:10). One of the heads (possibly "the first of the heads") has been mortally wounded (by a sword: 13:14) but the wound has healed and the beast has recovered. The

---

[6] See Bauckham, *Climax*, 446–47.

number of the name of the beast is given as 666, which is probably a form of riddle known as gematria. According to the most popular interpretation it is an allusion to the emperor Nero: if the Greek name "Neron Kaisar" is transliterated into Hebrew, the numerical values of the Hebrew letters add up to 666.[7]

The ten horns are characteristic of the fourth beast in Daniel's vision; the features of the leopard, bear, and lion derive from the other three beasts. The ten horns are ten kings who will receive authority "for one hour, together with the beast" (17:12). They will be "of one mind" and will hand over their power to the beast – an alliance which was anticipated when the sixth bowl was poured on the Euphrates. The kings and the beast will hate the harlot and destroy her. As such they will be instruments of divine purpose; but in the end they will be conquered by the Lamb (17:13–17). The "one hour" of their authority may be equated with the "one hour" of Babylon's destruction (18:10, 17, 19). A brief note, finally, identifies the prostitute as "the great city that has dominion over the kings of the earth." Whereas the beast is associated with the political and military power of Roman imperialism, the prostitute, Babylon, represents the corrupting influence of Rome as an economic and cultural force.[8]

In a parody of the description of God as one "who is and who was and who is to come" (1:4, 8; 4:8) it is said that the

---

[7] Cf. Bauckham, *Climax*, 384–407. Note the characterization of Nero as a beast in non-biblical sources (Bauckham, *Climax*, 409–10). Five emperors preceded Nero (Julius, Augustus, Tiberias, Caligula, Claudius). If Nero is the sixth king, then he currently "is" (17:10); if he is the beast, then he "is not" (17:8). The wounding and healing of one of the heads is not necessarily in the real past. If Revelation is genuinely prophetic, the healing of the wound could refer to the recovery of Rome from the chaos following Nero's suicide without requiring a late date of composition (see Bauckham, *Climax*, 442–43). Possibly John historicizes the myth of Nero's return in the re-establishment of imperial power through the Flavian dynasty (Bauckham, *Climax*, 444–48).

[8] Cf. Bauckham, *Climax*, 343.

beast "was and is not and is to come" (17:8; cf. 17:11). The "was" may refer to the limited period of forty-two months during which the beast blasphemed God and conquered the saints and ruled over every tribe and people and tongue and nation (13:5–8). This corresponds to the period in which Israel is at war with Rome (11:2), the two witnesses proclaim judgment against Jerusalem (11:3), and the woman is in the wilderness (12:6, 14). It would be reasonable to associate the judgment on Jerusalem with Nero, who gave the order for Vespasian to invade Judea (*J.W.* 3.1.1–3 §1–8; cf. *Sib. Or.* 5:150–151). The antipathy of the beast towards the saints, however, may have more to do with the persecution of Christians in Rome. If the beast (and one of the heads) is Nero, at least in this incarnation, then it is also tempting to understand the "is to come" as an allusion to the widely held superstition of *Nero redivivus*. Nero was reported to have committed suicide in A.D. 68, but the rumor spread that he had not died but had fled to Parthia, from where he would lead a Parthian army against Rome.[9]

The beasts introduce a dimension to the conflict that was absent from the preceding chapters. The afflictions that come upon Israel are directly initiated by divine action – either the opening of the seals or the blowing of the trumpets by the angels. Now, however, Rome takes on a much more prominent role. The allegory of the dragon and the beasts marks the transition from the story about Israel to the story about Rome.

Judgment on Rome

The camera of John's prophetic imagination cuts abruptly from the second beast to a view of the Lamb on Mount Zion, accompanied by 144,000 who had "his name and his Father's name written on their foreheads" (14:1). The image of the Lamb standing on Mount Zion evokes

[9] See Bauckham, *Climax*, 423–31.

Psalm 2:6: "I have set my King on Zion, my holy hill." This king, we have seen, will break the nations "with a rod of iron and dash them in pieces like a potter's vessel" (Ps. 2:9). The verse has been used already in the letter to the church in Thyatira with reference to the believer "who conquers and who keeps my works until the end": "to him I will give authority over the nations, and he will rule them with a rod of iron, as when earthen pots are broken in pieces, even as I myself have received authority from my Father" (Rev. 2:26–27). This makes it clear that the 144,000 who stand with the Lamb on Mount Zion are those who have conquered, who have remained "faithful unto death" (Rev. 2:10–11). They have "conquered the beast and its image and the number of its name" (15:2). They have replicated Christ's faithfulness and therefore receive the same reward: they have been "redeemed from mankind as firstfruits for God and the Lamb" (Rev. 14:4) and will rule with him. They are also, we may assume, the "people of the saints of the Most High" in Daniel's vision, to whom is given "the kingdom and the dominion and the greatness of the kingdoms under the whole heaven" (Dan. 7:27). As will be seen later, they are that privileged group of believers who will participate in the "first resurrection."

What follows, through to the end of Revelation 18, is the enactment of judgment on Rome. Three angels announce the judgment on "Babylon the great" and on those who worship the beast (14:6–11). There is a further call for the "endurance of the saints" (14:12–13). Then "one like a son of man," seated on a "white cloud," initiates the reaping of the harvest of the earth. Two angels gather the grapes from the "vine of the earth" and throw them into the "great wine press of the wrath of God" which is "outside the city" (14:14–20). The imagery is drawn from Joel's vision of the judgment of those nations which earlier were used as instruments of divine judgment on Jerusalem:

> Let the nations stir themselves up and come up to the Valley of Jehoshaphat; for there I will sit to judge all the surrounding nations.

> Put in the sickle, for the harvest is ripe. Go in, tread, for the winepress is full. The vats overflow, for their evil is great. (Joel 3:12–13)

The seven bowls of judgment poured out on the earth bring to an end the "wrath of God" (15:1). Judgment comes upon those who "bore the mark of the beast and worshipped its image" (16:2). The turning of the sea and rivers to blood points to the reason for the judgment: "they have shed the blood of saints and prophets, and you have given them blood to drink" (16:6). This theme is central to the judgment: Babylon the great is depicted as a prostitute "drunk with the blood of the saints, the blood of the martyrs of Jesus" (17:6). It sounds the closing note: "in her was found the blood of prophets and of saints, and of all who have been slain on earth" (18:24). The kingdom of the beast is thrown into darkness (16:10). Foul spirits like frogs incite the kings of the world to assemble for battle "on the great day of God the Almighty" at a place "that in Hebrew is called Armageddon" (16:13–16). The river Euphrates is dried up to allow passage for the kings from the east, in preparation for the battle that is described in 19:19, when "the beast and the kings of the earth with their armies . . . make war against him who was sitting upon the horse and against his army" (cf. 17:12–14).[10]

In the end, as in the Old Testament visions of judgment on the city, this Babylon is left desolate: "a dwelling place for demons, a haunt for every unclean spirit, a haunt for every unclean bird, a haunt for every unclean and detestable beast" (18:2; cf. Jer. 50:39). This is not the end of the world. The kings of the earth will stand far off and weep over the great city; the merchants of the earth will lament because no one buys their goods anymore; shipmasters and sailors will cry out when they see the

---

[10] Since this looks like an alliance *with* rather than *against* Rome, this is probably not to be understood as an allusion to the Nero *redivivus* legend (against Caird, *Revelation*, 206).

smoke of her burning (18:9–19). This evocative image of those who have a vested interest in the prosperity of the city wailing over its downfall has been adapted to extraordinary effect from Ezekiel's prophecy of the fall of Tyre (Ezek. 27:27–36). There is no need to take the details literally; but the implication cannot be avoided that what John wants to convey is the political and commercial impact of this judgment. He may also want us to remember that the prince of Tyre, much like the little horn of Daniel's vision and Paul's man of lawlessness, had boasted, "I am a god, I sit in the seat of the gods" (Ezek. 28:2).

The Defeat of the Beast and the Binding of Satan

The fall of Babylon is celebrated in heaven: "he has judged the great prostitute who corrupted the earth with her immorality, and has avenged on her the blood of his servants" (19:2); and there is a reiteration of the proclamation that "the Lord our God the Almighty reigns" (19:6; cf. 11:15; 12:10–12). Added to this, however, is a new announcement about the marriage of the Lamb (19:7–9).

The bride has been clothed with "fine linen, bright and pure," which is interpreted as the "righteous deeds of the saints" (19:8). These saints are presumably not the universal church but the 144,000 who have been "redeemed from mankind as firstfruits for God and the Lamb" (14:4). Their "righteous deeds" consist essentially in the fact that they kept themselves pure (14:4–5) and remained faithful to the point of death, thus conquering "the beast and its image and the number of its name" (15:2; cf. 12:11). As we have seen already, it is through the faithfulness of their testimony that the "salvation and the power and the kingdom of our God and the authority of his Christ have come" (12:10; cf. 11:15). So although the bride is the church as a whole (or at least the whole church at the moment of victory over the beast), what has made the bride "ready" and the marriage possible is specifically the faithful endurance of those believers who faced persecution and death.

The Word of God on a White Horse

The great harlot has been defeated, but there still remains the beast, which had gathered an alliance of the "kings of the whole world" (16:14). The immediate conflict in which these kings are engaged is a "battle on the great day of God the Almighty" at Armageddon (16:14, 16). Since the beast and the ten kings are clearly implicated in the fall of Babylon (17:16–17) and their assembling at Armageddon is followed by the destruction of the city, it is likely that this is a "battle" (literal or otherwise) against Rome rather than against God, whatever the precise significance of the name Armageddon. But although the alliance appears to have been instrumental in the overthrow of the harlot, more fundamentally it stands in opposition to God. In the end, they will "make war on the Lamb" and be defeated by him, "for he is Lord of lords and King of kings, and those with him are called and chosen and faithful" (17:14).

This is the background for the appearance (after the overthrow of Babylon/Rome) of the one who is called "Faithful," "Word of God," and "King of kings and Lord of lords" (19:11–16). A number of important themes converge in this description of Christ.

First, there is the motif of victory over death. The name "Faithful" implies this; and the robe he wears is "dipped in blood." He is also said to have a "name written that no one knows but himself," which is reminiscent of the 144,000, who have the name of the Lamb written on their foreheads, and who sing a new song which no one else can learn (14:3; cf. 2:17). Moreover, the warrior Christ on the white horse is accompanied by the "armies of heaven, arrayed in fine linen, white and pure (*bussinon leukon katharon*)," also mounted on white horses. The description of the clothing recalls the "fine linen, bright and pure" (*bussinon lampron katharon*) in which the Bride is dressed, suggesting that these armies are the saints who have remained faithful and have overcome death.

Secondly, there is again reference to Psalm 2, which

combines the ideas of the universal rule of God's anointed and the execution of God's wrath. This restates the conviction that the Son of Man will acquire sovereignty over the nations and that those powers that have opposed the saints will be judged.

Thirdly, the rule of Christ is expressed in violent and militaristic terms: he "makes war," he will "strike down the nations," he will rule them "with a rod of iron," he will "tread the wine press of the fury of the wrath of God the Almighty." But this terminology must be qualified in two respects. On the one hand, many of these expressions are Old Testament allusions, whose purpose is to draw into the vision the larger argument of the prophetic text. On the other, this rule is implemented by means of the word of God. The "sharp sword" with which he will "strike down the nations" is not held in his hand but issues from his mouth (cf. Isa. 11:4; Joel 2:11; 2 Thess. 2:8; Heb. 4:12).[11] The victory envisaged is that of truth, specifically the truth of the gospel, over the ideological and religious forces that opposed the church.

It is the Word of God, then, the proclamation of the good news about Jesus Christ, which defeats the beast in battle (19:17–21). The "beast and the kings of the earth" are gathered to make war against the "King of kings and Lord of lords" and the army of those who have also overcome death (19:19).[12] But the beast is captured and with the false prophet is thrown alive into the "lake of fire that burns with sulfur" – just as the fourth beast "was killed, and its body destroyed and given over to be burned with fire" in Daniel 7:11. The rest are slain by the sword that issues from the mouth of Christ.

Satan is Bound for a Thousand Years

Earlier Satan had been cast down to earth. Having been

---

[11] Arguably 2 Thess. 2:8 belongs to the same prophetic expectation.
[12] The feast of birds in Rev. 19:17–18 comes from Ezek. 39:17–20.

prevented from pursuing the woman, he "went off to make war on the rest of her offspring" (12:17). Now, however, without much ado, he is thrown into the pit and bound there for a period of a thousand years, "so that he might not deceive the nations any longer, until the thousand years were ended" (20:3). The force which had first opposed righteous Israel (12:1–7) and then, through the activity of the beast, had provoked persecution of the saints and opposition to the Lamb, has been removed from the world. With this comes the first resurrection: those who had been "beheaded for the testimony of Jesus and for the word of God" and who had not worshipped the beast came to life and "reigned with Christ for a thousand years." John's vision follows the pattern of Daniel 7: he sees the thrones that Daniel describes in verse 9; then judgment is given to the martyrs just as it is given in Daniel 7:22 to the saints of the Most High against whom the horn on the head of the fourth beast made war.[13]

This is the culmination of an argument – perhaps the main argument of the book – that has appeared at a number of points in John's vision: that those who suffer and die on account of their faith in Christ during the coming period of persecution will be part of the first resurrection and will reign with Christ for a thousand years. We saw earlier that each of the seven letters concludes with a promise to the one who conquers, couched in terms that anticipate the later development of the theme. For example, he "will not be hurt by the second death" (2:11), which is exactly the promise that is made to those who will share in the first resurrection: "Over such the second death has no power, but they will be priests of God and of Christ, and they will reign with him for a thousand years" (20:6). The participation of the martyr in the messianic reign is expressed in the most decisive terms: he will be given "authority over the nations, and he will

[13] The reasons for identifying those seated on the thrones with the souls of the martyrs are given by Aune (*Revelation*, 1084–85).

rule them with a rod of iron, as when earthen pots are broken in pieces" (2:26–27; cf. 12:5; 19:15). They are the 144,000 redeemed first from Israel, then from the world, who are sealed against the destructive power of the wrath of God. They have "conquered the beast and its image and the number of its name" (15:2). They are those who have suffered for the sake of the kingdom of God – for the sake of the acknowledgement, in the heavens, in the earth, and under the earth, that it is Christ and not the beast who is sovereign over all things. They are those who were willing to share in the sufferings of the Christ in order to share in his resurrection. They are the "wise" who must live through the affliction of the time of the end, but who will be "refined, purified, and made white" (Dan. 11:35). They are the oppressed saints of the Most High who appeared to Daniel in a vision of the night as "one like a son of man." They are those who have suffered for the sake of the kingdom of God – the acknowledgement in the world that it is Christ and not the beast who is sovereign over all things.

John's notion of a "first resurrection" encapsulates more clearly than anything else in the New Testament the central contention of this study – that *for the most part* the eschatological narrative is driving towards a goal not at the end of history but at the turning of the ages. For the most part, but not entirely. Remarkably, John is able to see beyond the horizons of New Testament history and has more to disclose.

Ten

The Church in the Age that Has Come

Let us imagine first-century Judaism as a ship – a splendid but badly run ship in which the officers and crew mistreat the passengers and squabble and fight over who should have control of the vessel. Blinded by their obsessions and jealousies, no one on the bridge notices that the ship is drifting towards a ferocious eschatological storm. When one or two men raise the alarm, they are seized as trouble-makers, brutally beaten, and thrown overboard. As the winds tear at the rigging and waves wash across the deck, a few brave souls decide to heed the warnings; they lower a lifeboat and take their chances on the rough seas. To the passengers and crew who stay on board this seems a reckless and disloyal move – and at times those clinging desperately to each other in the belly of the small boat, as it pitches and rolls, wonder if they have made the right choice. Some are swept overboard, some die from exposure and hunger. They cry out to the dark heavens, praying that the storm would cease. But they do not give up hope; they believe they have done the right thing. Then from a distance they watch in horror as the ship strikes rocks and sinks with massive loss of life – they are appalled, but they also feel vindicated. Eventually the wind drops, the waves subside. The lifeboat runs ashore on a sandy beach. They have come to the end of the end; they have survived. This is the beginning of a new age.

This is an imperfect parable. It does not tell us why

things on board the ship of Judaism had deteriorated to such a state; it does not tell us enough about why some took the risk of abandoning the security of the ship, where their hope came from, or how they loved one another. It fails to mention the fact that, when eventually they staggered ashore, there were strangers among them, people whose names had not been on the original passenger list – rescued perhaps from other ships caught in the storm. It tells us nothing about the fate of those who died. Had hope failed them? Perhaps we should have mentioned the ghostly figure, stained with the pallor of his drowning, who approached the lifeboat, walking across the troubled surface of the sea.

But the story may help to fix in our minds the thought that the central action of New Testament eschatology has not all been reserved for a grand finale at the end of *our* world. This was not *our* storm, it was not *our* ship; we are merely the descendants of those who survived. Why should not the authors of the New Testament tell a story about *their* future, for the sake of the men and women known to them who faced ostracism, reviling, beatings, the confiscation of their property, the heavy weight of official contempt for their beliefs, imprisonment, and possibly death? Is it not a matter of immense historical – and indeed spiritual – hubris to suppose that when they evoked this vivid drama of judgment given in favor of the Son of Man, it was not of immediate and concrete relevance to the communities of Christ's followers in Judea or Macedonia or Achaia?

What they saw, in effect, was not an end to history but a transition, a redefinition, a restructuring, a long and tumultuous process stretching out ahead of them: the emergence of a movement of renewal within Israel; confrontation with the power structures of Judaism; the announcement of these things in the pagan world; the painstaking development of communities of believers in which distinctions of gender, class, and race were nullified (in principle if not always in practice); the destruction – in a way the *self*-destruction – of Israel; and the confrontation with, and eventual "victory" over, the power structures of paganism and the imperial cult, the lawlessness that opposed the living God. What would drive and sustain this process was the faithfulness of the "elect." What this faithfulness entailed, however, was the suffering, death, resurrection, and public vindication of the Son of Man – pre-eminently as the individual figure of Jesus, the "firstfruits," the "head of the body," the "founder of their salvation," but also in the form of the saints of the Most High who suffered with him and in him.

At the back of this historical process is a typological narrative, told in Daniel, about Israel in crisis. The nation is still languishing under the consequences of the judgment that saw Jerusalem made desolate and the people deported to Babylon. Although the city has been rebuilt, these are troubled times; transgression has not been finished; they still await an everlasting righteousness and peace with God (cf. Dan. 9:24). As matters come to a climax, a desecrating pagan presence intrudes right to the heart of the nation's worship, inviting connivance and compromise from some, inciting faithful and determined resistance from others. Those who remain loyal to the God of their fathers inevitably suffer at the hands of their enemies, but they persist stubbornly in their belief that they will not be abandoned, that the sanctuary will not be left desolate for ever, that sooner or later God will intervene to rescue and restore – not because of Israel's righteousness, far from it, but because of his mercy. This critical belief is captured in a powerful vision of a judgment scene in which the beast that oppresses Israel is destroyed; sovereignty is taken from the little horn, the epitome of hostility to God embodied in some real political figure or régime; and the kingdom is given to a glorious human figure, the representation of those who suffered for the sake of the living God but who now "shine like the brightness of the sky above" (Dan. 12:3). It is an everlasting kingdom that will embrace all nations. Never again will the people of the Most High be subjugated and terrorized by a godless and satanic power. This is the victory that will bring Israel's long exile to an end. This is the heart of salvation.

The Heart of Salvation

We should remind ourselves that salvation in the Old Testament is a very worldly notion. It denotes God's intervention to rescue the people from a difficult or dangerous situation and restore them to wholeness: salvation is health, safety, peace, prosperity, military victory, deliverance; it is the continuing well-being of the people. Only in extreme instances does salvation require rescue beyond death in the form of resurrection, and then this is bound up with the fate of the nation.

The eschatological crisis that marked the transition between the old Israel and the new brought salvation as resurrection to the fore because the continuation of the community required faithfulness and steadfastness to the point of death. But we should not lose sight of the fact that salvation is the response of God to a particular set of concrete circumstances. So in the New Testament salvation must be interpreted, in the first place, in relation to the eschatological watershed of the coming of the kingdom of God (the destruction of Jerusalem, the defeat of Roman imperial power, the emergence of the church, the confession of Israel's Messiah as Lord among the nations) and the experience of God through the Spirit in the context of the "new covenant" community. The apocalyptic narrative that we have reconstructed suggests that this idea of "salvation," which is so critical for our understanding of what it means to be "church," must be explicated in three distinct ways. Any account of *personal* salvation should be developed from this eschatological starting point.

First, Israel needed to be saved – from the lingering consequences of the exile, from its subjection to a foreign power, from the daily brutalities of oppression, from injustice and unrighteousness in its midst, from the prospect of war and the imminent destruction of its system of worship, its beloved city, its whole way of life. This is what Joseph was promised by the angel: the son to be born to Mary would "save *his people* from their sins" (Matt. 1:21; cf. Luke 1:68–75).

Jesus' death at the hands of the Gentiles (Matt. 20:19; Luke 18:32) is, then, a death for Israel or in the place of the nation, a ransom for many in Israel (cf. Matt. 20:28; Mark 10:45). As the Son of Man figure he pre-empts the suffering of the "saints" who are "in him" or who belong to him; he takes upon himself the destructive force of the wrath of God against Israel and overcomes it. His words in Gethsemane, "let this cup pass from me" (Matt. 26:39), are a reference to the Old Testament cup of divine judgment on the people (cf. Ps. 75:8; Isa. 51:17, 22; Jer. 49:12; Lam. 2:13 LXX, cf. 4:21; Ezek. 23:31–34; Hab. 2:16). Understood from within the eschatological narrative this is not a universal judgment for a universal state of sinfulness that he faces but judgment for the particular sin of Israel's persistent rebellion against God. Crucifixion represented most graphically Rome's punishment of a rebellious nation. Peter is conscious of the historical urgency motivating the preaching of the gospel when he exhorts the crowds on the day of Pentecost, "save yourselves from this crooked generation" (Acts 2:40). It is in this context of catastrophic judgment on Israel that he asserts, "And it shall come to pass that everyone who calls upon the name of the Lord shall be saved" (Acts 2:21).

Salvation in this respect consisted in the survival and re-emergence of the people of God – those who could legitimately claim to have inherited the blessing and the calling of Abraham. The community of Jesus' disciples was not crushed when the house of Israel collapsed; it was not beaten into apostasy or irrelevance by pagan and imperial persecution.

Secondly, the manner of Israel's salvation opened up a new possibility – the inclusion of Gentiles in the people of God. Because the pagan world in its idolatry and unrighteousness, and especially in its antipathy towards the God of Abraham, Isaac, and Jacob, was also under judgment, salvation for the Gentiles meant salvation from the wrath of God and from the destruction of the dominant culture of the ancient world. More positively, it meant that those who until that point had been "alienated from the commonwealth of Israel and strangers to the covenants of promise, having no hope and without God in the world" (Eph. 2:12), now had access to this community. This was *Paul's* "gospel." It was promised through the prophets (Rom. 1:2); it concerned the Son of God, descended from David, who died and was raised from the dead (1:3–4); but the reason for proclaiming it was "to bring about the obedience of faith for the sake of his name *among all the nations*" (1:5). The object of Paul's work "in the priestly service of the gospel of God" was that the Gentiles should be an acceptable offering to God, "sanctified by the Holy Spirit" (Rom. 15:16).[1] So too in Galatians: the gospel that he preached was precisely that the nations would be justified by faith and would become offspring of Abraham, heirs according to promise (3:8, 14, 29).

His important statement in Ephesians 2:8–9 about salvation by grace through faith and "not a result of works" belongs to a larger argument about the reconciliation of Gentiles to God and their incorporation into a "holy temple in the Lord," which is the "dwelling place for God by the Spirit" (2:21–22). The "good news" for the Gentiles was not that they could be individually reconciled to God by inviting Jesus into their hearts, or be assured of life in heaven when they died. It was the announcement that the dividing wall of the law, which had kept them from sharing in the life and privileges (and responsibilities) of the people of God, had been torn down so that Jews and Gentiles could become *one body* (Eph. 2:14–16). To be "saved" was to become *part of a redeemed community*, a

[1] For this sense of *hē prosphora tōn ethnōn* see Moo, *Romans*, 890, and the majority of commentators.

community not under the wrath of God, a new humanity, in which the Spirit of God was active, which experienced the life of the age that comes after the eschatological crisis (cf. Acts 13:46–48), which was not under the power of Satan (cf. Acts 26:18). To be justified was to be recognized as having the right relationship with God that Israel had lacked (cf. Dan. 9:7, 18), as being no longer in the wrong, as having the righteousness that had been reckoned to Abraham because he had trusted in God, and therefore as having a legitimate and inalienable interest in the future of the people of God (cf. Rom. 9:8). Jesus' death provided for Israel's righteousness; Gentiles subsequently became participants in that.

Thirdly, for those who suffered from the hostility of the pagan world – and indeed from the enemy within Israel – salvation is formulated as an emulation of Christ's victory over evil and death. In this respect, people hoped to *escape from* the ordeal that they had to endure for the sake of the gospel; they hoped to be raised from the dead, to bear the image of the man of heaven, to be taken up into the air, to be with the Lord, to be seated with him at the right hand of the Father, to reign with him during the coming age. This was an appropriate hope for "heaven" – but in an important respect it was exceptional, the means by which the larger hope of the restoration of the people of God was secured.

All Israel will be saved?

There is one outstanding question that we need to address. Paul shared Jesus' conviction that Israel as a nation was under judgment, that time was running out, and that unless there was some extraordinary national change of heart, this judgment would be realized in devastating form in the not too distant future. Jesus on the whole appears to have been highly pessimistic about the likelihood of national Israel escaping catastrophe, but we find in Paul the remarkable statement, at the climax to his lengthy discussion of the fate of his people, that "all Israel will be saved" (Rom. 11:26). What did he mean by this?

He has argued at a number of points in Romans 9 – 11 that a division has come about in Israel: "not all who are descended from Israel belong to Israel" (Rom. 9:6); it is the children of the promise, not the children of the flesh, who are "counted as offspring" of Abraham (9:8); only a remnant of Israel will be saved, chosen by grace (9:27; 11:5); the elect obtained what it sought, but "the rest were hardened" (11:7); branches have been broken off the olive tree (11:17–24).[2] When he repeats the point, therefore, immediately following the parable of the olive tree, that "a partial hardening has come upon Israel" and then states that "*all* Israel will be saved," he can only mean that this division within the nation will be healed. The branches that were broken off because of their "unbelief" will be grafted back in; they will be reconnected to the root because they have become "children of the promise." This will come about as a consequence of the inclusion of Gentiles among the descendants of Abraham, which will make Israel jealous (11:11, 14), but "all Israel" here is still only Israel – Paul is certainly not talking about the church, and the inclusion of Gentiles is, as far as this argument is concerned, a secondary matter.[3]

We are having to cut a rather long story short here, but I would suggest that best sense is made of this passage if we read Romans 11:25 as something of a parenthesis: Paul interrupts his argument in order to explain the "mystery" at the heart of this analogy, that it has become possible for Gentiles to be grafted *contrary to nature* (11:24) into a cultivated olive tree. The salvation of "all Israel," then, is not made directly dependent upon the inclusion of the full number of Gentiles, which is difficult to explain, but is a

---

[2] Note Jer. 11:16 LXX: Israel was called a "fair olive tree," but "at the sound of its being cut (*peritomēs autēs*) a fire was kindled against it; great is the affliction upon you; its branches have become useless."

[3] Cf. Moo: "all Israel" has a corporate sense, denoting the nation at that moment in time (*Romans*, 722–23; cf. Witherington, *Jesus, Paul*, 122–23).

prospect that emerges quite naturally from the metaphor: for the lopped branches to be restored to the tree so that it becomes *whole* again would constitute the salvation of *all* Israel. If this is the case, then the statement "all Israel will be saved" inherits the conditionality of the olive tree metaphor. Israel will be restored to wholeness when the branches are re-engrafted – because "God has the power to graft them in again." But this is by no means a foregone conclusion: it will happen only "if they do not continue in their unbelief" (11:23).

What has happened to the wrath of God in this process? Paul jumps from the partial hardening of Israel to the salvation of all Israel, but these were "vessels of wrath prepared for destruction" (9:22). So the question arises: Is Israel saved before this destruction (thus escaping it) or after it? The answer is found in the argument constructed from the Scriptures in Romans 11:26–27, which makes two straightforward claims: first, that the deliverer will come from Zion and eradicate "ungodliness" from Israel (11:26); secondly, that this removal of Israel's sins will provide the basis for a new covenant (11:27). The key text is the Septuagint translation of Isaiah 59:20–21 ("the deliverer shall come for the sake of Zion, and shall turn away ungodliness from Jacob; and this shall be my covenant with them, said the Lord"), which Paul has altered at a crucial point: the deliverer will come not "for the sake of" Zion (*eneken Ziōn*) but "from" Zion. To this he has appended a clause from Isaiah 27:9 LXX: "when I shall take away his sin."

The reasons for the modification are not hard to find. Psalm 13 LXX (cf. Ps. 52 LXX), from which Paul has already quoted in support of his argument that all people are under the power of sin, Jews and Gentiles alike (Rom. 3:9–12), is very close thematically to Isaiah 59:9–20: God sees the iniquity that is in the world; there will be a great terror; he will act on behalf of the righteous; and in verse 7 the psalmist asks, "Who will bring *from* Zion the salvation of Israel?" Similar statements are found in Psalms 20:2; 50:2; 110:2.

The general principle again applies: we need to read not only the quotation but also the context from which it was taken. In the background is the story in Isaiah of a reprobate nation, separated from God by its iniquities (Isa. 59:2), in which "Justice is turned back, and righteousness stands afar off" (59:14). The Lord sees that there is no one to intervene and arms himself for battle against his adversaries. People from east and west will come to fear the name of the Lord, for "the wrath will come from the LORD as a violent river with fury" (Isa. 59:19 LXX). A redeemer will come (cf. Isa. 49:7, 25–26; 52:9; 54:5) and remove ungodliness from Jacob; God will make a new covenant with Israel mediated through one who is given the Spirit (59:21; cf. 54:10; 55:3); Jerusalem will become a light to the peoples of the earth; the scattered children of Israel will be gathered together; and the nations will come in submission, bringing gifts (59:20 – 60:22). For, the Lord says, "in my wrath I struck you, but in my favor I have had mercy on you" (60:10; cf. Rom. 11:30–32).

In Paul's encapsulation of this complex narrative, stubborn, unrighteous Israel is destined for destruction – God has put up with their sin for some time, but he will not do so forever. Nothing will happen until enough Gentiles have been grafted on to the decimated stem of the olive tree – enough, presumably, to secure its survival, corresponding to Jesus' statement that the "gospel of the kingdom will be proclaimed throughout the whole world" before the end comes (Matt. 24:14; cf. Mark 13:10). Then God will come and deliver Israel from its sins, destroy his enemies, banish ungodliness from Zion, and establish a new covenant with the redeemed people that will make them a light to the whole world (cf. Isa. 60:1–5). Whatever exactly is meant by "all Israel," it is Israel *after* God has struck it in his wrath and ungodliness has been banished.

There is little thought here of the part played by a foreign power in the execution of the wrath of God against Israel. But ungodliness (*asebeia*) is next to lawlessness (*anomia*), and although Paul's argument here is quite different from that of 2 Thessalonians 2:3–12, it may be possible to superimpose the one scenario upon the other. The two word groups are often used in the Greek Old Testament as virtual synonyms (e.g., Isa. 13:11; Jer. 2:29; Ezek. 22:11); Isaiah 27:9 LXX, which Paul cites in Romans 11:27, tells how the "lawlessness (*anomia*) of Jacob will be taken away." The Daniel narrative demonstrates the potential for complicity between a lawlessness that intrudes from outside and unfaithfulness on the part of Israel: the forces of Antiochus will defile the holy place, remove the perpetual sacrifice, and offer in its place an abomination of desolation. They will "defile a covenant among a hard people" (Dan. 11:31–32 LXX). The hardening of Israel, which is the effect of God giving them a "spirit of stupor" (Rom. 11:7–8), is then the counterpart to the "strong delusion" that God sends in 2 Thessalonians 2:11.

This superimposition of the two narratives may also have a bearing on how we understand the statement that "all Israel will be saved" (*pas Israēl sōthēsetai*). It may correspond to statements about the salvation of Israel in Daniel 12:1. The Greek texts diverge somewhat, but the readings are suggestive: "in that day all the people shall be lifted up (*hupsōthēsetai pas ho laos*), whoever is found registered in the book" (LXX); "in that time your people shall be saved (*sōthēsetai ho laos sou*), everyone found written in the book" (Theod.). The salvation of Israel when the deliverer comes from Zion is the salvation of Israel following the great affliction provoked by the Antiochus figure. As in Daniel the rescue of the people is accompanied by a resurrection of many from the dead, so the salvation that Paul envisages for Israel is equivalent to "life from the dead" (Rom. 11:15).

The question, therefore, was whether at the coming of the Son of Man, at the point when those in Christ would be vindicated in the world, this community would in some way include Israel as a national entity. If the Jews did not persist in their unbelief following divine judgment, then the descendants of Abraham according to the promise would retain an essentially Jewish identity. If not, the church would become in effect a Gentile institution, which, of course, is what happened.

After the fire

Salvation is for the sake of what comes after. We can illustrate this rather neatly from 1 Corinthians 3:10–15, where Paul speaks of a "day" that will disclose the quality of the work done by the apostles and others as they have built upon the foundation of Jesus Christ. The work will be tested by fire: certain types of material will survive the fire, other types will be burned up. We would normally understand this as a reference to the final judgment.[4] Our primary interest would be in the fate of the worker: What sort of reward will be gained? What loss will be suffered in the event of the building being destroyed? What does it mean to be saved "only as through fire"? The argument we have pursued in this book, however, suggests a rather different reading. The fire is the real and distressing eschatological crisis that Paul believed the churches (not least the church at Corinth) faced in the coming years. Only those communities built on the foundation of Jesus Christ – the Son of Man who suffered and overcame – and constructed of durable, non-flammable materials would survive persecution and whatever forms of social and political turmoil were likely to attend the "end of the ages" (1 Cor. 10:11). Verses 16–17 may add to this a further thought: those forces that destroy the "temple of God" in Corinth, like the forces that would destroy the temple of God in Jerusalem, will themselves be destroyed. If the destruction of the temple corresponds to, and is an analogy for, the testing of what is built on the foundation of Christ, we have a natural reiteration of a familiar eschatological pattern: a day of testing or judgment that begins with the household of God (cf. 2 Pet. 4:17), followed by judgment upon the enemies of God's people.

---

[4] Cf. Thiselton, *First Corinthians*, 312.

So the teaching of the apostles had this objective: to ensure that the church was strong enough to withstand the coming onslaught, to stand firm against opposition and temptation, and not be put to shame when eventually those who oppose it are defeated and Christ is publicly vindicated in the world.

And now we find ourselves in the aftermath of the eschatological crisis, in the age that has come. The satanic power that posed such a great threat to the church in the early centuries has been overcome through the proclamation of the gospel and the faithfulness of believers and is now bound in the abyss. Evil has not been finally eradicated, death remains an inescapable fact of life, opposition to the gospel has not been finally ended; but Christ is confessed as Lord throughout the world, above all powers in heaven, on earth and under the earth, and it will be a "thousand years" before the church again faces that sort of threat to its existence (Rev. 20:7–9). The grace of God and the faithfulness of his saints has got us to the point where we can start being his people in the world, demonstrating throughout the "coming ages" the reality of the "immeasurable riches of his grace in kindness toward us in Christ Jesus," doing the "good works" for which we were created (Eph. 2:7, 10). Christ died so that there might be a viable people of God in the world, a temple of the Holy Spirit, a priesthood to mediate between humanity and the living God, a holy nation.

The thesis that we have worked out in this book – if it survives the fire of critical judgment – must have significant implications for the life, work and worship of the church that cannot be explored here. We will need to think carefully about how we define the significance of Jesus for the church today. If we are going to talk about the divinity of Christ, this apocalyptic story of the Son of Man – which in many respects is the argument that connects the prophet from Nazareth with the Christ who is worshipped – must somehow be taken into account, celebrated, retold – not suppressed in the interests of a rationalized or simplified Christology. We will need to re-evaluate our understanding of "personal salvation" in the light of an eschatological narrative that is much more clearly linked to place and time than our highly individualistic and existentialist modern notions of what it means to be saved. We will probably need to develop a mode of spiritual life that is much broader in its scope, much more earthy in its orientation, much more imaginative and resourceful in its dealings with the world. We will certainly want to recover a sense of what it means for us to have inherited the promise to Abraham and the calling to be present in the world for the sake of God – because so much was suffered so that we might be the renewed, Spirit-inspired people of God in the world, a blessing to all the families of the earth. How are we to understand mission if in an important sense salvation as deliverance from the wrath of God and the resurrection of some to be with the Lord is behind us, while ahead, beyond a final judgment, lies not the ethereal landscape of heaven but a new creation, *new heavens and a new earth* – in which the dwelling of God is with humankind, in which there is no more suffering and death, from which injustice and depravity have been abolished, where human society is healed? To many readers it will appear that the argument of this book has removed the incentive for mission. On the contrary, I think it should make us all the more urgently aware of our calling to be a people for God's purposes in the world.

Final Judgment

We need to wind things up. The New Testament is for the most part not interested in a final judgment in any absolute sense. Judgment is a matter of enormous importance but it is confined within the foreseeable future: judgment on Israel, judgment on the immediate enemies of the people of God, judgment on the idolatrous pagan world. The "Day of the Lord" is never the end of the world – it is always a day of reckoning, a day of rescue, and a day of renewal, *in the midst of history*. Of course, these distinctions cannot be made too sharply. There is an inevitable bleeding of language, an overflow of imagery, between the different contexts;[5] and there is bound to be a sense in which prophecies of the imminent overturning of the current religious and political order provide the outline and colors for any ultimate vision of judgment – just as the metaphor of new creation is used both to make sense of the renewal of Israel and to embody a more fundamental and universal hope that sin and death will not have the final say. In this sense, because of the Spirit of God and the precedent that Scripture itself sets, we cannot say that New Testament eschatology is a closed book.

We are bound to ask, at this point, whether this might not also be true of the image of the Son of Man coming on the clouds of heaven – not least because this represents for many believers a hope too deeply ingrained, too deeply traditional, to be easily consigned to the past. Even if originally this prophetic vision had to do with the victory of Christ and those in him over the massive political-religious opposition of Roman imperialism, can it not still embody for the church today the hope we have that our trust in God, the Father of our Lord Jesus Christ, will be vindicated?

The question will be whether it really says what we want to say about the future. There is no allusion to the coming of the Son of Man as such in John's description of the final defeat of Satan and death, the judgment of all the dead, and the appearance of a new heaven and a new earth with the new Jerusalem at its center. Conversely, Daniel's vision of the deliverance of Israel entails an ending to "the shattering of the power of the holy people" (Dan. 12:7) but not the transformation of creation. The "coming soon" of Revelation 22:7, which evokes the *parousia* motif, relates to events *before* the thousand years, within the horizon of John's readers, not to the final renewal of creation. This is

---

[5] 2 Pet. 3:10–13 is the best example of this.

not accidental. The vision of the Son of Man has to do fundamentally with judgment upon the pagan oppressor and the transfer of the kingdom to those who, despite their suffering, remain faithful to the God of Israel. The New Testament has applied this vision to Jesus and to those who participate in his sufferings: the kingdom is God's reign in the coming ages, realized through the suffering and vindication of his saints, a reign of self-giving obedience and love. It remains a valid paradigm through this period because evil and death have not been finally defeated, because other kingdoms vie for sovereignty, because the temptation to find a broader, easier path is ever-present. This is what it means to confess as Lord over our lives the one who supremely gave himself for others – and perhaps, where the same willingness to suffer for the sake of Christ is asked of the church, we may be right to invoke the hope that God will vindicate and deliver. But at the point when evil and death are finally eradicated, when all things are put in subjection, this kingdom of the Christ becomes unnecessary and can be handed back to God the Father (1 Cor. 15:24, 28). So, at the very end, the vision of the Son of Man coming on the clouds of heaven in fact ceases to be relevant.

Looking beyond the foreseeable future, beyond the destruction of the beast and the drastic curtailment of satanic activity, John describes a period of a thousand years, at the end of which Satan, having been released from the abyss, will again deceive the nations and gather them for battle against the "camp of the saints and the beloved city" (Rev. 20:7–9). These nations are said to be "Gog and Magog" (20:8). Ezekiel was instructed to prophesy against "Gog, of the land of Magog" (Ezek. 38:2). The significance of this prophecy for John's vision is that in "the latter years" Gog would lead an army from the north against "the land that is restored from war, the land whose people were gathered from many peoples upon the mountains of Israel." He would "devise an evil scheme" and attack a prosperous and peaceful nation (38:10–12); but God would "enter into judgment with him," and Gog would be destroyed by "torrential rains and hailstones, fire and sulfur" (38:22; cf. Rev. 20:9). This judgment is presented as perhaps a final vindication of God before the nations: "So I will show my greatness and my holiness and make myself known in the eyes of many nations. Then they will know that I am the LORD" (Ezek. 38:23). In John's vision of this last conflict the nations are consumed by fire from heaven and the devil is thrown into the lake of fire and sulfur, where the beast and the false prophet are, to be "tormented day and night forever and ever" (Rev. 20:10; cf. Matt. 25:41).

The disappearance of earth and heaven at this point is swift and painless. They simply flee away from the presence of the one seated upon the great white throne. There is a finality to this annihilation that is missing from other visions of cosmic destruction in the Bible, which for all their violence and horror retain a sense of a world that continues beyond the day of God's wrath.[6] All the dead, the greatest and the least, are assembled before the throne and a number of books are opened, including the book of life. John does not consider the possibility that some might be alive at that time, in contrast to the *parousia* visions, which take very seriously the impact of this event on the living. He is gazing far beyond the horizons of the New Testament's outlook on the future.

The dead have been held in storage, so to speak, by Death and Hades until this point and are now given up; some are given up by the sea (Rev. 20:13). They are then "judged by what was written in the books, according to what they had done." Death and Hades – the last enemy – are thrown into the lake of fire, which is the second death;

---

[6] Aune draws a comparison with texts such as Judg. 5:4–5; Pss. 18:7–15; 68:7–8; Micah 1:3–4, and others (*Revelation*, 1101), but the imagery and mood of these texts is really quite different; Zephaniah speaks of the fire of God's wrath that will consume the earth (1:18; cf. Aune, *Revelation*, 1117), but the effect is not total destruction but desolation (2:5–7).

anyone whose name is not found written in the book of life is also thrown into the lake of fire (20:12–15; cf. 21:27). There appear to be two conflicting criteria of judgment here. On the one hand, people are judged according to what they have done: "the cowardly, the faithless, the detestable . . . murderers, the sexually immoral, sorcerers, idolaters, and all liars" will be consigned to the second death (21:8; cf. 21:27). On the other, we are told that anyone whose name is not found in the book of life will be thrown into the lake of fire – seemingly with no consideration given to whatever good or evil he or she may have done.

The "book of life" contains the names of those who will live. Not to be listed in the book of life, or to have one's name expunged from it, means death. In an attempt to atone for Israel's sin of worshipping the golden calf, Moses says falteringly to God: "if you will forgive their sin – but if not, please blot me out of your book that you have written" (Exod. 32:32). The Lord's answer is that it is those who have sinned whose names will be removed from the book, the outcome being that a plague is sent upon the people because they made the calf – *life* is taken from them (32:35).[7] The image is found in Revelation 3:5: those who overcome among the believers in Sardis will not have their names blotted from the book of life. This is the "book of life of the Lamb that was slain"; the names recorded in it were written "before the foundation of the world" (Rev. 13:8; cf. 17:8).[8] Whether the singular book of life confirms or supersedes the judgment that is reached on the basis of what a person has done is difficult to say. But we cannot diminish the moral and spiritual implications of this scene. There is no place for wickedness in the new creation. This is surely the point of the two statements about the wicked who shall be destroyed in the "lake that burns with fire and sulfur" (Rev. 21:8) or shut outside the gates of the city, denied access to the tree of life (22:14–15).

---

[7] Cf. Ps. 69:28; Isa. 4:3; and Aune, *Revelation*, 224.
[8] Also Luke 10:20; Phil. 4:3.

The lake of fire that burns with sulfur poses a problem in more ways than one. The motif is not paralleled exactly in the Old Testament or Jewish literature.[9] Sulfur is closely associated with the destruction and contamination of Sodom and Gomorrah and similar acts of divine judgment (Gen. 19:24; Deut. 29:23; 3 Macc. 2:5). Psalm 11:6 says that "fire and sulfur . . . will be the portion of the wicked." Isaiah describes a fire that has been prepared for the king of Assyria that is kindled with sulfur (Isa. 30:33). When Edom is judged in a "year of recompense for the cause of Zion," its streams are turned into pitch and its soil into sulfur, and its land becomes burning pitch (Isa. 34:9). We then have a statement that is echoed at two points in Revelation that are crucial for the debate about eternal punishment: "Night and day it shall not be quenched; its smoke shall go up for ever" (34:10). Those who worship the beast and its image are "tormented with fire and sulfur," "the smoke of their torment goes up forever and ever," and they "have no rest, day or night" (Rev. 14:10–11); and the devil, the beast, and the false prophet are tormented "day and night forever and ever" (Rev. 20:10). The lake may be the antitype of the "sea of glass" that is before the throne of God in John's first vision of heaven (Rev. 4:6), but of greater significance is the "stream of fire" that issues from the throne of God in Daniel's vision of judgment against the four beasts (Dan. 7:10).

I would suggest, from this, that John has used the image of the lake of fire in two distinct ways. It has been constructed, in the first place, from a number of Old Testament texts that describe devastating and lasting judgment upon the enemies of God's people – Assyria, Edom, Greece – and which must be understood in historical terms. It is then applied to the envisaged judgment upon Rome, in which the three "mythical" figures (the devil, the beast, and the false prophet) and those who worship the beast are all implicated. We may still choose to take the torment literally, but we need,

---

[9] Cf. Aune, *Revelation*, 1065–66. Aune finds a collocation of the "lake of fire" and the "second death" in Egyptian mythology.

first, to recognize that this judgment is limited in its scope and, secondly, to remind ourselves that recourse to Old Testament types inevitably generates a certain *indirectness* – we are taken on a literary detour and we have to ask why. Are we supposed to read this as a quasi-literal description of eternal suffering? Or is the language intended to place the predicted collapse of the imperial cult in the same category as other acts of divine judgment? When the image occurs a second time we have moved beyond the historical to a final judgment, which may explain the shift of emphasis from torment to destruction.[10] The lake of fire is no longer a place of suffering but the means by which everything that does not belong in the new creation is destroyed.

New Heavens and New Earth

If John's vision takes us beyond the third horizon of a judgment of all the dead into an utterly unfamiliar world in which evil and death have been abolished, we might have expected to see a marked discontinuity in the language and imagery. What in fact we find is both discontinuity and continuity. The vision of a new creation in which there is no more suffering and death goes beyond the antecedent Old Testament visions. When Isaiah makes use of the metaphor of the creation of new heavens and a new earth to describe the restoration of Israel and the complete forgiveness of the nation's sin ("the former things shall not be remembered or come into mind": Isa. 65:17), he foresees the prosperity of the righteous but not the abolition of death: "the young man shall die a hundred years old" (65:20).[11] The new

---

[10] Sulfur is also a constituent in the judgment on Gog in Ezek. 38:22.

[11] Isa. 25:8 may be taken to refer to a final defeat of death, but the context suggests that this has in view death as "evidencing the curse imposed in consequence of sin" (Motyer, *Isaiah*, 209). LXX reads differently ("death has prevailed and swallowed up, and again God has taken away every tear from every face"), but essentially confirms this interpretation: there will be forgiveness of sins and an end to the punishment.

creation is not utterly different. It embodies an ideal that is recognizable to the Jewish mentality that was giving shape to the new self-understanding of the people of God – so that it can say something about identity and purpose and hope for *this* present world.

Immediately following the appearance of a new heaven and a new earth John sees "the holy city, new Jerusalem, coming down out of heaven from God, prepared as a bride adorned for her husband" (21:2). The imagery of the adorned bride is drawn from Isaiah 49:18, where it is used as a metaphor for a rebuilt Jerusalem: the once forsaken city is adorned by the returning exiles, who far outnumber those who were taken away (49:19–21), just as a bride is adorned for marriage.[12] He sees the same thing again a few verses later when he is taken by an angel in the Spirit to a "great, high mountain," from where he sees the "holy city Jerusalem coming down out of heaven from God, having the glory of God, its radiance like a most rare jewel, like a jasper, clear as crystal" (21:10–11). This is one of the seven angels that had poured out the bowls of God's judgment on the world (15:1 – 16:21). Another had taken him in the Spirit into the wilderness to see an analogous vision of the harlot city Babylon.

What follows is an elaborate description of this pristine and fabulous city that draws especially on Ezekiel's elaborate vision, "in the twenty-fifth year of our exile," of the temple and Jerusalem (Ezek. 40 – 48). It is the place of God's dwelling in the midst of people (Rev. 21:3; cf. Ezek. 43:7; 48:35; cf. 37:27). Its twelve gates, three on each side, are inscribed with the names of the twelve tribes of Israel (21:12–13; cf. Ezek. 48:30–34). The angel carries a measuring rod of gold with which he measures the city and its gates and walls (21:15–17; cf. Ezek. 40:3, 5 – 42:20). The river of the water of life flows "from the throne of God and

---

[12] The figure also occurs in Isa. 61:10, where "salvation" and "righteousness" are the decorations; but it is less certain here that the reference is to Zion (see Motyer, *Isaiah*, 504).

of the Lamb through the middle of the street of the city" (22:1–2; cf. Ezek. 47:1). The tree of life grows on either side of the river, and the "leaves of the tree were for the healing of the nations" (22:2; cf. Ezek. 47:12). It is remarkable, in view of the prominence of the temple in Ezekiel, that there is no temple in John's vision: "its temple is the Lord God the Almighty and the Lamb" (21:22). Nor is there any need for the sun or moon to provide light: "for the glory of God gives it light, and its lamp is the Lamb" (21:23; cf. Isa. 60:1, 19–20). This is the final prospect – not of vindication and kingdom, but of a profound, God-centered well-being in the midst of things.

You can discuss the issues raised in this book, and related matters, at www.opensourcetheology.net.

Bibliography

Allison, D. C., "Jesus and the Victory of Apocalyptic," in C. C. Newman (ed.), *Jesus and the Restoration of Israel* (Downers Grove: IVP; Carlisle: Paternoster, 1999), 126–41

Aune, D., *Revelation* (3 vols.; Dallas: Word, 1997–98)

Aus, R. D., "God's Plan and God's Power: Isaiah 66 and the Restraining Factors of 2 Thess. 2:6–7," *Journal of Biblical Literature* 96.4 (1977), 537–53

Bailey, D. P., "The Intertextual Relationship of Daniel 12:2 and Isaiah 26:19: Evidence from Qumran and the Greek Versions," *Tyndale Bulletin* 51.2 (2000), 305–12

Barr, J., "Paul and the LXX: A Note on Some Recent Work," *Journal of Theological Studies* 45.2 (1994), 593–601

Bauckham, R., *Jude, 2 Peter* (Waco, TX: Word, 1983)

—, *The Climax of Prophecy: Studies on the Book of Revelation* (Edinburgh: T&T Clark, 1993)

Beasley-Murray, G. R., *Jesus and the Last Days* (Peabody, MA: Hendrickson, 1993)

Best, E., *The First and Second Epistles to the Thessalonians* (London: A & C Black, 1986)

Blomberg, C. L., "Eschatology and the Church: Some New Testament Perspectives," in C. R. Trueman, T. J. Gray and C. L. Blomberg (eds.), *Solid Ground: 25 Years of Evangelical Theology* (Leicester: Inter-Varsity Press, 2000), 84–107

Bockmuehl, M., "1 Thessalonians 2:14–16 and the Church in Jerusalem," *Tyndale Bulletin* 52.1 (2001), 1–31

Brower, K. E., "'Let the Reader Understand': Temple and

Eschatology in Mark," in K. E. Brower and M. W. Elliott (eds.), *"The Reader Must Understand": Eschatology in Bible and Theology* (Leicester: Inter-Varsity Press, 1997), 119–43

Bruce, F. F., *1 and 2 Thessalonians* (Waco, TX: Word, 1982)

Caird, G. B., *The Language and Imagery of the Bible* (London: Duckworth, 1980)

—, *The Revelation of St. John the Divine* (London: A & C Black, 1984)

Caragounis, C. C., "Kingdom of God, Son of Man and Jesus' Self-Understanding I & II," *Tyndale Bulletin* 40.1 (1989), 3–23; 40.2 (1989), 223–38

Casey, M., "Idiom and Translation: Some Aspects of the Son of Man Problem," *New Testament Studies* 41.2 (1995), 164–82

Charlesworth, J. H. (ed.), *The Old Testament Pseudepigrapha*, I and II (London: Darton, Longman & Todd, 1983, 1985)

Collins, J. J., "The Son of Man in First-Century Judaism," *New Testament Studies* 38 (1992), 448–66

—, *Daniel* (Minneapolis: Fortress Press, 1993)

Collins, R. F., *First Corinthians* (Collegeville, MN: The Liturgical Press, 1999)

Craigie, P. C., *Psalms 1–50* (Waco, TX: Word, 1983)

Cullmann, O., "Le Caractère Eschatologique du Devoir Missionnaire et de la Conscience Apostolique de S. Paul: Étude sur le *katechon* (*–ōn*) de II Thess.2.6–7," *Revue d'Histoire et de Philosophie Religieuses* 16 (1936), 210–45

Dixon, P. S., "The Evil Restraint in 2 Thess 2:6," *Journal of the Evangelical Theological Society* 33.4 (1990), 445–49

Dunn, J. D. G., *Romans* (2 vols.; Dallas: Word, 1988)

—, *The Theology of Paul the Apostle* (Grand Rapids/Cambridge: Eerdmans, 1998)

Eastman, S., "Whose Apocalypse? The Identity of the Sons of God in Romans 8:19," *Journal of Biblical Literature* 121.2 (2002), 263–77

Ehrman, B. D., *Jesus: Apocalyptic Prophet of the New Millennium* (Oxford/New York: Oxford University Press, 1999)

Elderen, B. van, "Early Christianity in Transjordan," *Tyndale Bulletin* 45.1 (1994), 104–109

Elias, J. W., *1 & 2 Thessalonians* (Scottdale, PA: Herald Press, 1995)
Ellicott, C. J., *Commentary on the Epistles of St. Paul to the Thessalonians* (Grand Rapids: Zondervan, 1957)
Ellis, E. E., "New Testament Teaching on Hell," in K. E. Brower and M. W. Elliott (eds.), *"The Reader Must Understand": Eschatology in Bible and Theology* (Leicester: Inter-Varsity Press, 1997), 199–219
Evans, C. A., "Jesus and the Continuing Exile of Israel," in C. C. Newman (ed.), *Jesus and the Restoration of Israel* (Downers Grove: InterVarsity Press; Carlisle: Paternoster, 1999), 77–100
—, *Mark 8:27 – 16:20* (Nashville: Thomas Nelson, 2001)
—, "Defeating Satan and Liberating Israel: Jesus and Daniel's Visions," *Journal for the Study of the Historical Jesus* 1.2 (2003), 161–70
Fee, G. D., *The First Epistle to the Corinthians* (Grand Rapids: Eerdmans, 1987)
—, *Paul's Letter to the Philippians* (Grand Rapids: Eerdmans, 1995)
Fletcher-Louis, C. H. T., "The Destruction of the Temple and the Relativization of the Old Covenant: Mark 13:31 and Matthew 5:18," in K. E. Brower and M. W. Elliott (eds.), *"The Reader Must Understand": Eschatology in Bible and Theology* (Leicester: Inter-Varsity Press, 1997), 145–69
Frame, J. E., *The Epistles of St. Paul to the Thessalonians* (Edinburgh: T&T Clark, 1912)
France, R. T., *The Gospel of Mark* (Grand Rapids/Carlisle: Eerdmans/Paternoster, 2002)
Fredriksen, P., *Jesus of Nazareth, King of the Jews: A Jewish Life and the Emergence of Christianity* (London: Macmillan, 2000)
Fudge, E. W., and R. A. Peterson, *Two Views of Hell: A Biblical and Theological Dialogue* (Downers Grove: InterVarsity Press, 2000)
Giblin, C. H., *The Threat to Faith: An Exegetical and Theological Re-Examination of 2 Thessalonians 2* (Analecta biblica 31; Rome: Pontifical Biblical Institute, 1967)

—, "The Millennium (Rev 20:4–6) as Heaven," *New Testament Studies* 45.4 (1999), 553–70

Goldingay, J. E., *Daniel* (Dallas: Word, 1987)

Green, G. L., *The Letters to the Thessalonians* (Grand Rapids/Leicester: Eerdmans/Inter-Varsity Press, 2002)

Hagner, D. A., *Matthew* (2 vols.; Dallas: Word, 1993, 1995)

Harrison, J. R., "Paul and the Imperial Gospel at Thessaloniki," *Journal for the Study of the New Testament* 25.1 (2002), 71–96

Hawthorne, G. F., *Philippians* (Waco, TX: Word, 1983)

Head, P. M., "The Duration of Divine Judgment in the New Testament," in K. E. Brower and M. W. Elliott (eds.), *"The Reader Must Understand": Eschatology in Bible and Theology* (Leicester: Inter-Varsity Press, 1997), 221–27

Hooker, M. D., *The Gospel According to Mark* (London: A & C Black, 1991)

Horsley, R. A. (ed.), *Paul and Empire: Religion and Power in Roman Imperial Society* (Harrisburg, PA: Trinity Press International, 1997)

Jewett, R., "The Agitators and the Galatian Congregations," *New Testament Studies* 17 (1971), 198–212

Kim, S., "The Jesus Tradition in 1 Thess 4.13–5.11," *New Testament Studies* 48.2 (2002), 225–42

Kreitzer, L. J., *Jesus and God in Paul's Eschatology* (Sheffield: JSOT Press, 1987)

Lane, W. L., *The Gospel of Mark* (Grand Rapids: Eerdmans, 1974)

Leaney, A. R. C., *The Gospel According to St Luke* (London: A & C Black, 1966)

Lincoln, A. T., *Ephesians* (Dallas: Word, 1990)

Marshall, I. H., "Son of Man," in J. B. Green, S. McKnight and I. H. Marshall (eds.), *Dictionary of Jesus and the Gospels* (Downers Grove/Leicester: InterVarsity Press, 1992), 775–81

—, *1 and 2 Thessalonians* (Vancouver: Regent College Publishing, 2002)

Martin, R. P., *James* (Waco, TX: Word, 1988)

Mearns, C. L., "Early Eschatological Development in Paul:

The Evidence of I and II Thessalonians," *New Testament Studies* 27. (1981), 137–57

Menken, M. J. J., 22 *Thessalonians* (London/New York: Routledge, 1994)

Moo, D., *The Epistle to the Romans* (Grand Rapids/ Cambridge: Eerdmans, 1996)

Moore, A. L., *The Parousia in the New Testament* (Leiden: Brill, 1966)

Morris, L., *1 & 2 Thessalonians* (London: Tyndale, 1976)

—, "Man of Lawlessness and Restraining Power," in G. F. Hawthorne, R. P. Martin and D. G. Reid, *Dictionary of Paul and his Letters* (Downers Grove/Leicester: InterVarsity Press, 1993), 630–42

Motyer, J. A., *The Prophecy of Isaiah* (Leicester: Inter-Varsity Press, 1999)

Moule, C. F. D., "'The Son of Man': Some of the Facts," *New Testament Studies* 41.2 (1995), 277–79

Munck, J., *Paul and the Salvation of Mankind* (London: SCM Press, 1959)

Nicholl, C., "Michael, the Restrainer Removed (2 Thess. 2:6–7)," *Journal of Theological Studies* 51.1 (2000), 27–53

Nolland, J., *Luke* (3 vols.; Dallas: Word, 1993)

O'Brien, P. T., *Colossians, Philemon* (Waco, TX: Word, 1982)

Peerbolte, L. J. Lietaert, "The KATÉXON/KATÉXŌN of 2 Thess. 2:6–7," *Novum Testamentum* 39.2 (1997), 138–50

Perriman, A. C., "The Pattern of Christ's Sufferings: Colossians 1:24 and Philippians 3:10–11," *Tyndale Bulletin* 42.1 (1991), 62–79

Plevnik, J., *Paul and the Parousia: An Exegetical and Theological Investigation* (Peabody, MA: Hendrickson, 1997)

Poirier, J. C., "The First Rider: A Response to Michael Bachmann," *New Testament Studies* 45.2 (1999), 257–62

Proudfoot, C. M., "Imitation or Realistic Participation?" *Interpretation* 17 (1963), 140–60

Richard, E. J., *First and Second Thessalonians* (Collegeville, MN: The Liturgical Press, 1995)

Ridderbos, H., *Paul: An Outline of His Theology* (ET London:

SPCK, 1977)

Rubenstein, R. E., *When Jesus Became God* (San Diego/New York/London: Harcourt, 1999)

Sanders, E. P., *The Historical Figure of Jesus* (London: Penguin, 1993)

Schoeps, H. J., *Paul: The Theology of the Apostle in the Light of Jewish Religious History* (Philadelphia: Westminster Press, 1959)

Silva, M., "Old Testament in Paul," in G. F. Hawthorne, R. P. Martin and D. G. Reid, *Dictionary of Paul and His Letters* (Downers Grove/Leicester: InterVarsity Press, 1993), 630–42

Slater, T. B., "One Like a Son of Man in First-Century CE Judaism," *New Testament Studies* 41.2 (1995), 183–98

Stanley, C. D., *Paul and the Language of Scripture* (Cambridge: Cambridge University Press, 1992)

Still, T. D., *Conflict at Thessalonica: A Pauline Church and its Neighbours* (Sheffield: Sheffield Academic Press, 1999)

—, "Eschatology in Colossians: How Realized is It?" *New Testament Studies* 50.1 (2004), 125–38

Tannehill, R. C., *The Narrative Unity of Luke-Acts: A Literary Interpretation* (Minneapolis: Fortress Press, 1990)

Thiselton, A. C., *The First Epistle to the Corinthians* (Grand Rapids/Carlisle: Eerdmans/Paternoster, 2000)

Thompson, L. L., *The Book of Revelation: Apocalypse and Empire* (New York/Oxford: Oxford University Press, 1990)

Townsend, J. T., "II Thessalonians 2:3–12," *Society of Biblical Literature Seminar Papers* 19 (1980), 233–46

Wall, R. W., "The Acts of the Apostles," in L. E. Keck, et al. (eds.), *The New Interpreter's Bible*, X (Nashville: Abingdon Press, 2002)

Wallis, W. B., "The Problem of an Intermediate Kingdom in I Corinthians 15:20–28," *Journal of the Evangelical Theological Society* 18.4 (1975), 229–42

Wanamaker, C. A., *Commentary on 1 & 2 Thessalonians* (Grand Rapids: Eerdmans; Exeter: Paternoster, 1990)

Water, R. Van De, "Reconsidering the Beast from the Sea

(Rev. 13.1)," *New Testament Studies* 46.2 (2000), 245–61
Wenham, D., "Paul and the Synoptic Apocalypse," in R. T. France and D. Wenham (eds.), *Gospel Perspectives: Studies of History and Tradition in the Four Gospels*, II (Sheffield: JSOT Press, 1981), 345–75
—, *Paul: Follower of Jesus or Founder of Christianity?* (Grand Rapids/Cambridge: Eerdmans, 1995)
White, J. R., "'Baptized on Account of the Dead': The Meaning of 1 Corinthians 15:29 in its Context," *Journal of Biblical Literature* 116.3 (1997), 487–99
Whiteley, D. E. H., *The Theology of St Paul* (Oxford: Basil Blackwell, 1972)
Williams, D. J., *1 and 2 Thessalonians* (Peabody, MA: Hendrickson, 1995)
Witherington, B., *Jesus, Paul and the End of the World* (Downers Grove: InterVarsity Press, 1992)
—, "Transcending Imminence: The Gordian Knot of Pauline Eschatology," in K. E. Brower and M. W. Elliott (eds.), *"The Reader Must Understand": Eschatology in Bible and Theology* (Leicester: Inter-Varsity Press, 1997), 171–86
Wright, N. T., "Jerusalem in the New Testament," in P. W. L. Walker (ed.), *Jerusalem Past and Present in the Purposes of God* (Cambridge: Tyndale, 1992)
—, *The New Testament and the People of God* (London: SPCK, 1992)
—, *Jesus and the Victory of God* (London: SPCK, 1996)
—, *The Resurrection of the Son of God* (London: SPCK, 2003)
—, and M. Borg, *The Meaning of Jesus* (London: SPCK, 1999)

Scripture Index

Old Testament

Genesis
11:5 154
12:3 49
15:18 201
16:10 194
17:4 194
19:24 199, 242
24:56 142
28:12 75
28:14 49, 75
39:20 142
49:8 187
49:9 186
49:10 187

Exodus
4:22 69
7:20–21 199
8:11 72
9:18 34
9:20 200
9:25 199
9:26 200
10:12–20 201
10:14 34
10:22 199
10:23 200
11:6 34
19:4 212
19:6 183
19:10–18 154
19:11 154
19:20 154
21:6 83
23:31 201
25:31–35 208
26:35 208
31:14 145
32:32 241
32:35 241
34:5 154

Leviticus
23:29 72

Numbers
4:18 145
11:25 154
19:19 194
19:20 145
20:3 88
23:19 51
31:19–20 194
31:24 194
35:30 209

Deuteronomy
13:13 138
15:9 138
17:6 209
18:15 72
18:19 72
19:15 209
28:15–68 127
28:25–26 127
29:23 242
30:1–6 74
31:15 154
32:16–17 203
32:18 212
33:2 154

Joshua
6 198
22:22 139

Judges
2:18 110
5:4–5 240
5:19–20 45
19:22 138
20:13 138

1 Samuel
1:16 138

2:12 138
22:2 101

2 Samuel
4:5–7 78
16:7 138
20:1 138
22:5 138
22:18 157

1 Kings
1:34 198
1:39 198
13:34 158, 160
17:1 207
20:13 138, 139
21:10 138
21:13 138

2 Kings
1:10–12 208
5:9 76
9:13 198
21:3 42
21:5 42
23:4–5 42
23:10 91

1 Chronicles
15:24 198
29:30 34

2 Chronicles
18:18 42
28:3 91
29:19 139

Ezra
8:31 157

Nehemiah
2:19 139
3:4 149
6:6 139
9:28 157
12:41 198

Job
10:15 76
15:23 37
16:9 90
25:6 51
31:9 76
34:18 138
35:8 51
38:17 95
39:30 36

Psalms
2:1 210
2:2 210
2:6 217
2:7 69, 212
2:7–9 177
2:8–9 210
2:9 212, 217
6:7 110
8:4 51
8:6 176
9:14 95
9:18 94
11:6 110, 242
13 232
18:1 157
18:4 138
18:7–15 240
18:17 157
18:48 157
20:2 232
22:1 6
24:7–10 76
31:15 157
33:6 42
33:19 117
34:15–16 90
36:12 90
36:28 158
38:14 72
44:13–14 110
47:5 198
48:15 94
50:2 232
50:3–5 75
51:7 120
65:8 43
68:7–8 240
69:28 241
71:17 49
73:1 120
73:3 120
73:11 120
75:8 228
76:9 120
78:5 120
78:11–12 110
79:16 52

79:18 52
82 45
88:23 133
88:47 120
89:5 61
89:7 61
90:4 123
97:1 125
97:3 125
97:5 125
97:10 125
97:11 125
98:6 198
101:21 110
102:9 120
104:24 52
106:18 95
110 176
110:1 179
110:1–2 59
110:2 177, 232
111:9–10 90
118:151 117
122:5 63
137:8–9 159
144:3 51
144:18 117

Proverbs
1:26–27 158
6:12 138
21:7 158
30:27 156

Isaiah
2:6 191
2:6–8 203
2:17 191
2:19 191
2:20–21 203
2:21 191
3:1–5 191
3:14–15 96
4:3 241
5:24–26 89
5:30 45
10 41
10:1–3 96
10:20–27 160
11:3–4 161
11:4 160, 187, 221
11:10 187
11:10–12 160
11:12 47, 48, 187, 192
13–14 41
13:4–22 44
13:6 117
13:7–9 23
13:9–11 41
13:10 44, 199
13:11 234
14:11 94
14:12 200
14:12–15 61
14:13–14 133
14:13 200
14:15 200
18:3 47, 48
22:12 207
23:17 78
24:3 110
24:4–5 65
24:18–21 65
24:21 45
24:21–23 41, 44
25:8 196, 243
26:18–19 165
27:9 232, 234
27:12–13 155
27:13 74
28:14–19 122
29:5–7 209
29:6 25, 157
29:11 185
29:19–20 96
30:19 90
30:33 242
31:4–7 155
32:11 207
33 41
34:1–4 190
34:4 41, 44, 124
34:8 124
34:9 242
34:10 242
34:12 88
38:10 95
38:18 94
41:11 29
41:17–18 96
42:1 69
43:6 75
47 41
47:11 88
48:20 45
49:5–6 195

49:7 233
49:9–10 195
49:10 195
49:18 244
49:19–21 244
49:22 47, 48
49:25–26 233
50:5–8 86
51:1 87
51:2 87
51:3 86
51:4–6 65
51:12 51
51:17 228
51:22 228
52:6 54
52:8 54
52:9 233
52:11–12 45
52:13–53:12 141
52:13 141
53:11 141
54:5 233
54:10 233
55:3 233
56:2 51
58:1 198
58:9 54
58:12 54
59:2 233
59:9–20 232
59:14 233
59:19 233
59:20–60:22 233
59:20–21 232
59:21 233
60:1 245
60:1–5 233
60:8 166
60:10 233
60:19–20 245
61:10 244
63:18 34, 124
64:1–2 124
65:2 65
65:17 124, 243
65:19 65, 90
65:20 243
66:6 156
66:7–9 212
66:9 143
66:14–15 158
66:15 124
66:19 47
66:19–20 47
66:20 75
66:21 65
66:22 66, 124
66:23 65
66:24 65, 92, 93

Jeremiah
1:14–15 201
2:19 139
2:29 234
4:5 155, 198
4:8 207
4:16 25
4:19 155
4:19–21 198
4:21 48
4:23 65
5:14 207
6:1 198
6:17 198
6:24 25
6:26 207
7:9 203
7:31 91
7:32–34 91
7:33 37
8:2 203
8:16–19 202
9:14–15 203
9:15 199
10:2 44
10:22 25
11:16 231
12:4 110
12:11 110
12:12 33
14:12 189
14:16 25
15:2 188
15:2–3 189
15:3 37
15:4 203
15:5 189
15:19 72
16:4 37
16:15 72
17:17–18 117
19:3 91
19:7 37, 91
19:10–11 91
21:1–2 87

21:5	87
21:8	87, 88
21:8–10	87
22:23	23
23:8	72
23:15	199
23:19	25
24:6	72
25:11–12	11
25:26	78
27:19	72
27:26	34
27:43	25
28:27	47
28:36	29
28:55	158
29:10	11
30:8	25
30:29	25
31:2	196
31:2–3	158
31:7	195
31:8	158, 195
31:9	195
31:10	195
31:12	196
31:13	196
31:31–34	75
31:32	158
31:36	65
32:31	158
32:37–40	75
38:8	195
38:12	196
41:20	37
42:15	67
44:7	145
48:40–42	23
49:9	79
49:12	228
49:22	23
49:36	192
50–51	41
50:6	45
50:8	45
50:28	45
50:39	218
50:40	51
51:6–10	45
51:25	200
51:27	198, 201
51:34–35	159
51:45–46	45
51:50–51	45
51:57	45
51:63–64	202

Lamentations

2:13	228
2:16	90
4:12	191
4:21	228

Ezekiel

1:1	184
1:5–12	184
1:22	184
1:24	184
1:26	184
1:28	184
2:3	185
2:9–10	184
2:10	184
4:1–7	51
5:1–4	51
5:11	189, 203
5:11–12	192
5:12	188
6:14	158
7:2	192
7:15–16	32
9:2	192
9:3–4	192
9:5–6	192
11:22–23	21
12:2	51, 77
13:17	51
14:8	145
14:16	158
14:21	189
16:55	72
17:2	51
20:3–4	51
20:32	49
21:2	51
21:3	118
22:2	51
22:11	234
22:27–31	96
23:31–34	228
26:16	191
27:27–36	219
27:35–36	191
28:2	133, 219
28:6	133
28:9	133

30:3 117
32:7 199
32:7–8 41, 44
33:3–4 155
33:3–6 198
33:27 189
34:12 196
34:13 75
37:9–14 52
37:20–28 196
37:27 194, 244
38 41
38:2 239
38:10–12 239
38:14–23 209
38:19 25
38:20 78
38:22 240, 243
38:23 240
39:17–20 221
40–48 244
40:1–2 205
40:3 244
40:4 205
40:5–42:20 244
43:2 36
43:2–7 205
43:7 244
43:7–9 203
43:10 205
47:1 245
47:12 245
48:30–34 244
48:35 244

Daniel
1:1–7 10
1:5 63
1:17 11
1:20 11
2:44 11
3:29 11
4:2–3 11
4:22 164
4:34–35 11
4:36 72
5:21 11
5:26 11
6:9–11 194
6:26–27 11
7:1 54
7:2 192
7:3–8 54
7:8 54, 133
7:9 54
7:10 242
7:11 161, 221
7:11–12 54, 60
7:13 12, 50, 52, 53, 54, 59, 166
7:13–14 48, 55, 61
7:14 56, 60, 69, 169, 187
7:18 61, 64, 143, 169
7:20–21 54
7:21 178, 209, 214
7:21–22 82, 142
7:22 54, 55, 61, 64, 67, 143, 187, 222
7:23 82
7:25 54, 59, 133, 178, 214
7:25–27 68, 142
7:27 55, 61, 64, 169, 179, 187, 217
8:4 164
8:10 45, 133, 164
8:10–12 61
8:12–14 34
8:13–14 205
8:19 11
8:23–24 133
8:24 61
8:25 164
8:26 185
9:3–19 71
9:4–15 11
9:7 230
9:12 33
9:16 11
9:18 11, 230
9:24 12, 71, 226
9:24–26 11
9:26 12, 34, 122, 136, 140, 145
9:26–27 41
9:27 12, 30, 145
10:4–5 185
10:5–6 204
10:13 45
10:14 203
10:21 12, 185
11:4 192
11:12 164
11:13 83
11:27 83
11:28 12
11:30 12

11:30–39 146, 147
11:31 12, 30, 140, 185
11:31–32 234
11:31–39 140
11:32 12, 141, 146
11:32–33 141
11:33 12, 142, 146, 150, 194
11:35 12, 142, 147, 148, 194, 223
11:36 12, 133, 147, 164, 185
11:37 164
11:40–41 12
11:45 151
12:1 33, 117, 156, 164, 185, 193, 234
12:1–2 165, 167
12:1–3 105, 141, 176, 186
12:2 12, 85, 164, 175
12:3 12, 150, 152, 194, 226
12:4 185, 186, 204
12:6–7 204
12:7 34, 185, 205, 238
12:9 186, 193, 204
12:10 141, 142, 186
12:11 30, 140, 205
12:12 27, 147

Hosea
5:8 198
6:2 62
7:12 25
8:1 198, 201
8:1–5 203
8:4–6 201
9:6 158
10:5–8 203
10:8 191
11:11 72

Joel
1:8 207
1:9–20 201
1:13 207
1:15 45, 117
2:1 117, 198, 201
2:2 33, 34, 191, 201
2:4 201
2:6 45, 201
2:9 79
2:10 41, 45, 65, 199
2:11 191, 221
2:12–20 45
2:15 198
2:27–32 46
2:30 65, 199
2:30–31 45
2:30–32 41
2:31–32 46
3:12–13 218
3:15 199
3:15–16 41
3:16 65
4:14 117

Amos
2:6–7 96
3:2 49
4:1–2 96
5:18–20 117
6:3 117
8:1 207
8:4–14 96
8:9 45

Obadiah
1:1–2 25
1:12–13 158
1:15 117

Micah
1:3 155
1:3–4 240
4:9–10 23
4:10 157
5:1–14 203
5:9 145
5:13 145
7:4 90
7:6 7, 26, 90

Nahum
1:11 138
1:15 138

Habakkuk
1:1–2:3 41
1:2 128
1:4 126
1:5 121
1:6 202
1:8 37, 202
1:12 126
1:13–17 126

2:1	126
2:3–4	127, 128
2:4	126, 127
2:5	126
2:6	126
2:6–19	126
2:16	228

Zephaniah

1:2–3	78
1:7	117
1:14	117
1:14–16	191
1:18	240
2:5–7	240

Haggai

2:6	65
2:6–7	41
2:21	65
2:21–22	41

Zechariah

1–4	208
1:8–11	188
2:4	76
2:5	205
2:6	192
2:6–8	45
2:6–13	75
2:10	75
2:11	75, 208
3	208
3:8	208
4	208
4:2–3	208
4:6	208
4:6–10	208
4:12	208
6:1–8	188
6:11–13	208
8:23	85
9:9	156
9:14	36, 156, 198
12:3	34, 205
12:10–14	49
12:12	49
13:1	49
14	41
14:4	19
14:5	45, 80, 165
14:8–9	80
14:17	49

Malachi

3:2	191

New Testament

Matthew

1:21	228
3:7	20, 94, 118
3:10	93, 94
3:12	93
5:13	151
5:18	66
5:22	92
5:29–30	92
6:13	157
7:13–14	88
7:19	93
7:24–27	18
8:11–12	89
10:6	77
10:6–7	81
10:17–18	26
10:17–23	26
10:22–23	27
10:23	18, 26, 39
10:26–31	26
10:28	93
10:32	93
10:32–33	63
10:34–36	90
10:34–39	26
10:38	169
10:40	81
10:42	81
11:23	94
12:24–32	59
12:32	59
12:39	48
13:11	84
13:22	84
13:37–42	93
13:39–40	84
13:41	81
13:47–50	93
13:49	84
15:27	95
16:4	48, 49
16:18	94
16:27	67, 81
16:28	67, 68, 99
17:1–8	68
17:9	68

17:11 72
18:8 94
18:9 92
19:16 85, 168
19:21 168
19:28 63, 84, 169, 172, 192
19:29 85
20:19 228
20:21–23 177
20:28 228
21:28–32 20
21:33–46 20
21:45 89
22:1–14 20
22:7 89
22:13 89
22:43–45 176
23:2–3 20
23:5–12 20
23:15 92
23:29–39 119
23:33 20, 92
23:34–36 190
23:37–39 19, 21
23:38 77
24:3 19, 46, 50, 83
24:4–6 132
24:4–8 23
24:6–8 188
24:7 121
24:8 27
24:9 26
24:9–14 26
24:10–12 26, 138
24:11–12 27
24:13 27
24:14 27, 233
24:15 8, 30, 132
24:15–22 30
24:16–18 79
24:21–22 33
24:23–26 35
24:24 44
24:26–27 39
24:27 35, 51, 58
24:28 36, 201
24:29 38, 190
24:29–35 38
24:30 47, 49, 50
24:30–31 76
24:31 47, 74, 156
24:33 76
24:34 39
24:35 64
24:36 41
24:37 37, 51
24:37–39 79
24:38–39 79
24:39 37, 51
24:40–41 79
24:43 79
24:45–51 78, 89
25:1–12 79
25:1–13 89
25:14–30 78, 89
25:24 78
25:31–46 28, 80
25:35–36 110
25:40 28, 82
25:41 94, 240
25:45 82
25:46 85, 94
26:39 228
26:61 64
26:64 58, 61
26:64–65 48
27:11 63
27:40 64
27:46 6
27:52–53 86
28:20 85

Mark

3:28–29 59
3:29 60
4:11 84
4:19 84
4:26–29 18
7:28 95
8:18 51
8:34 169
8:38 68, 81
9:1 99
9:2–8 68
9:9 68
9:12 72
9:13 26
9:42–48 92
9:43 92
9:45 92
9:47 92
9:48 92
10:17 85, 168
10:29–30 83
10:30 85, 169
10:45 228

12:1–12	20
12:35–37	176
13:2	19
13:3	19
13:4	18
13:5–7	132
13:5–8	23
13:5–23	39, 40, 43
13:8	27, 121
13:9	26
13:9–13	26
13:10	27, 233
13:11	27
13:12	7, 26
13:13	27
13:14	8, 30, 132
13:14–16	79
13:14–20	30
13:17	57
13:19	57
13:19–20	33
13:21–22	39
13:21–23	35
13:24	57
13:24–25	38, 190
13:24–27	40
13:24–31	38
13:26	39, 47, 48, 50
13:26–27	76
13:27	74, 156
13:28	40
13:28–29	40
13:29	76
13:30	39
13:30–31	78
13:31	64
13:32	41, 57, 78
13:34–37	78
14:58	64
14:62	58
14:62–64	48
15:29	64
15:34	6
16:19	177

Luke

1:32–33	13
1:53	96
1:68–75	228
1:70	72
1:71–75	72
1:72–73	71
1:74	157
3:7	94, 118
3:8	96
3:9	94
3:17	93
4:25	67, 207
4:42	142
5:35	18
6:20	97
8:15	149
9:23	169
9:26	81
9:27	99
9:28–36	68
9:51	51
10:15	94
10:17	179
10:20	179, 241
10:25	85
11:29	48
11:30	48
11:47–51	119
12:5	93
12:8–9	60, 63
12:10	59
12:37	18
12:39	79
12:42–48	78
12:49,	67
12:51	67
12:51–53	90
13:4–5	88
13:23	89
13:23–24	88
13:28–29	89
13:31–35	21
13:33	207
14:16–24	96
16:1–9	29
16:4	29
16:8	85
16:8–9	29
16:9	29
16:14	95
16:19–23	95
17:20–37	21, 30
17:21	36
17:23	35, 36
17:24	35, 36
17:26–27	79
17:26–29	79
17:26–32	39
17:28–30	79
17:30	37, 61, 64, 67

17:34–35 79
17:34–37 37
17:37 201
18:1–8 29
18:2–8 116
18:7–8 67
18:18 85, 168
18:29–30 83, 169
18:30 85
18:32 228
18:32–33 62
19:11 90
19:12–27 78
19:12–28 89
19:20–24 90
19:27 90
19:43–44 30
19:44 49
20:9–19 20
20:41–44 176
21:5 19
21:8–9 132
21:8–11 23
21:9–11 188
21:11 23, 121
21:12 26
21:12–19 26
21:13–15 27
21:16 26
21:17 26
21:19 27
21:20 30
21:20–24 30
21:21 79
21:23 67, 78, 101, 118
21:24 34, 41, 205, 206
21:25–26 38, 190
21:25–33 38
21:26 42
21:27 47, 50
21:28 76
21:31 76
21:32 39
21:33 64
21:34–35 79
21:35 78
21:36 63, 69
21:37 19
22:28–30 63
22:29–30 172
22:30 169, 192
22:69 58
23:28–30 98
23:30 191
23:43 86
23:44 67
24:4–5 70
24:7 70

John
1:51 61, 75
2:19 64
4:14 195
5:7 52
5:25 156
5:27 47
5:28–29 86
7:38–39 195
11:25 86
11:51–52 74
11:52 75
14:3 70
15:6 93
21:22 70, 99

Acts
1:6 72
1:10–11 70
2:17–21 46
2:21 228
2:32–36 177
2:33–34 59
2:36 77
2:40 228
3:13–15 73
3:19–21 71
3:21 71, 72
3:22–25 72
3:23 72
3:25 71, 73
5:31 59
5:36 121
7:4 67
7:34 110
7:42 77
7:54 90
7:55–56 59
8:39 164
10:45–47 112
11:27–30 121
13:40–41 121
13:46–48 230
14:22 106
15:14 75
15:14–18 75
17:1–9 102

17:6 53
17:26 34
17:30–31 123
18:1–17 101
18:2 120
21:21 139
21:38 24
23:6 105
23:10 164
24:15 105, 171
26:6–7 105
26:8 105
26:18 230
28:15 163
28:20 105

Romans
1:2 229
1:3–4 229
1:4 58, 212
1:5 229
1:16 126
1:17 126
1:18 123, 127
2:5 123
2:8 123
2:9 119, 125
2:28–29 75
2:29 74
3:9–12 232
5:2–5 109
6:4 58
6:8 174
8:2 108
8:16–17 108
8:17 108, 172
8:18 111
8:18–19 149
8:19 111
8:20–21 110
8:23 110, 111
8:28 172
8:29 110, 111, 170
8:29–30 172
8:34 59, 177
8:35 109
8:36 110
8:37 111
8:38 100
8:38–39 180
9:6 231
9:8 230, 231
9:22 119, 232
9:27 231
9:27–33 121
9:31–32 119
9:33 121
10:1 121
10:3–4 119
11:5 231
11:7 231
11:7–8 234
11:11 231
11:14 231
11:15 234
11:17–24 231
11:23 232
11:24 231
11:25 231
11:25–26 209
11:26 231, 232
11:26–27 232
11:27 232, 234
11:30–32 233
13:1–2 140
13:4 118
13:11 115, 179
13:11–12 115
14:10 166
15:16 229
16:5 167
16:20 116, 179

1 Corinthians
1:7 118
1:7–8 154
1:8 154
3:10–15 235
3:16 135
3:16–17 235
3:17 135, 136
3:22 100
4:5 154
4:8 172
4:9 102, 104
4:13 102
5:3 53
5:5 154
6:2 172
6:9–10 172
7:1 100
7:20 100
7:26 100
7:28 101
7:29 113
7:29–31 113

7:31	113
9:24–27	106
10:5	114
10:11	84, 114, 235
10:13	115
11:2	149
11:30	101
15:2	149
15:3	64
15:3–4	70
15:5–7	171
15:20	170
15:20–24	167, 170
15:21–22	170
15:23	154, 197
15:23–24	170
15:24	239
15:24–28	176
15:28	239
15:29	104
15:31–32	102
15:43	58
15:49	107
15:50	172
15:51–52	116, 176
16:15	167
16:17	53

2 Corinthians

1:5	105
1:14	154
2:14	104
3:5–18	75
3:18	107
4:4	107
4:10	104
4:14	166
4:16	104
5:1	104
5:8	104
6:9	104
6:10	143
6:14–16	137, 138
6:14–18	135
6:16	75, 135
7:6–7	53
10:2	53
10:10	53
10:11	53
11:23–27	109
12:2	164
12:4	86, 164
12:10	109
13:2	53
13:10	53

Galatians

2:20	42
3:8	229
3:11	127
3:14	229
3:29	229
4:3	42
4:6–7	108
5:21	172

Ephesians

1:3	181
1:10	34
1:14	172
1:18	172
1:20	59
1:20–22	180
1:20–23	56
1:21	181
2:3	118, 123
2:6–7	181
2:7	10, 236
2:8–9	229
2:12	229
2:14–16	229
2:21–22	229
3:8	181
3:19	181
5:5	172
5:6	117, 118, 181
5:16	117
6:10–17	178
6:11–12	178
6:13	117, 178, 181
6:17	178

Philippians

1:19–21	104
1:23	104, 106
1:28	112
1:29–30	102, 107
1:29–30	109
2:7–8	107, 173
2:8	107
2:9	180
2:9–11	56
2:10	180
2:12	53
2:16	108
3:5	105

3:8–9 105
3:8–10 173
3:10 104
3:10–11 104
3:11 105
3:14 107, 173
3:20–21 173
3:21 107
4:3 241
4:5 117

Colossians
1:12 172, 181
1:13 180, 181
1:18 111, 170
1:22 166
1:24 103
1:28 166
2:1 107
2:3 181
2:8 42
2:10 181
2:12 180
2:15 180
3:1 59, 180, 181
3:1–4 177
3:4 149, 163, 181
3:6 118, 123, 181
3:24 172

1 Thessalonians
1:6 102, 103
1:9–10 118, 157
1:10 122, 174
2:2 106, 107
2:13–16 120
2:14 102, 112
2:15–16 119, 121
2:16 120
2:19 154
3:3–4 106
3:5 108
3:13 154, 165
4:5 141
4:13–18 174
4:15 106, 116
4:15–17 115, 153, 154, 171
4:16 154, 165
4:16–17 164, 165
4:17 116, 162
5:1–2 130
5:2 154
5:2–10 122
5:3 122
5:10 116
5:21 143, 149
5:23 142, 149, 150, 154

2 Thessalonians
1:4–5 142
1:4–10 112, 157
1:5 106
1:6 159
1:6–7 165
1:6–10 116
1:7 40, 159
1:7–8 157
1:7–10 153
1:8 141
1:9 157, 158
1:9–10 160
1:11 142
2:1 156, 164
2:1–2 117
2:1–8 10, 57, 130
2:2–3 132
2:3 139, 140
2:3–4 133, 135
2:3–7 122, 131, 132, 133, 134, 209
2:3–10 100, 142, 178
2:3–12 234
2:4 135, 136
2:5 131
2:6 146, 148
2:8 40, 151, 154, 221
2:8–9 160
2:8–10 157
2:9–10 166
2:10–14 141
2:11 234
2:13 166
2:13–14 142
2:14 158, 163, 167
2:15 149

1 Timothy
2:6 34
4:1 140
6:12 107
6:14–15 154
6:15 34

2 Timothy
1:8 154
1:10 162

1:16 72
2:11–12 172
2:11–13 174
4:1 154, 172
4:6 106
4:7 107
4:8 106, 154
4:18 172

Titus
2:12–13 154

Hebrews
1:3 59, 177
1:13 59
2:5–8 180
2:8–9 180
3:6 149
3:14 149
4:12 221
7:25 177
8:1 59, 177
8:1–2 177
9:26 84
10:12 59, 177
10:13 177
10:25 117
10:32–34 128
10:32–39 127
10:36 127
10:37–38 128
10:39 127
12:1 107
12:2 59, 177
12:22 75
12:23 111

James
1:1 192
5:3 128
5:7–9 129
5:8 117
5:9 76
5:17 207

1 Peter
1:1 192
1:7 154
1:13 154
2:1–20 178
2:9 195
2:21 178
3:22 180
4:5 175
4:6 175
4:7 117, 175
4:12 180
4:17–18 175
5:4 175
5:8 29, 178
5:8–9 106

2 Peter
1:16 69
1:16–19 68
1:19 69, 123, 125
2:4–10 124
2:9 124
3:4 69, 129
3:5–7 124
3:6 124
3:7 123
3:8–9 123
3:10 123, 154
3:10–13 238
3:12 123, 124
3:13 124
3:14 123
4:17 235

1 John
2:18 117
2:28 154
5:5 147

Jude
23 164

Revelation
1:1 182, 204
1:2 190
1:3 182
1:4 182, 215
1:5 111, 182, 183
1:6 183
1:7 182, 183
1:8 215
1:9 183, 184, 190
1:12–13 208
1:12–20 184
1:13 52
1:13–16 183
1:15 184
1:17 184
1:18 182, 183
1:20 208

2:7 86, 111
2:10–11 217
2:11 111, 147, 183, 222
2:17 183, 220
2:26 111, 147
2:26–27 183, 217, 223
3:5 111, 147, 183, 241
3:12 111, 147, 183
3:21 111, 147, 172, 183
4:1–2 184
4:6 184, 242
4:6–8 184
4:8 215
5:1 184
5:3 185
5:5 111, 186
5:5–6 193
5:9–10 187, 195
5:10 187
6:2–8 188
6:8 189
6:9 189
6:10 189
6:11 190
6:15 191
6:17 191
7:1 191
7:2–3 192
7:4 192
7:9–16 193
7:14 190, 193
7:15 194
7:16 195, 196
7:17 195, 196
8:5 198
8:7 199
8:7–12 198
8:11 199
8:13 200
9:1 201
9:1–12 201
9:2 201
9:4 201
9:7 201
9:8 201
9:13–11:13 207
9:14 201
9:20 201
9:20–21 202
10:1 55
10:1–2 203
10:1–3 204
10:5–6 204
10:7 204, 210
10:10–11 204
11:1–2 204
11:2 207, 216
11:3 204, 207, 216
11:4 208
11:6 207
11:7 209, 214
11:8 199, 207
11:11–12 209
11:13 209
11:15 198, 210, 219
11:18 210
12:1–13:18 211
12:1–7 222
12:5 164, 223
12:6 208, 212, 216
12:7–10 179
12:9 144
12:10 219
12:10–12 219
12:11 111, 213, 219
12:14 208, 212, 216
12:15–16 212
12:17 211, 213, 222
13:1 214
13:5 214
13:5–6 214
13:5–8 216
13:8 241
13:12 211
13:14 214
13:15 197
13:16–17 197
14:1 216
14:1–5 193, 196
14:3 197, 220
14:4 167, 197, 217, 219
14:4–5 219
14:6–11 217
14:7 209
14:10–11 242
14:12–13 217
14:14 52
14:14–20 217
15:1–16:21 244
15:1 218
15:2 111, 217, 219, 223
16:2 218
16:5–7 190
16:6 218
16:9 209
16:10 218

16:13–16	218
16:14	220
16:16	220
16:18	34
17:3	214
17:6	218
17:7–18	214
17:8	215, 216, 241
17:9	214
17:10	214, 215
17:11	216
17:12	215
17:12–14	218
17:13–17	215
17:14	220
17:16–17	220
17–18	221
18:2	218
18:6	159
18:9–19	219
18:10	215
18:17	215
18:19	215
18:24	218
19:2	219
19:6	219
19:7–9	219
19:8	219
19:10	190
19:11–16	197, 220
19:11–21	161
19:12	183, 197
19:15	183, 223
19:17–21	221
19:19	218, 221
20:1–3	179
20:2	143
20:3	222
20:4	190
20:4–6	172, 175, 197
20:6	183, 222
20:7–9	236, 239
20:8	239
20:9	240
20:10	240, 242
20:12	183
20:12–15	170, 241
20:13	240
21:2	244
21:2–3	183
21:3	244
21:7	111, 147
21:8	241
21:10–11	244
21:12–13	244
21:15–17	244
21:22	245
21:23	245
21:27	241
22:1	183
22:1–2	245
22:2	245
22:6	182
22:7	238
22:14	183
22:14–15	241

Index of Ancient Sources

Septuagint and Apocrypha

Baruch
3:19 94
4:11 90

Epistle of Jeremiah
60 36
64–67 44

1 Esdras
9:6 100

2 Esdras
4:42 23

4 Ezra
2:27–29 91
5:5 45
6:25 27, 83
7:27 27
13:1–3 55
13:24 175

Judith
10:18 52

3 Kingdoms
13:34 192, 194
20:13 172, 173

1 Maccabees
1:11 13, 141
1:14–15 13
1:26 110
1:41–57 137
1:52–53 137
1:54 30
1:59 30
1:62–64 147
1:63–64 13
1:64 118
2:15 140
2:28 33
3:16 139
3:42 88
3:45 34
3:51 34
4:60 34
9:27 34
11:14 139
17:11–15 13

2 Maccabees
2:21 162
3:1 145
3:4–40 145
3:24–26 162
4:34 145
5:2–3 24
5:2–4 162
5:11 139
6:7 101
6:12 158
6:23 95
7:9 168
7:23 168
7:38 168
8:17 137
12:22 162
13:6 88, 158
13:11 72
15:2 101
15:12 145
15:27 162

3 Maccabees
1:16 100
1:18 110
2:5 242
3:16–18 53
4:2 110
5:8 162
5:51 95, 162
6:9 137
6:29–30 158

6:31	95
6:34	158

4 Maccabees

1:11	111
4:24	137
5:13	101
5:37	101
6:24	101
8:14	101
8:22	101
8:24	101
9:6	101
9:8	158
9:9	159
9:21	110
9:23	107, 112
10:11	159
10:15	158
11:20	107, 112
12:12	159
13:15	107, 159
15:29	107, 112
16:16	107, 112
16:16–19	13
17:11	107, 112
17:11–12	107
17:12	168

Sirach

11:13	76
16:18	65
17:32	42
20:11	76
39:28	83
39:30	158
43:7	83
51:3	90

Tobit

4:9	101
14:5	34, 83

Wisdom of Solomon

1:12	158
1:13	88
1:14	158
3:1–8	63
3:7	111
4:11	154
5:4–5	63
13:1–3	45
16:13	95
18:7	88
18:13	158

Old Testament Pseudepigrapha

Ascension of Isaiah

4:2	139
4:2–3	139

Assumption of Moses

12:4	83

2 Baruch

12:3–4	41
53:8–10	36
54:21	83
69:4	83
83:7	83

1 Enoch

1:1–4	154
24:6	156
25:3	154
62:4	23

Jubilees

1:17	85
1:26	85

Odes of Solomon

16:14	42

Psalms of Solomon

2	141
8:1	158
17:11	141
17:11–20	141
17:11–22	132
17:24	161

Sibylline Oracles

3:796–808	24
5:33–34	139
5:150–151	216

Testament Levi

6:11	119

Testament Moses

8.1	34

Dead Sea Scrolls

1QM 1:11–12 34
1QM 2:15–4:17 48
1QM 14:2–3 194

Josephus

Against Apion
1.135–36 139

Antiquities of the Jews
3.5.2 54
3.8.5 54
9.4.3 54
10.11.7 9, 31
11.3.9 84
18.8.1–9 138
20.5.1 121
20.5.3 120
20.8.6 24
20.9.1 147

Jewish War
Proem 4 34
2.10.1–4 139
2.12.1 120
2.13.4 24
2.13.5 24
2.17.8 35
2.20.1 28
3.1.1–3 216
4.3.10 32
4.4.5 24
4.6.3 31
4.9.3–8 35
5.12.3 24
5.13.7 24
6.4.1 31
6.4.5 32
6.5.3 16, 24, 35
6.6.1 31
6.9.4 34
7.82 139

Life
43 139

Philo

De Vita Mosis
2.65 84

De Praemiis et Poemis
117 156

Classical and Church Fathers

Cicero
Ad Atticum
8.16.2 163

Suetonius
Claudius
25.4 120
Tacitus
Historiae
5.13 24, 25

Eusebius
Historia ecclesiastica
2.23.4–18 147
3.5.3 33

Hope for Ever

The Christian View of Life and Death

Stephen S. Smalley

1-84227-358-2

Hope in relation to life and death, is on any showing a topic of great importance. It seeks to make sense of history, with its evil and suffering as well as its good. Moreover, the topic forces us to give a full account of God, the Father of our Lord Jesus Christ. God is perceived accordingly not simply as Mind behind a cosmic order, but as the Lord who is sovereign and active in his creation. The doctrine of hope pushes enquirers to the intellectual and spiritual limits of theological investigation, and helps them to answer questions about the meaning and purpose of life, and the nature and consequences of death.

As Christians we have a hope that is for ever. In this timely and accessible book, Stephen Smalley focuses on the theology of hope in its Christian and biblical perspective, and shows how the eschatological character of hope is a balance and a tension between the past, present and the future.

When Will These Things Happen?

A Study of Jesus as Judge in Matthew 21–25

Alistair Wilson

1-84227-146-6

This study seeks to allow Matthew's carefully constructed presentation of Jesus to be given full weight in the modern evaluation of Jesus' eschatology. Careful analysis of the text of Matthew 21–25 reveals Jesus to be standing firmly in the Jewish prophetic and wisdom traditions as he proclaims and enacts imminent judgement on the Jewish authorities then boldly claims the central role in the final and universal judgement.

Atonement for a 'Sinless' Society

Engaging with an Emerging Culture

Alan Mann

1-84227-355-8

'Sin doesn't really exist as a serious idea in modern life,' wrote the journalist Bryan Appleyard. He is not alone in his views. 'Sin' has become just as tainted, polluted and defiled in the postmodern mind as the word itself indicates.

Atonement for a Sinless Society is about an encounter between two stories: the story of the postmodern, post-industrialized, post-Christian 'sinless' self and the story of Atonement played out in the Passion Narrative. Alan Mann charts a way through the apparent impasse between a story that supposedly relies on sin and guilt to become meaningful, and one that fails to recognize the plight of humanity as portrayed in this way.

Drawing on cultural commentators, narrative therapists and contemporary theologians, Alan Mann shows that the biblical narrative needs to be re-read in the light of this emerging story so that it can speak meaningfully and sufficiently to an increasingly 'sinless' society.